CHSP
HUNGARIAN STUDIES SERIES
NO. 11

WITHDRAWN

EDITORS
Peter Pastor
Ivan Sanders

THE HUNGARIAN REVOLUTION OF 1956

— Myths and Realities —

László Eörsi

Translated from the Hungarian by
Mario D. Fenyo

 Social Science Monographs, Boulder, Colorado
Center for Hungarian Studies and Publications, Inc.
Wayne, New Jersey

Distributed by Columbia University Press, New York

2006

EAST EUROPEAN MONOGRAPHS
NO. 693

Originally published as *Mítoszok helyett – 1956 –*
© 2003 by Eörsi László
© 2003 by Noran Könyvkiadó Kft.

© 2006 by Eörsi László
© 2006 by the Center for Hungarian Studies and
Publications, Inc.
47 Cecilia Drive, Wayne, New Jersey
07470–4649
E-mail: pastorp@mail.montclair.edu

The translation from the Hungarian original was supported by a grant from Magyar Könyv Alapítvány [Hungarian
Book Foundation] (www.hungarianbookfoundation.hu)

Library of Congress Control Number 2006902699
ISBN 0–88033–591–2

Printed in the United States of America

CONTENTS

FOREWORD

Earlier versions of the essays in this volume have been published between 1994 and 2002 in various periodicals. They need to be collected not just because of their common theme—all are related to the Hungarian Revolution of 1956—but also because every one of them is surrounded by legends, wrapped—to a greater, or lesser extent—in myths. We must not live with illusions; it has oft been shown that to struggle against the voices of sirens, bent on enhancing some story or other or, on the contrary, to denigrate the reputation of some revolutionary hero, usually for the sake of some base political motive, is a struggle like that of Sisyphus. Yet it may be a worth while enterprise, after all, to publish the results of research, factual as they may be, for there are those who, after all, are interested in what really happened. Of course, the myths are interesting for their own sake, as long as we keep in mind that they belong to another "genre."

Legends surrounding 1956 were budding already in the first days of the revolution, mostly as a consequence of a dearth of information. Perhaps the best known among these is the one created in defense of Prime Minister Imre Nagy, according to which he was forced to introduce martial law and a curfew by the Stalinists, at the point of a gun.

Immediately after the defeat of the revolution by force of arms the legends, born out of despair and bitterness, often exaggerated the number of tragic endings. The most common of these was the fiction of Minister of Defense Pál Maléter's resistance in the mountains of Bakony, which will be discussed in the essay on the Bástya csoport [Bastion Group].

As we know, in the party-state, the political leaders and their acolytes fatally falsified the goals and history of the revolution; it may be said, with some oversimplification, that they reduced the whole revolution to the lynchings that took place on Köztársaság [Republic] Square, in front of the Party headquarters.

Since the change of regime in 1990, partly as a result of the importation of further legends from emigration, the most far-fetched and ill-intentioned fabrications have obtained signal success with the public. Perhaps the legend of the "elicited revolution" is the best known. The essence of this legend is that the Soviet leadership, with the Hungarian Party leaders in its wake, deliberately provoked the revolution, in order to deal with it. The assumption is absurd, if only because the sequence of events, down to the uprising itself, could only hurt the basic interests of the Soviet Union. Moreover, there is not a single archival source to support such an interpretation. Nevertheless, this myth has gained wide acceptance, and not only among the unread and ill-informed. The fabrications devised with a political ulterior motive became entrenched between 1992 and 1994, and again since 1998, on the initiative of the right-wing and extreme right-wing parties. Much like the works of authors under János Kádár, but with an opposite agenda, masses of writings and documentaries have appeared without any nuanced descriptions, with banal, biased interpretations.

To uncover the facts, the reconstruction of the history of armed movements in 1956 initiated from below—which is the subject of my study—I have used primarily archival sources, with the required critical approach. It has become my conviction over the years, that these sources are more reliable by several orders of magnitude than the totality of oral tradition. Therefore I often become embroiled in vain disputes with those who advocate perhaps the most commonly accepted legend, according to which the trials following 1956 were on the model of the Stalinist show trials of an earlier decade. The truth is that the record of interrogations, the confessions, the testimonies, the signed denunciations allow us to reconstruct particular events, provided we remain aware that the authorities have distorted these documents in the form of charges, sentences and propaganda coups.

***

I have been studying the uprising of 1956 since the change of regime in 1990. So far I have written a detailed account of happenings in four areas of Budapest: Ferencváros, Angyalföld, Józsefváros and Széna Square. The chapter "The Siege of Budapest, 1956" may be considered a brief summary of a monograph yet to be written. Valid studies have already been written about the conflicting role played by József Dudás in 1956, so I have made use of secondary works in this instance, more so than in the other chapters. This chapter is the least definitive, for important sources may yet come to light.

The other studies deal with the period immediately following the defeat of the revolution. Undoubtedly the greatest debates in various media were elicited by the story of Ilona Tóth and her death sentence. Was her trial a show trial? I am engaged in an ongoing dispute with various historian colleagues on this topic, with no resolution in sight.

The story and tragedy of Péter Mansfeld is perhaps the most often mentioned topic in the recollections of 1956. Not by coincidence, since he happened to be the youngest victim of the reprisals. Yet the cruelty of the reprisals cannot justify the distortions propagated even by some of our political leaders.

The chapter on the "Bástya" Group deals with the resistance of that group, by participants whose names have not been forgotten.

Of course, this choice of topics must be accepted as some kind of excuse, for a number of other events from 1956 could have been included in this study, on the basis of the parameters we have set. The simple, pedestrian explanation of their omission is that the documents are in the process of being revealed, or research has not even begun. Thus this volume may be considered the first in a series.

Demonstration on the grand boulevard

Széna Square

The burning of communist literature

Üllői Road

Calvin Square

The Szabad Nép building

"We are restoring order. Only a military occupation can ensure a government that will back us."

THE SIEGE OF BUDAPEST, 1956

"We knew what we were fighting for; they, on the other hand, were obeying a mistaken, criminal command."

THE WEAKENING OF COMMUNIST POWER: THE ANTECEDENTS OF THE REVOLUTION

The death of Iosif Stalin in 1953 opened a new epoch for the oppressed countries of the Soviet empire. The signs of change were most obvious in the case of Hungary

By 1953 the real income of the overwhelming majority of Hungarian workers had dropped by some 20 percent in relation to 1949. The mandatory political meetings had increasingly undermined the morale of the workers, as the morale of the peasantry, subjected to repeated requisitions, was further undermined by forced collectivization.

Nikita S. Khrushchev and the Soviet Party leadership realized that the policies of forced industrialization, collectivization and general sovietization have generated deep discontent in the relatively modernized region of East Central Europe, leading to a potential explosion in the case of Hungary. In June 1953, only two months after the death of Stalin, Khrushchev and company secretly summoned first secretary of the Party and prime minister, Mátyás Rákosi, along with other Hungarian leaders, to Moscow. They were expected to practice self-criticism for the relentless Stalinist policies they pursued until that time (albeit those policies had been prescribed by the Kremlin) and were instructed to elaborate a program catering better to the needs of the population. Rákosi was ordered to cede the chair of prime minister to Imre Nagy, who had been relegated into the background, but who had criticized the Party leaders for the same reasons.

All this was typical of the conditions in those days: within the Soviet sphere, only the Kremlin could authorize even favorable changes.

After the dressing-down in Moscow the Central Committee of the Hungarian Workers' Party (MDP) held a meeting. At this point the most prominent leaders, the foursome of Mátyás Rákosi, Ernő Gerő, Mihály Farkas, and József Révai, were in the crossfire of attacks, because of their economic policies as well as their disregard of the laws and due process. Thus the process of destalinization began in July 1953, with the prime ministry of Imre Nagy. Forced collectivization came to a halt, the notorious "kulak lists" were eliminated, acts of lawlessness gradually ceased: no more forced labor camps, and the show trials were under review. All this made Imre Nagy extremely popular, even though Rákosi and company were increasingly hampering the reforms.

For about a year and a half there was mudslinging between Rákosi and Imre Nagy, and their respective followers. The stakes were rather high. Rákosi's arbitrary rule and his role in setting up the show trials tied him to the Stalinist regime. He knew that the reforms would lead to his political demise. Nagy, on the other hand, believed it was possible to build socialism without resorting to terror. Of the Communist leaders at that time he was the only one who tolerated dissent, and indeed made it possible for non-Communists to play a role in politics. (Those outside the Party, however, could accomplish nothing in public affairs, because the decisions had to be sanctioned by the Party and its apparatus, even at the local level.)

Rákosi, relying on the Party apparatus, did everything in his power to isolate Nagy. The prime minister could count on the goodwill of the common people and the support of the intelligentsia. The new government program amounted to a real liberation; it was an admission that the self-extolling propaganda of the Party did not correspond to reality, and this was officially recognized. Even though the professional elite among the Communists did not dare or was unable to break with the dogmatic ideological approach, the majority of the staff of Party daily *Szabad Nép* attacked Rákosi and company openly. The most outspoken, however, were quickly removed by the Party officials.

During the premiership of Nagy in 1953–54 the standard of living rose, there was progress in agriculture and the production of consumer goods. Steps were taken to restore due process. Beginning with 1954, victims of the show trials of the previous years who were still alive, including János Kádár, the future leader, were released from confinement. The issue of these fake trials and the rehabilitation of the victims was still a taboo topic, mainly because Rákosi was directly involved.

Upon his return from Moscow at the end of November Rákosi already knew that the hardliners were once again in the saddle: they disapproved of the admission of West Germany into NATO, as they did of the thaw initiated by Imre Nagy. They had decided to "restore order" in Hungary. Rákosi briefed the Political Committee, which once again, opted to back him against Nagy. In January 1955, once again, the situation was resolved in Moscow, in the presence of the two antagonists. This time the Soviet Party leaders directed their severe criticism at Nagy's "rightist deviation," although he refused to indulge in self-criticism and stood by his convictions, then and later.

From then on Rákosi's efforts were directed at excluding Nagy from political life, not without success. He identified the main danger as residing in "rightist, anti-Marxist, anti-Party, and opportunist" views. The Party apparatus increasingly rallied to Rákosi's side. In April 1955 Nagy was relieved of all his offices and eventually expelled from the Party.

The Party officials wanted to restore the powers Rákosi had before June 1953, but they had to realize that the era of "classical Stalinism" had passed. Since the thaw the tools of terror could no longer be used indiscriminately, the Stalinist ideology was no longer unequivocal. Nor did they succeed in removing Nagy completely from public life, since he retained many disciples, and found increasing numbers of followers among the youth (e.g., the Petőfi Circle). The opposition group formed in this manner, although it had no formal existence, launched the first significant anti-Stalinist reform movement in East Central Europe and, for over one year, from the summer of 1955 to the fall of 1956, played an increasingly significant role in Hungarian politics, resulting unintentionally in the Revolution of 1956.

The effectiveness of this opposition movement was promoted by the international conjuncture, the atmosphere of moderation, the Soviet-Yugoslav rapprochement and, finally, the Twentieth Congress of the CPUSSR in March of 1956, where Khrushchev spoke at length about Stalin's terrible crimes, and demanded that the Stalinist ideology be discredited.

This marked the end of Rákosi's political career for it became obvious that his person was the main obstacle to reform. During the spring and summer of 1956 there were more and more demands for the resignation of the hated tyrant. At the meetings of the opposition the problems of the country were openly discussed, with two exceptions: dependence on the Soviet Union and one-party rule remained taboo subjects even then, implicitly, by consensus rather than by explicit statements.

The bloody events in Poznan, in Poland, at the end of June (the beating of the workers during their protest, resulting in fifty dead and about three hundred wounded) spurred the Hungarian leaders to take a firmer stand. But then the Soviet leaders, upon the intervention of President Tito of Yugoslavia, forced Rákosi to resign, put him on an airplane and flew him to Moscow. He was replaced by the second in command, the old confidant of Moscow, Ernő Gerő, whereas János Kádár became the new second in command, as the secretary of the Central Committee.

The Soviet and Hungarian administrations did not undertake more meaningful changes. The Hungarian Party leaders had lost all credibility in front of public opinion, while the people began to lose their sense of fear. Ernő Gerő was hardly more popular than Rákosi had been, but he was less intimidating. His feelings of unsteadiness became evident after only a few weeks.

In September the rehabilitation of the victims of the Communist regime became unavoidable. Gerő and Kádár were hoping to carry out the process quietly, out of the limelight, but Júlia Rajk demanded an open, ceremonial reburial, along with a complete moral rehabilitation of her husband, László Rajk, executed in 1949. She had the backing of the entire opposition within the Party and other social forces. Gerő and company dared not deny her wish.

The reburial of the remains of Rajk revealed the criminality of the Communist regime to millions. At the same time, the masses sensed the feelings of insecurity, the paralysis of the establishment. We may consider that day as the opening salvo of the revolution. But the revolution was not dominated by the same forces as the movement for reform.[1]

THE OUTBREAK OF THE REVOLUTION

In the fall of 1956 a structurally fatally flawed Communist regime confronted a growing opposition within the Party—an opposition which was aware of the backing of the masses. This opposition expected the realization of reforms by a change of leadership within the establishment.

In October 1956, when Władisław Gomułka became the Party leader in Poland, despite opposition from the Soviet Central Committee, the Hungarian opposition saw its tendencies vindicated. The ordinary citizen felt the time for action had come, for if one took a determined stand it seemed even the Kremlin could be forced to compromise.

The movements of university students also gathered momentum throughout the country, contributing to the weakening of the Party establishment. They created independent organizations, distancing themselves from the centralized Stalinist network of institutions; they formulated their demands in points of programs, presenting these to industrial plants, to local and national political bodies. They signaled they were prepared to act, if necessary, by means of student strikes and demonstrations.

The programs included reforms, such as the appointment of Nagy as premier, the summoning of a Party congress, the reassessment of the practice of requisitions and of piecework. By then, however, democratic and national objectives were added as well, to include a multiparty system, free elections, civil rights, economic independence, etc. There were even demands for the withdrawal of Soviet troops.

The delegation dispatched to the state radio, however, was denied permission to read the demands regarding the withdrawal of troops and free elections. Hence the idea of a demonstration for the next day, October 23, arose. Its main content was to express sympathy for the transformation in Poland and to stress various points of the program.

The Party leadership, however, was determined to stop the demonstration, by force if necessary. Others within the establishment, such as Sándor Kopácsi, the chief of police of Budapest, sympathized with the opposition, and objected to police intervention. The Party leadership grew hesitant; first it gave instructions to the forces of law and order to prepare for action but, since the demonstrators were going ahead regardless, and there were protests from the Writers' Union, the Petőfi Circle, the editors of the *Szabad Nép* and the student delegations, it backed down, the ban was lifted.

The number of participants grew by leaps and bounds, and the mood became radicalized. Therefore the Party leaders asked the reluctant Imre Nagy to speak to the crowd assembled in front of the Parliament building. Nagy met the crowd around nine in the evening. His speech, however, caused major disappointment; there was not a word about meeting any of the demands. Neither the Political Committee nor Nagy realized that the demonstration had reached a more advanced stage.

Then the demonstrators toppled the statue of Stalin. Since the program still could not be read over the radio, and Party Secretary Gerő rudely criticized the mass movement, labeling it a "nationalist demonstration," the people present became determined to present their demands over the air. The secret police, however, fired into the crowd, whereupon the demonstrators placed the radio station under siege, with the help of weapons obtained from military detachments sent to put them down, from the reserves in the factories, from police patrols, and from the barracks. This was the beginning of the armed uprising.

The Soviet troops stationed in the country, responding to Gerő's plea for help, were mobilized and headed toward the capital. The insurgents, however, took up the fight against them, and thus the unsystematic struggle became a struggle for liberation.[2]

THE SOVIET ARMED FORCES IN HUNGARY

The stationing of Soviet troops in Hungary was made possible by an arrangement among the Allied forces.[3] This agreement was confirmed in 1947 by the terms of the peace treaty between the Soviet Union and Hungary, which stated that the Soviet forces will remain in Hungary as long as their forces are stationed in Austria. Even though the Soviets evacuated Austria, the Warsaw Pact treaty of 1955 sanctioned the Soviet military presence. From then on the equivalent of about four divisions were stationed in Hungary.[4]

On October 23 Ambassador Yuri Andropov[5] felt that the situation in Budapest "was extraordinarily dangerous," and requested the intervention of the army over the phone.[6] The preparations for this intervention were discussed by Khrushchev, the first secretary of the Central Committee of the Soviet Communist Party,[7] with Gerő, the first secretary of the Hungarian Workers' Party.[8] Minister of Defense Georgy Zhukov[9] was given orders to occupy Budapest. (The situation in the other cities and in the villages did not appear as serious.)[10] On the next day, between 2 and 4 A.M., Soviet units, amounting to almost a division in strength, were pouring into the capital from all directions: 6,000 troops, 290 armored vehicles, about 120 army trucks and 156 pieces of artillery.[11] The repression of the "counterrevolutionary uprising" was entrusted primarily to the Special Army Corps under Lieutenant General Piotr Lashchenko, stationed at Székesfehérvár.[12]

It was already obvious that this strategy of the political leadership based on a show of force would not achieve its objective.[13] The Soviet and Hungarian political and military leadership did not expect to encounter serious resistance in Budapest. It soon became clear, however, that the discontented masses will not content themselves with knocking over Soviet monuments. The armored vehicles, in particular, were vulnerable in street fighting at close quarters. This force proved insufficient, even though it was able to guard most of the public buildings. On the 25th three further divisions arrived in Budapest from the Soviet Union and Romania, with effectives totaling twenty thousand.[14] After intense fighting and serious losses the Soviet Party leadership decided to withdraw its troops from Budapest. The decision was largely the outcome of the changed assessment by the Hungarian political leaders. As a condition for the withdrawal it was decided, in agreement with the Hungarian side, that the Soviet troops will be replaced by Hungarian forces, and the rebels will surrender their weapons to those forces. On October 30, the formations directly engaged were withdrawn; the entire operation was concluded by noon of the following day. (The area around the Parliament building was the last one to be vacated by the Soviet forces.)[15] According to several sources, a number of tanks concealed themselves in the Népliget [People's Grove] and elsewhere; in other words, the withdrawal was not complete.

On this same day—partly due to pressure from the Chinese leaders—Nikita Khrushchev and company decided in favor of renewed aggression. By then fresh Soviet units were filtering across the border, in spite of the objections of Prime Minister Imre Nagy.[16] On November 1, in response to the invasion, Nagy officially withdrew Hungary from the Warsaw Pact and declared the country to be neutral. On November 2 and 3, at the news of Soviet maneuvers, Hungarian military units took up firing positions in the suburbs and outlying districts—at the Juta Hill, at Nagykőrösi and Határ Roads, around Soroksár, at Jászberényi and Kőbányai roads, on Máté Zalka Square, at the Élessarok, and in the Chaikovsky Park.[17] The two politicians handpicked by Moscow, János Kádár[18] and Ferenc Münnich,[19] were heading to the Kremlin the next day, while the Soviet forces were tightening their ring around Budapest.

At dawn on November 4, on the basis of orders issued by the commander in chief of the Warsaw Pact forces, Konev,[20] the Soviets launched operation Whirlwind, with the participation of KGB forces led by Ivan Serov[21] personally. Armed resistance was attempted once again, mainly by civilians.[22] Western or United Nations assistance remained an illusion; the Soviet forces, enjoying enormous supremacy in arms, completed the siege of Budapest, entailing considerable destruction, by November 11.[23] The forces were to leave finally, thirty-five years later, without a fight.

THE FORMATION OF INSURGENT GROUPS

From the moment the revolution broke out more and more groups of insurgents formed across the entire territory of the capital city. Their personnel may be estimated at 15,000 altogether. Their membership was drawn mainly from among young workers and unskilled workers, who had been harassed, and became embittered, humiliated during the Stalinist regime. Many among the older participants had been held in Soviet prisoner of war camps. The majority sympathized with the demands of the revolutionaries. They took up arms to end the dictatorship and secure the country's independence, after eight years of terror. The overwhelming majority opted for a rather vaguely defined "true socialism" and rejected any notion of the restoration of the preceding regime. Others joined the revolutionaries out of a desire for adventure, to acquire weapons[24] or to seek opportunities for future success. The outstanding feature of their activities, especially in the first few days, was their spontaneity, for the fighters were far from belonging to the best informed or the most conscious social strata.

Beginning with the night of October 23 insurgents gathered, usually in small groups, mainly in working class districts, having procured handguns, weapons from the police, from the military, or collected bottles filled with fuel. They found natural–born leaders to fight against Soviet forces assembling nearby.[25] The strongest groups of resistance formed in the eighth and ninth districts, on Baross Square, Széna Square, at Pesterzsébet, and Csepel. The majority of the population backed the groups, whose personnel changed almost by the hour. At the beginning their main activity was struggle against the Soviets—and, to a much lesser extent, against the state security forces, the ÁVH, other forces of law enforcement and the military; the lack of a sense of proportions in this endeavor was quite obvious to any outsider. In the first stage of the revolution, even ordinary soldiers were reluctant to take on the risk of fighting on the side of the insurgents; thus the revolutionaries remained the underdog as regards their numbers, their weaponry,[26] and their training, throughout. They compensated for these deficiencies by their enthusiasm, their ingenuity.[27] The "holy street kids"[28] managed to lead the revolution to victory, to the amazement of the world, against an enormous superiority of force—even if only temporarily.[29]

INSURGENTS DURING THE CEASEFIRE

The circumstances of the insurgents changed considerably after October 28, when the central leadership accepted the resolution of the Party's Political Committee assessing the events as a revolution, as a freedom fight. The number of groups and their effectives increased considerably at this time; military officers would join as advisors and trainers; the insurgents were also joined by rank and file soldiers, then by politicians, and common criminals released from jail. (Some insurgent groups liberated jails under the assumption that political prisoners were housed there). A National Guard was established with the participation of military, police, and civilian personnel, as the outcome of negotiations and centralization. The commander in chief was General Béla Király,[30] his deputy the Colonel of the

Police Sándor Kopácsi, chief of police of Budapest.[31] On November 2 and 3 the guard representatives elected an executive committee of ten members, the majority civilians. Thus the groups of insurgents, now functioning as units of the National Guard, acquired a legal framework. To prevent chaos they agreed that all those who applied for the guard— if older than eighteen—will be issued an armband and an identification card signed by Kopácsi, whereas all others will be disarmed. (Of course, these measures were not carried out completely.)

The members of the National Guard were promised a regular salary and uniforms. The leaders organized their group in conformity with military hierarchy—into companies and squads—and set up patrols, enforced discipline, tried to prevent—sometimes unsuccessfully—dereliction of duty. In this period the main task of the armed groups was to maintain order, security, and assist in the distribution of provisions to the general population. Moreover, they tracked down the henchmen of the Rákosi dictatorship—mainly members of the ÁVH and Party leaders— so that independent courts of law might eventually judge them.

Almost everywhere "special groups" (they operated under a various names) were formed to capture the guilty, with the help of the general population. (Sometimes the denunciations were mistaken, or deliberately malevolent). The National Guard conducted house-searches in the case of suspects, as prescribed, to collect weapons and uniforms. (There is little doubt that among those conducting searches there were some who "found" other objects of value as well). The units of the National Guard established loose ties with the revolutionary committees in the inner city, while in the suburbs a closer relationship existed.

A special group was formed, from October 30 on, in the building of the *Szabad Nép*. The building had become the base of the technician József Dudás,[32] who was in the Communist underground during the Horthy era. The "Hungarian National Revolutionary Committee" he had established was headquartered there with the approval of the workers' council at the site. The "National Committee" comprised not only fighters, but had the backing of some intellectuals and had access to printing equipment. Dudás, however, was constantly seeking separate ways and became isolated from other armed units. Eventually almost every group refused to cooperate with him.

The only significant combat during the days of the ceasefire also took place on October 30: the siege of Party headquarters on Köztársaság Square, in Budapest. The besiegers came mainly from the seventh and eighth districts. It was commonly believed that the building was still the headquarters of the already dissolved ÁVH and of the antirevolutionary Party apparatus. Armored units of the Hungarian military, dispatched to protect the building, backed the besiegers by mistake.[33] The crowd took over the building with their help and, in a blind rage, lynched about twenty of those they captured, mostly small fry members of the ÁVH.

ARMED RESISTANCE AFTER NOVEMBER 4

As a consequence of the attack by the Soviet forces the number of insurgent groups and the effectives of each diminished, even though there were a few freshly organized units. Several units of the National Guard dissolved upon hearing the news of the aggression. The military personnel were often the first to leave, even before any armed confrontation, either because they realized the hopelessness of the struggle, or because they felt exasperated by the lack of discipline and the chaotic conditions, or because more radical civilian leaders acquired greater influence, at their expense. This was the tendency not only in the central districts, where officers functioned as advisors or were fully integrated, but also in the outlying boroughs, in Csepel, Pesterzsébet, and Újpest, although troops partook in the armed conflict in large numbers, as separate units. From the start the majority of higher ranking officers, thus the deputy commander of the National Guard, Colonel Sándor Kopácsi, felt armed resistance had no prospects of success. General Béla Király, the commander of the National Guard, withdrew with his men to the hills of Buda. The insurgents gradually lost the support of the population, a sense of despair and distrust took over: the feverish hunt for traitors sometimes resulted in tragedies. The insurgents who held out were counting on the intervention of the United Nations or forces from the West. Resistance lasted longest in Pesterzsébet (November 10–11), but fighting continued at the Schmidt Palace in Óbuda, in the area of Saint Ladislas Square in Újpest, at the Élessarok in Kőbánya, in Erzsébetváros, at the centers of Józsefváros and Ferencváros. Much smaller units of freedom fighters held out in the days November 7 to 10, almost to the bitter end. Several of the captured insurgents, or those suspected of insurgency, were shot on the spot,[34] others were deported to the Ukrainian towns of Uzhgorod or Stry in the USSR. Many of the dissolved units continued to resist, even without weapons, against the resuscitated old regime, both within and outside the country.

THE PRINCIPAL FIGHTING UNITS

The Insurgents at the Corvin Passage

The battles resulting in the largest number of casualties were fought along Üllői Road which separates the boroughs of Józsefváros and Ferencváros, between the grand boulevard and Nagyvárad Square, and between Boráros Square and Baross Street along the grand boulevard.

Groups of insurgents had formed in this area already during the first days of the revolution, taking up combat—as elsewhere—with bottles of fuel, machine guns, and hand grenades against the Soviet tanks. The most severe encounter took place at the intersection of the boulevard and Üllői Road; it was here that the Soviets suffered their greatest losses—some twenty to twenty-five tanks and about 150 troops. The greatest fame surrounded the group that gathered at the strategically located Corvin Movie Theater, under the command of the warehouse supervisor László Iván Kovács.[35] Their effectiveness was such that the Hungarian political and military leaders were contemplating the annihilation of this base, with the help of the Soviets, already on October 25; the operation, scheduled for October 28, was cancelled mainly thanks to the intervention of Prime Minister Imre Nagy. Of course, the insurgents in the neighboring eighth and ninth districts, including the soldiers at the Kilián barracks, were instrumental in the success of the group at the Corvin. Let us refer to all the groups in the neighborhood as the Corvin group.

Representatives of the group entered into negotiations with those "from the other side of the barricades" before ceasefire was declared. The Soviet high command and the representative from the Ministry of the Interior tried to convince the insurgents to lay down their arms, in exchange for safe-conduct. The leaders of the Corvin group, however, came up with a ten-point counterdemand. These indicated, among other things, that they would have preferred the writer Péter Veres to form an interim government, instead of Imre Nagy. (Indeed, Nagy was not very popular in those days, because of his declaration of martial law and the campaign mounted by Radio Free Europe against him.)

During the ceasefire negotiations the representatives of the Corvin group were given a prominent role. On a number of occasions, and at different venues, they discussed with political, military and police leaders. At Party headquarters, the side confronting the leaders of the MDP [Hungarian Workers' Party] reached a consensus: they would recognize the government of Nagy, provided the government disbanded the ÁVH and provided those who took part in the fight were granted amnesty. They were promised that their appeal would be broadcast. Since that did not happen, there was no surrender. The majority of the insurgents agreed that they would not lay down their arms unless and until the Soviet troops withdrew from Budapest. After the withdrawal, however, they collaborated with the military and the police in restoring order. After October 31, a military-type organization became more evident. The command at the Corvin remained the most influential group until the end; it had the largest numbers of representatives on the law enforcement committees and at the meetings of the National Guard.

Despite the warning signs, the Soviet attack on November 4 caught the 1,500 to 2,000 National Guardsmen at the Corvin by surprise. They were led at this time by the agronomist Gergely Pongrátz.[36] The invaders focused on this area first and foremost, targeting the Corvin theater and the Kilián barracks. They soon began to lay mines, against which there was no defense. Although the Corvin group had captured two or three tanks, we are not aware that these were ever used in action, although it did make good use of its five or six artillery batteries and some fifteen machine guns.

After a resistance which lasted a day or two the Corvin group and some other groups in the vicinity evacuated their base. Several smaller groups in the area continued the armed struggle until November 7–8. During November the Corvin group disabled about six tanks, and about twenty-five to thirty combatants were killed on each side. (Of course, there were several victims among the general population as well.)[37]

The Insurgents in the Ninth District

Two rather large groups of insurgents assembled on the other side of Üllői Road, in the heart of Ferencváros, already on October 24. One along Berzenczey Street under the command of the machinist István Wágner (alias "Göndör"—curly), which became known as the Göndör group, the second on October 25–26 on Tompa Street commanded by the toolmaker János Bárány (alias "Bordósapkás Jancsi"—Johnny with the crimson cap). These groups confronted not only the Soviet forces but, on several occasions, Hungarian police and military units as well. On October 27, at the service station on Tűzoltó [Firefighter] Street, another group was formed on the initiative of construction foreman István Angyal,[38] made up of some from the Berzenczey Street and other as yet unorganized fighters from the district. The three groups destroyed about ten tanks, and almost fifty Soviet soldiers fell in combat against them. Angyal and his fellow commander, the film director Per Olaf Csongovai (alias "Csolaf"),[39] played an important role in the ceasefire negotiations thanks to their friends and contacts with the intelligentsia. Csongovai even became a member of the Executive Committee of the National Guard. The civilian fighters were represented by the group from Tűzoltó Street at the constituent meeting of the Revolutionary Committee of Defense. Their commanders who, by the way, were much more sophisticated politically than most insurgents, openly claimed to be Communists. Among the leaders they tried to keep in touch with János Kádár first, for they considered the Party leader their best bet for consolidating a new, democratic, socialist system. On the other hand, the group from Tompa Street, according to the few sources available to us, were counting on Zoltán Tildy.

In the first half of the ceasefire period all three groups expanded or changed their base. The group from Tűzoltó Street occupied the service station of the ÁVH across the street, the group from Berzenczey Street transferred to the dormitory for policewomen on Ferenc Square, those from Tompa Street split into two groups. One part transferred to the student hostel on Ráday Street after János Bárány got in touch with Lajos Petrák, the leader of the Revolutionary Youth Alliance—a front for the Communist MDP. Later on Petrák and his companions, more savvy politically, were able to influence Bárány. The group that stayed on Tompa Street was led by the instrument technician Lajos Mezei. Among the National Guard units formed in the district only the one on Ferenc Square adopted a military hierarchy.

The attack launched on November 4 caught the National Guard unit of the ninth district fast asleep, even though they knew that Soviet troops were filtering into Hungary continuously. The group from Tűzoltó Street clashed with the invaders on Nagyvárad Square, Üllői Road, and on Mester and Viola Streets. There were twenty-two or twenty-four ÁVH recruits within their ranks who had been taken into custody during the ceasefire. During the fighting the commanders of the groups kept trying to make contact with the Soviet military and the Hungarian political leaders to negotiate a ceasefire. They succeeded in sitting down at the table with the Soviets, but rejected the unconditional surrender offered to them as their only choice.

The Göndör group confronted Soviet troops on Ferenc Square, and on Viola Street, alongside those from Mester Street, Kálmán Thaly Street and Tűzoltó Street. Those from the Tompa Street and Ráday Street exchanged fire with the invading tanks on both sides of Ferenc Boulevard. The revolutionaries of the ninth district defended themselves against the overwhelming force for four days, with nothing but handguns and bottles of fuel. (The pressure on the Kilian barracks was so heavy already on November 4, that its defenders were forced to flee that same day. Some of them joined the civilian insurgents and fought to the end.) Armed resistance in Ferencváros had ceased for all practical purposes by November 8. The insurgents from Ferencváros set seven or eight tanks on fire during November, and both sides suffered about ten to fifteen casualties.

A small portion of the insurgents from districts eight and nine continued the struggle by producing leaflets, engaging in strikes, organizational activities.

The Insurgents in the Seventh District

The only place in the seventh district where there was a sizable resistance group in the first days of the revolution was in the area of the Eastern [Keleti] Railway Station. The headquarters of the insurgents were at number 19 Baross Square. From October 28, under the command of Gyula Pásztor and Sándor Pásztor (not related) their activities became increasingly coordinated. There are almost no sources regarding their combats in October. They were joined by a number of university students, who engaged in a great deal of propaganda activity using mimeograph machines and stencils. Other insurgents had also made use of these devices, but not to that extent. When the national guard was formed, the command of the group was taken over by the technician László Nickelsburg, but the two Pásztors continued to play important roles, as did the sewer cleaner László Balogh (alias "Pipó"). This group participated in the liberation of the inmates of the Central Prison on November 1.

Between October 27 and 29 a number of new groups were formed in the district. The district's revolutionary committee had its headquarters in the District Council building on Csengery Street, under the chairmanship of István Hegedűs, delegated by the Party. The armed group that was led by transportation worker Lajos Steiner took up residence in the same building.[40] Thus the insurgents were influenced by several Party officials or police officers, but the composition of the group kept changing. Steiner's group removed many secret files from one of the police stations, but there remained no time to make use of these.

The "Farkas" or "Wesselényi" group was under the command of the heat insulation installer Dezső Kovács (alias "Susogó" —whisperer or "Farkasgazda" —wolfmaster) and the technician Ferenc Drbál[41]; splitting from the fighters in the District Council building they first moved to the headquarters of the district police and later, on the 30th, to a building on Wesselényi Street. Since the FKgP [Smallholder Party] needed that space, they moved to Almássy Square on November 1. They exchanged this base on November 3 in favor of the Royal Hotel on the grand boulevard, for strategic reasons. Since the leaders of the group felt they could not carry out their National Guard activities without professional training, they got in touch with János Solymosi and Colonel Károly Döbrentei, who gave them advice and guidance.

At the district police, and Party headquarters two sizable National Guard group were formed, under the leadership of police First Lieutenant László Csabai, later László Bencze, or dispatcher József Nemeskéri and Major József Drabant. The majority of the members in the first group had come over from the police, and from the military in the latter, also referred to as the Kossuth group. The groups in the district were organized into companies, sections, squads.

In addition, there were smaller armed groups stationed in the EMKE restaurant, the New York coffeehouse, the KIOSZ [National Alliance of Craftsmen] building on Hársfa Street, on Klauzál Square, and on Garai Street. Altogether some one thousand or twelve hundred freedom fighters.

The leaders of the larger groups in the district were included in the discussions regarding the formation of the National Guard. Ferenc Drbál became a member of the executive committee.

The revolutionaries of this district were preparing for the Soviet attack: on November 3 in the afternoon the district commanders of the National Guard and their military advisors met at the Baross Square base and worked out a defense plan; the meeting was chaired by Nickelsburg. They agreed that the Baross Square group would secure the area around Eastern Railway Station, the "Farkas" group would move to the Royal Hotel and, together with those at the Party headquarters, would be keeping an eye on the section between Majakovszkij Street and Rákóczi Avenue along Lenin Boulevard, as well as the area around Almássy Square. The area formed by Hársfa, Majakovszkij, Rottenbiller and Wesselényi Streets would be watched by Steiner and his group. The commanders approved the plan (albeit they could not agree on the choice of commander in chief in the district).

The resistance by the largest group, with some four to five hundred effectives, collapsed relatively early. Contributing to this may have been the fact that commander Nickelsburg—probably upon seeing the endless row of Soviet tanks on the move—changed his mind about taking up the fight. He resigned and left, since his fellow commanders did not agree with him. The tanks shot up the base and the surrounding buildings, and most of the insurgents soon gave up the resistance, but others dispersed and caused severe losses to the Soviets along Rákóczi Avenue, at the Bethlen Movie Theater, in the City Grove and along György Dózsa Avenue. (Their bases were on Jenő Landler Street, Garai Square and in the Exhibition Hall.) Smaller units fought until November 9.[42] According to one source, those from the Baross Square, with nothing but light weapons and bottles of gas at their disposal, inflicted mortal wounds on fifteen Soviet soldiers and destroyed three military vehicles.

The insurgents fought successfully for several days along the section of Lenin Boulevard. After November 6 the so-called Revolutionary Military Council, with Lajos Steiner, Ferenc Drbál and three other officers, guided the resistance and coordinated the activities of the groups. Their headquarters were in the building of the Ministry of Transport and Postal Services, next to the Royal Hotel. They were joined from the neighboring districts by the Vajdahunyad Street group led by József Sipos, and part of the Eötvös Street group. The insurgents, numbering about five hundred fighters in each group, resisted until November 9 or 10, then about one hundred fled to Szabadság Mountain in Buda, in the hope of continuing the fight under the command of General Király.[43] But it was too late for that.

Under the leadership of István Klauber there was a group of National Guardsmen from Zugló, made up of about forty or fifty men from the seventh district, armed with two machine guns. The thirty or forty fighters from the base on Thököly Avenue ambushed a Soviet unit, inflicting losses of thirty to forty troops and seven or eight tanks.

The largest number of unarmed insurgents came from the district. They were active in distributing leaflets in widely dispersed areas and in trying to organize abroad, in order to prevent the consolidation of the Kádár regime.

The Insurgents at Széna Square

The group at Széna Square was formed on October 26–27; it was to become the number one stronghold on the Buda side. They erected barricades against the Soviet tanks, reinforced by railway cars switched over via the tram tracks from the nearby Southern Railway Station. The leader of the group was the fifty-nine-year old chauffeur, János Szabó.[44] In any case, the fighting in this area was not nearly as intense as the one at the Corvin Passage, for instance. Before the ceasefire the leaders at Széna Square contacted the officers at the Bem barracks, who in turn tried to convince them to lay down their arms. The insurgents showed no inclination to do so. Following this episode a Soviet-Hungarian attack temporarily dispersed the armed civilians from the area.

On November 4 Soviet armored detachments made their appearance at the Southern [Déli] Railway Station. The insurgents, numbering about fifteen hundred, tried to delay the Soviets. Thereafter some of their subunits withdraw to the nearby Buda borough of Pesthidegkút. At the village of Solymár, however, the Soviet forces surrounded the group from Széna Square. Even then they did not surrender, but were able to escape, at the cost of severe losses. Thereupon János Szabó dissolved the group.[45]

The Insurgents at Csepel

In the first days of the revolution the civilian insurgents were confronting not Soviet forces, but Hungarian armed units. On November 4 the Soviets immediately occupied some of the firing positions of the artillery regiment stationed at Csepel, a large industrial complex on an island in the Danube. Along these, there were others they had never relinquished since their first attack on October 26–27. The batteries remaining in Hungarian hands were gathered at strategically important positions by the command of the local National Guard. The commander of the troops was First Lieutenant Sándor Kőrösi,[46] whereas the leader of the civilians was István Buri.[47] They could not even agree on basic strategic goals, inasmuch as Kőrösi was intent only on a defensive posture, while Buri was arguing in favor of attacking the Soviet armored units passing by. Since the civilians were in the majority, they launched attacks and caused serious damage to the invaders. Finally the officers, too, joined the resistance; thanks to their relatively strong firepower (in comparison with other groups of insurgents). They even fired at Soviet aircraft. Their mortars were aimed at the runway of the military airport at Tököl. The insurgent group, numbering about 350, disabled seven or eight tanks and hit an aircraft. Before the infantry assault, they blew up the roads leading to the area, thus delaying the Soviet attack. Later, they prevented the penetration of armored units by piling up trucks and tankers from the Csepel Ironworks. The increasingly heavy attacks by the Soviet forces once again divided the defenders; the officers saw no sense in continuing the struggle. In the morning of November 9 the Soviets eliminated all armed resistance here.[48]

The Insurgents at Pesterzsébet

Across from Csepel, on the other side of the spur of the Danube dividing the island from Pest, insurgents gathered spontaneously at the boroughs of Pesterzsébet, Pestlőrinc, and Soroksár; they confronted the Soviets during the first days of the revolution, trying to prevent them from reaching the center of the city. The group at Pesterzsébet chose the chemical engineer László Oltványi[49] as their leader, eventually as the head of the district's National Guard. Other armed groups active in the vicinity joined Oltványi's group. Thus the centralization of the command of the armed revolutionaries was initiated at Pesterzsébet, even before the ceasefire.

On November 1 and 2, the National Guard at Pesterzsébet received significant military support: an anti-aircraft artillery unit with six batteries and a sharpshooter battalion with two machine guns took up positions on the Juta Hill and the Soroksár Road, to prevent the return of Soviet forces to Budapest. On November 4, after Oltványi assigned positions to the National Guardsmen, the civilian and military forces clashed with the Soviets at several locations, in a synchronized operation. They were particularly successful at the Juta Hill. In addition to handguns, the civilian forces had at their disposal, two antiaircraft batteries and one rocket launcher, and could even aim at Soviet tanks from a distance.

The freedom fighters at Pesterzsébet made the Soviet advance perilous by blowing up the asphalt cover of the road. This was where armed resistance around the capital city lasted longest; but here too they were outnumbered, and by November 10–11 resistance was over.[50]

EPILOGUE

As a consequence of armed clashes, 1,945 Hungarians—insurgents and residents—were killed in 1956. The almost 17,000 wounded were treated in the hospitals, clinics and other healthcare facilities in Budapest. Two hundred and twenty-nine persons were sentenced to death and executed, in consequence of their activity in 1956. One hundred and seventeen of them, or around 51 percent, received the death penalty for participation in armed activity.[51] According to our estimates, about one third of the defenders of Budapest left the country after the defeat of the revolution.

The Soviet army lost 670 personnel—85 officers and 555 regular troops—and suffered 1,500 wounded (according to other estimates, the number of wounded was 1,251). More than half of their losses were inflicted on units of the Special Army Corps during their operations in October.[52] Among the more important weaponry, the Soviets lost about 40 tanks and mechanized batteries, 30 to 35 armored vehicles, almost 20 canons, 4 rocket launchers, and about 10 antiaircraft artillery pieces.[53]

NOTES

1. György Litván, "A forradalomhoz vezető út" [The road leading to revolution], in *Az 1956-os magyar forradalom* [The Hungarian Revoluton of 1956], ed. György Litván (Budapest: Tankönyvkiadó, 1991), pp. 10–30.
2. János M. Rainer, "A forradalom napjai" [The days of the revolution], in *Az 1956-os magyar forradalom*, ed. Litván, pp. 34–48; see also the relevant documents in the Appendix, pp. 189–191.
3. Combats in which the participants were Hungarian on both sides, the firing squads—of which the one on October 25, on Kossuth Square was the most regrettable—and other atrocities are not discussed in detail; nor do I discuss the negotiations and the pertinent political situation. Numerous studies and other publications have already been published on these aspects. This writing deals only with the fight of the insurgents and of the Soviet troops. My sources include Éva Gál, András B. Hegedűs, György Litván, and János M. Rainer, eds., A *"Jelcin-dosszié"* [The "Yeltsin Dossier"] (Budapest: 1956-os Intézet, 1993); Viacheslav Sereda and Aleksandr Stikalin, eds., *Hiányzó lapok 1956 történetéből* [Miss-

ing Pages from the History of 1956] (Budapest: Móra, 1993); Jenő Györkei and Miklós Horváth, eds., *Soviet Military Intervention in Hungary 1956* (Budapest: Central European University Press, 1999); Viacheslav Sereda and János M. Rainer, eds., *Döntés a Kremlben* [Decision in the Kremlin] (Budapest: 1956-os Intézet, 1996).

4. Jenő Györkei and Miklós Horváth, "Additional Data on the History of Soviet Military Occupation," in *Soviet Military Intervention*, ed. Györkei and Horváth, p. 8.

5. Andropov, Yuri V. (1914–1984), a member of the CPUSSR since 1939, Soviet ambassador to Budapest from July 1954 to March 1957. Member of the Central Committee, CPUSSR since 1961, head of the KGB from 1967. First secretary of the CPUSSR since 1982, chairman of the Supreme Soviet since 1983.

6. Györkei and Horváth, "Additional Data," in *Soviet Military Intervention*, ed. Györkei and Horváth, p. 11.

7. Khrushchev, Nikita S. (1894–1971). Joined the Communist Party in 1918. Member of the Central Committee from 1934 to 1966, First Secretary of the Ukrainian Communist Party from 1938 to 1949, and of the Soviet Communist Party from 1953 to 1964. In 1964 was relieved of his functions in a putsch-like coup.

8. Ernő Gerő (1898–1980). Member of the Communist Party of Hungary since 1918, in 1931 appointed to the Komintern's Executive Committee, fought in the Spanish Civil War. Editor of *Új Hang* [New Voice] and propagandist for the Red Army. A leading political figure in Hungary from 1945 to 1956, elected first secretary of the Party in July 1956, but removed from that position on October 25. Transported to Moscow on October 18, could not return to Hungary until 1961. Expelled from the Party in 1962.

9. Zhukov, Georgy, Z. (1896–1974). Member of the Soviet Communist Party since 1919. Deputy to the commander in chief during World War II, Marshall of the Soviet Union since 1943, member of the Central Committee from 1953, minister of defense between 1955 and 1957, alternate member of the Presidium of the Central Committee. Removed from leadership in 1957 and sent into retirement.

10. Alexandr M. Kirov, "Soviet Mililitary Intervention in Hungary, 1956," in *Soviet Military Intervention*, ed. Györkei and Horváth, p. 11. According to Kirov, in the summer of 1956 the Soviet military leadership prepared a plan (code-name "Wave"), for the "Special Army Corps's Participation in the Restoration of Order on Hungarian Territory." Between October 9 and 16 the troops were on the alert. Measures were introduced even on Soviet territory "in case events get out of hand in Hungary." p. 132.

11. Györkei and Horváth, "Additional Data," in *Soviet Military Intervention*, ed. Györkei and Horváth, p. 11; see also Appendix, pp. 190–191.
12. Lashchenko, Piotr N. (1910–1992). Served in the Red Army from 1930. Was the commanding officer of the Special Army Corps stationed in Hungary in 1955–56.
13. As in Berlin in June 1953.
14. The military historian Miklós Horváth, relying on Soviet and other sources, writes "that the effectives of the five divisions of troops placed in radio preparedness and engaged in restoring order were 31,500 troops, 1,130 tanks and automotive batteries, 380 armored trucks, and 3,830 vehicles. The Ministry of the Soviet Armed Forces, placed the division of fighter planes and bombers stationed in Hungary in radio readiness, as well as one of the fighter plane divisions from the Carpathian Military District. Thus altogether 159 fighter planes and 122 bombers were ready for deployment." See *Új Honvédségi Szemle*, no. 10 (1996).
15. Györkei and Horváth, "Additional Data," in *Soviet Military Intervention*, ed. Györkei and Horváth, pp. 70–71; see also Appendix, p. 191.
16. Imre Nagy (1996–1958). POW on the Russian front in 1916. Fought in the Red Guard during the Civil War. Joined the Communist (Bolshevik) Party in 1920. Back in Hungary, joined the workers' movement. Lived in the Soviet Union between 1930 and 1945. Took on political roles in Hungary thereafter. Prime minister between 1953 and early 1955, then he was expelled from the Party. Became head of government once again when the revolution broke out. He declared an armistice, introduced a multiparty system, declared Hungary to be neutral and withdrew the country from the Warsaw Pact. On November 4 sought refuge in the Yugoslav Embassy. Later deported to Romania by the Soviets. Arrested on April 14, 1957, sentenced to death and executed on June 16, 1958.
17. Miklós Horváth, *1956—Katonia kronológia* [1956—Military Chronology] (Budapest: Magyar Honvédség Oktatási és Anyagellátó Központ, 1993), p. 53.
18. János Kádár (1912–1989). Took part in the Hungarian workers' movement since 1931. From 1945 a member of the Political Bureau of the Hungarian Communist Party, then deputy Party secretary. Minister of the interior between 1948 and 1950. Incarcerated between 1951 and 1954. Elected first secretary of the Party on October 25. State minister during the revolution, a founding member of the MSZMP (Hungarian Socialist Workers' Party). The Soviet leadership appointed him the head of the countergovernment. The top leader of the country from 1957 to 1988.
19. Ferenc Münnich (1986–1967). In exile in the Soviet Union until 1945, fought in the Spanish Civil War. Chief of police of Budapest from 1946

to 1949, then diplomat until 1956. Minister of the interior during the revolution. Became minister of the armed forces under Kádár, prime minister from 1958 to 1961. Member of the Central Committee from 1955 to 1960, member of the Political Committee until 1966.

20. Ivan Konev (1897–1975). Member of the Party since 1918. Marshal of the Soviet Union, commander in chief of the Central Army Group in 1945–46. Commander in chief of the Soviet ground forces in 1946–1950, and first deputy minister of defense. Reappointed in 1953 and held these posts until 1955. Commander in chief of the unified ground forces of the Warsaw Pact countries. between 1955 and 1960. Commander in chief of the Soviet army groups in Germany in 1961–62.

21. Ivan Serov (1905–1990). Joined the Party in 1926. Deputy commissar for the interior between 1941 and 1954, head of the KGB until 1958. Member of the Supreme Soviet of the Soviet Union from 1946 to 1962. Thereafter, however, he gradually lost the trust of the leadership. Was expelled from the Party in 1965.

22. Miklós Horváth, *1956 hadikrónikája* [The Military Chronicle of 1956] (Budapest: Akadémiai Kiadó, 2003), pp. 21, and 141. According to Horváth the effectives of the Hungarian People's Army were about 115,000 in this period: composed with the officer corps of 24,500. The non-commissioned officers with rank and file troops, plus students at officer and non-commissioned officer training schools amounted to 90,500. There were 20,000 civilian workers. The army had fifty-two tanks at its disposal in the capital before the revolution broke out, five of which were probably captured by the insurgents.

23. The Russian siege of Grozny in 1999 reminded us of 1956. The Chechens defended themselves more successfully, since they received considerable aid from the outside, their weapons were not as obsolete, the fighters fought with even more determination, and they were probably less worried about damage to their city. Another important difference is that the police and the military remained mostly passive in Hungary, while in Chechniya the insurgents had the opportunity to create an independent armed force over the years.

24. The most important of the arms depot was the Lámpagyár [Lamp Factory] on Soroksár Road, but the insurgents got hold of sizable arms supplies at the barracks on Timot Street, and at the police headquarters in the eighth and ninth districts.

25. According to some of the recollections, the Soviet troops began firing "for no particular reason," causing serious destruction on Ferenc Boulevard. It is much more likely, however, that the occupation forces were attacked by the insurgents equipped with Molotov cocktails as they were moving in.

26. Ernő Laurenszky, *A forradalom fegyverei—1956* [The Weapons of the Revolution] (Budapest: Magyar Honvédség, 1995). According to this study the Soviet-made weapons obtained from the Hungarian People's Army were about ten to fifteen years out of date. On October 27–28 the insurgents succeeded in obtaining weapons that were more up-to-date, including a number of artillery pieces and even some armored vehicles. According to several sources the Soviet troops were sometimes willing to hand over their tank for food or drinks. This, however, does not sound very likely, given the risks involved.

27. The best example is the disarming of tanks. (They had no difficulty dealing with armored vehicles riding on tires—these were open caskets. The tires were shot out or the personnel in the vehicle were easily picked out from above.) It was not easy, however, to hit armored vehicles on the move with the Molotov cocktails. Barricades were erected, also pots were strung across the road and moved around from the doorways by means of strings attached to the handles. The driver of the tank, whose range of vision was rather limited, would slow down, suspecting a land mine, making it easier for the pitchers of the cocktails to hit their target.

28. The expression is credited to Tibor Déry, noted Hungarian author.

29. In 1956 Time magazine named the Hungarian freedom fighter "Man of the Year."

30. Béla K. Király (1912). A highly decorated officer from World War II. He chose the Soviet side in 1945, was treated as a POW, but escaped from Soviet captivity. Joined the Hungarian Communist Party (MKP) in 1945. Major general from 1950, the commanding officer of the Zrínyi Military Academy. Was condemned to death in 1952, but his sentence was commuted to life imprisonment. He was released from prison in September 1956. During the revolution became the chairman of the Revolutionary Military Committee and the Revolutionary Defense Commmittee, and commander in chief of the National Guard, military commander of Budapest. In 1957 he was elected deputy chair of the Hungarian Revolutionary Council in exile. Settled in the United States, obtained a doctorate in history in 1962 from Columbia University. Published several volumes of memoirs. He returned to Hungary in 1990.

31. Sándor Kopácsi (1922–2001). Participated in the antifascist resistance. Joined the MKP in 1945. Chief of Budapest police since 1952. Arrested by the KGB on November 5, 1956. Sentenced to life in prison. Released in 1963. Emigrated to Canada in 1975, returned to Hungary in 1989. At that time he published an autobiographical novel, *Életfogytiglan* [Life Sentence] (Budapest: Bibliotéka, 1989).

32. The biography of József Dudás is in the following chapter.

33. Archives of the Institute of Military History (hereafter HL), 012/57, István Galó and fellow defendants.

34. No archival sources of such cases have been found so far.

35. László Iván Kovács (1930–1957). In 1944–45 lived on territory under German control, hence afterward his opportunities for education and position were limited. He shined as a soccer player at various places of employment. Joined the insurgents at the Corvin film theater, became their commander between October 25 and November 1. He was a regular participant in the armistice negotiations. On November 4 his rivals labeled him a traitor. In December he organized against the new regime. Arrested on March 12, 1957, was sentenced to death, and executed on December 30.

36. Gergely Pongrátz (1932–2005). Resettled to Hungary from Transylvania in 1945. Joined the Corvin group in October 1956. Became commander on November 1, but resigned on November 5 or 6. Joined the Hungarian Revolutionary Council in Vienna, lived in the United States and Spain. Became the vice president of the Association of Hungarian Freedom Fighters. Returned to Hungary in 1990 and accepted the leadership of several organizations pertaining to 1956. His memoirs were published in 1982: *Corvin köz, 1956* [The Corvin Passage] (Budapest: Pongrátz G., 1982).

37. HL, 432/58, György László Béla and fellow defendants; Archives of the Municipality of Budapest (hereafter, BFL), 451/89, József Nagy and fellow defendants; BFL, 2834/57, László Schmidt and fellow defendants; HL, 0039/58, Gyula Váradi and fellow defendants; BFL, 8046/58, Mária Wittner and fellow defendants.

38. István Angyal (1928–1958). Deported to Auschwitz in 1944. Expelled from the university in 1949 for political reasons. Thereafter worked at Sztálinváros (Dunapentele) as concrete installer and construction foreman. Participated in revolutionary activities throughout 1956, became the commander of the insurgents at Tűzoltó Street. From November 8 printed flyers at the hospital on Sándor Péterfy Street. Arrested on November 16, sentenced to death, executed on December 1, 1958.

39. Olaf Per Csongovai (1930–2005). Resettled in Hungary from Turkey in 1939. Joined the Communist Hungarian Workers' Party in 1949. Graduated from the university in 1955 and worked at the Hungarian Film Studios. Participated in all revolutionary activities in 1956. One of the leaders of the group on Tűzoltó Street. Reproduced flyers at the hospital on Sándor Péterfy Street. While in exile in Paris he mobilized public opinion against the death sentences in Hungary. A member of Trotskyist movements.

40. Lajos Steiner (1930–1958). Escaped to the German Federal Republic after the revolution, but returned to Hungary in 1957, counting on an amnesty. Arrested on June 25, sentenced to death, and executed on August 5, 1958.
41. Ferenc Drbál (1929–1991). National weightlifting champion. Emigrated to Munich after the defeat of the revolution.
42. Historical Office (hereafter TH),V–150381, Ministry of the Interior.
43. TH, V–150381. According to the records in the Ministry of the Interior, the Soviets suffered forty to fifty casualties in the fighting in the vicinity of the Royal Hotel on November 5, and one of their tanks was destroyed. According to my estimate, the combined forces in the seventh district—not counting those from Baross Square and smaller groups—inflicted twenty to forty casualties on the Soviets and burnt up four to seven tanks.
44. János Szabó (1897–1957), fought throughout World War I, became Red Army company commander in the Hungarian Soviet Republic of 1919. In 1944 moved from Transylvania to Hungary, working mainly as chauffeur. Joined the Hungarian Communist Party in 1945, but was expelled from its successor, the Hungarian Workers' Party (MDP). He was imprisoned for attempting to escape to the West. Joined the group on Széna Square on October 26, 1956. Arrested on November 19, sentenced to death, executed on January 19, 1957.
45. BFL, 627/89, Jenő Fónay and fellow defendant; BFL, 2382/57, László Rusznyák and fellow defendants; HL, 0115/57, József Dudás and fellow defendant. All we know about the Soviet losses is that five soldiers were killed at the Southern Railway Station.
46. Sándor Kőrösi (1932–1958). Volunteered for military service. Joined the MDP in 1951. On October 31, 1956, was assigned to Csepel at the rank of first lieutenant; he assisted in reinforcing the battle positions and in the resistance. Arrested on March 18, 1957, sentenced to death, executed on March 6, 1958.
47. István Buri (1914). Gendarme before 1945. Worked as a locksmith after the war. During the revolution he took part in occupying the police headquarters at Csepel, and became one of the commanders of the insurgents. After the revolution became one of the leaders of the Hungarian Revolutionary Council in Vienna; later, continued to organize from Genoa, Italy, settled in Australia. Was sentenced to death in absentia in 1958.
48. HL, 742/57, Sándor Kőrösi and fellow defendants; BFL, 3563/59, Károly Szente and fellow defendants.
49. László Oltványi (1915–1996). Before 1945 first lieutenant. Imprisoned by the state security, the ÁVH, in 1953. Helped found the Hungarian

Revolutionary Council in Vienna. Continued to organize from Genoa. Became president of the Association of Hungarian Freedom Fighters in Italy. Lived in Brazil from 1958 to 1968, then moved to the German Federal Republic. For his memoirs, see Oltványi, *Harcok Dél-Budapesten, 1956* [Combats in Southern Budapest, 1956] (Washington: Magyar Szabadságharcos Világszövetség, 1981).

50. BFL, 2593/75, Ferenc Gyergyói and fellow defendants; HL, 071/59, Béla Kálmán and fellow defendants; HL, 031/58, János Mecséri and fellow defendants; BFL, 1900/58, Sándor Okner, BFL, 9235/61, János Viniczai and fellow defendants.

51. 1956-os Intézet, *1956 Kézikönyve—Megtorlás és emlékezés* [Manual of 1956, Reprisal and Remembrance] (Budapest: 1956-os Intézet, 1996), pp. 303–305.

52. Kirov, "Soviet Mililitary Intervention," in *Soviet Military Intervention*, ed. Györkei and Horváth, pp. 187–188. The book includes other data, somewhat at odds with these.

53. Estimate based on Evgeny I. Malashenko, "The Special Corps Under Fire in Budapest—Memoirs of an Eyewitness," in *Soviet Military Intervention*, ed. Györkei and Horváth, pp. 273–276.

JÓZSEF DUDÁS AS REVOLUTIONARY

"Natural-born revolutionary"?
"Half-mad megalomaniac"?
"Fascist bandit"?

Mr. and Mrs. Dudás in the Szabad Nép building

One of the most controversial personalities of the October revolution was József Dudás. His close acquaintances, fellow-workers do not begrudge him superlatives, whereas many intellectuals and revolutionary leaders think of him as a demagogue, an extremist, a muddleheaded adventurer, or as a counterrevolutionary, a man of unbounded ambition, or even a Fascist.

Stories about Dudás rose into the foggy realm of legends already at the time of the revolution, and the picture has not become any clearer since.[1]

POLITICAL BACKGROUND

Dudás was born in 1912 at Marosvásárhely, Transylvania, into a working-class family.[2] In 1926, as an apprentice worker, he joined the worker's movement: "my social background and Romanian chauvinism, the hallmark of old Romania...awakened my political consciousness early in life, drawing me to the proletarian revolution; classless society, the free evolution of all ethnic groups, the socialist state...were the ideals and principles for which I was willing to make any sacrifice."[3] He joined the Kommunista Ifjumunkás Szövetség [Communist Junior Worker Alliance] (KIMSZ),[4] but the organization did not last under the harassment of the authorities. In 1932 Dudás participated in its reorganization, and he was drafted into the Romanian Communist Party. He took part in strikes and demonstrations; he was arrested once again in Timişoara [Temesvár] for organizing the general strike of 1934, sentenced to nine and a half year in jail. He actually was incarcerated for five and a half years at the Doftana prison until 1939.[5]

He moved to Budapest in 1940 after the Second Vienna Award, which returned Northern Transylvania to Hungary. He studied mechanical engineering, and took a job as mechanical engineer, without a diploma, with the Steelworks of Budapest, and later with the Cogwheel Works at Csepel. In 1944 he was in the antifascist underground. He became an organizer and leader of the Hazafiak Szabadság Szövetsége [Freedom Association of Hungarian Patriots].[6] He got in touch with the sections and leaders of the Magyar Front [Hungarian Front], including the Communist László Rajk and the Smallholder Zoltán Tildy. He was an organizer and an intermediary. At the same time he rejoined the workers' movement, got in touch with the Communist Pál Demény faction.[7]

He became a member of the delegation which started out on September 22, 1944, for Moscow, to negotiate an armistice. The risky journey made little sense, for the Soviet leaders were already aware of the arrival of Horthy's emissary, Colonel General Gábor Faragho, and his delegation, who crossed the front lines on September 28. No concrete agreement could be negotiated by Dudás and his companions. Upon his return Dudás was wounded, but continued to take part in the antifascist struggle. He was selected a member of the Magyar Nemzeti Felszabadító Bizottság [Hungarian National Committee of Liberation].

After liberation, Dudás elaborated a twelve-point program as a member of the plant committee at the Cogwheel Works. One of his objectives was to make sure that the owners, upon their return, do not curtail the rights the workers had acquired. He argued that all plants employing over five hundred workers should be placed under state control. He proposed a joint directorate of the two workers' parties [Socialist and Communist], and stood up to the leaders of the Hungarian Communist Party, whom he had criticized mostly from the left until then. He felt the lack of self-criticism was wrong, and the Party lacked a proletarian "core." Its ranks should be filled by industrial workers, at least 70 percent.[8]

He joined the Demény-Weisshaus faction which, unlike the leaders of the Hungarian Communist Party, backed his twelve-point program. He even sent this document to the Soviet commandant of the city, attempting to milk the contacts he made on his trip to Moscow, but there was no response.The sources are divided as to his membership in the Party,[9] but he did renew his contacts with the leaders of the Independent Smallholder Party, who welcomed him: they knew about his antifascist past, and entrusted him with establishing a workers' component of the party. Zoltán Tildy appointed him to a committee of experts

was put on an election list for the City Council. Later he was appointed to the party's executive committee. The views are divided as to
whether he had ever officially joined the Smallholders.[10] He got in
touch with Bálint Arany, a leader of the Magyar Testvéri Közösség
[Hungarian Fraternal Community], who had also been part of the
resistance. Dudás attended the meetings of the group, whereas Arany
came to the meetings of the Demény-Weisshaus faction[11]; they distributed leaflets. Of course, all this did not go unnoticed by the state
security agents; he was arrested early in January 1947, and spent three
months in internment camp. In May of 1948, however, the Communist
politician, László Rajk, intervened on behalf of his comrade in arms
and Dudás was released.

A few months later, however, he was detained again, this time at
Kistarcsa; later he was sent to the Hungarian gulag camp at Recsk.
Rajk, who had been arrested himself in the meantime, now testified
against him, probably under duress. Rajk testified that in the 1930s
Dudás had been an undercover agent for the police in Timişoara.[12] A
similar confession was elicited from Dudás in 1947 since, indeed, he
had worked undercover for the Romanian state security, the Siguranca, after 1931.[13] He was extradited in 1951 at the request of the
Romanian state security, to investigate his activities as an alleged
police informer, but in 1954 he was returned to Hungary for lack of
evidence. He was amnestied and rehabilitated. He abstained from politics until 1956. He got married. He worked full time as a technician
and at two part-time jobs.

THE FORMATION OF THE HUNGARIAN NATIONAL REVOLUTIONARY COMMIT-TEE AND THE TWENTY-FIVE-POINT PROGRAM

On October 23, 1956, Dudás participated in the
demonstrations but, after that, he did not leave his Buda apartment in
the Hűvösvölgy for days on end, fretting over the events. He went
downtown on the 27th, by which time the household was even out of
bread; he walked, since there was no public transportation. His preg-

nant wife accompanied him, and she shared with him the successes and failures of the ensuing days. While the women were queuing up in front of the bakery, Dudás took a look around Széna Square and its vicinity. At the Margaret Bridge he saw that the crowd had surrounded Péter Veres, the writer-politician, since some held him responsible for the sins of the Stalinist regime.

Outshouting everyone, Dudás came to the defense of Veres; then, from the top of a wrecked vehicle, spoke briefly about his past, stressing that he had been a political prisoner for years.[14] Then he spoke about how to realize the goals of the revolution; he insisted that power should be entrusted, instead of the indecisive government, to a governing body that represented the will of the people. His speech, replete with catchwords like "independence," "democracy," "national," won over the crowd. The cheering crowd accompanied him to Széna Square, where he was able to address a larger crowd. Since his ambitions were primarily political, he did not join the insurgents even when invited to do so, yet insisted that he was counting on their support. The next day, once again on the Széna Square—where it was rumored that "yesterday's speaker who had the qualities of a leader will 'take the stage' once again"—he delivered a well prepared speech to a huge crowd. The main goals of his program were already there in outline form. Finally he invited the crowd to select a hundred men for October 29, who would meet in the building on Leó Frankel Street and, by means of further voting, would inaugurate the revolutionary committee of the second district. The hundred men were duly appointed, each applicant stood on top of a wreck, and the crowd selected the most accomplished speakers by voice vote. János Szabó (alias "Uncle Szabó") the commander of the insurgents of Széna Square, was personally invited by Dudás to attend.

With the soldiers from the Bem barracks and under the armed guard of the group from Széna Square, organized by Dudás, they met on October 29, at 11 A.M., in the meeting room of the Second District Council building, in the presence of four to five hundred insurgents, to select the Hungarian National Revolutionary Committee [Magyar Nemzeti Forradalmi Bizottság]. Dudás proved to be the best prepared, the most convincing, and presented himself as "one of the leading figures of the revolution."[15] He sketched his twenty-five-point program[16] and the "Appeal" he had written. His principal demands were: The U.N.

Security Council should send an armistice committee to Hungary, along with economic and, if necessary, military aid, and recognize the committee as a belligerent; setting up a provisional government with the participation of Imre Nagy, János Kádár, Béla Kovács, freedom fighters and members of the committee; withdrawal from the Warsaw Pact; the evacuation of the Soviets; neutrality on the Austrian model; the immediate dismantling of the state security apparatus, the ÁVH, as already announced by the government; a student parliament; the creation of councils of workers, peasants and soldiers; freedom to travel in and out of the country; complete freedom of religion, press, and assembly; a multiparty system. In accordance with the twenty-five points the "present resolution" would be sent to all member states of the United Nations and to Hungarian leaders.[17] His appeal stressed the importance of the committee, given that the revolutionary forces across the country had no central organization, to centralize the scattered administration and then, evolving further, to contribute effectively to the transformation of the political and social order. Obviously, the government would negotiate only with such a top organization. Therefore, the committee undertook to summon a national congress of revolutionary delegations at the Sports Hall for November 1, at 10 A.M., with the participation of delegates with an unsullied past—that is, excluding all those who had served the Horthy and the Rákosi regimes. He asked the revolutionary organizations to get in touch with the committee assembled at the Second District Council building to elaborate the agenda and the proposals for the congress.[18]

Dudás became the chairperson of the committee, thirty-two members were selected, including the former officials of the council, with some members of the Communist MDP, priests, tradesmen, intellectuals and a few workers.

Dudás made good use of his political experience and his public speaking abilities; he felt instinctively, with the mass movement encompassing all social groups, that the revolution had gone beyond the goals of the indecisive government. He was able to win over the crowds by projecting to them the image of an energetic, able leader. During the revolution he was the only one to summarize the demands of the street, and to offer an overall program for society in general.[19] His radicalism, which was far from being extreme, impressed even the majority of the supporters of Nagy. His pragmatism was reflected in the fact that several points of his program became part of the government's program (multiparty system, coalition government, a national guard, neutrality). "He recognized that, much as at the end of World War II, an era had come to an end, atop the ruins of which the representatives of various political tendencies could struggle for power."[20] He felt that his own chances were good.

His rapid successes awakened his sense of mission, and his ambitions kept growing. First and foremost he wanted the revolutionary forces under his direction, and since his popularity among the Széna Square group went unchallenged, he felt his goal could easily be accomplished.

TAKING OVER THE OFFICES OF THE *SZABAD NÉP*

At the conclusion of the meeting, Dudás set out in the vehicle of the Széna Square group to get his program and "Appeal" printed. (He never returned to the second district, and barely maintained contact with the organization on Leó Frankel Street by telephone.) He was accompanied by university student András Kovács as a volunteer aide-de-camp and by the electrician György Márton, who were to play important roles in the following days. Dudás drove first to the Parliament to negotiate with Imre Nagy, on the basis of this twenty-five points, but the prime minister was too busy to receive him.[21]

Then Dudás went looking for a printing shop, to have his program printed out in many copies. In the evening he met with success at the headquarters of the *Szabad Nép*, and the Szikra Press.[22]

By then Dudás had about a hundred armed men. In addition to the printshop and the printers, the building also housed a telephone central, with an international network. Dudás decided to use this location as the base of the Hungarian National Revolutionary Committee. He read his program to the staff of the daily. Our sources are contradictory regarding the reaction of the staff—probably the impact on the blue-collar workers was favorable, on the journalists less so.

Then he reached an agreement with the military detachment, reduced in numbers, to guard the premises together. At the same time several soldiers under the command of Sergeant Gyula Andrásy arrived expressly to offer Dudás and the printers their backing. Then Dudás focused on getting his program and his "Appeal" printed, and thought, probably for the first time, about launching a newspaper. The circumstances for such an undertaking had to be conducive. Chaos prevailed in the building, which hampered the work of the printshop. "When we went there" as András Kovács, the leader of the armed group, recalls, "there was a bunch of people, I do not want to say a mob, but complete confusion prevailed, people were coming and going, armed and unarmed, it was bedlam....We created order, we kicked some out, we set guards at the entrance, in other words, we shook up the company somewhat."[23]

Dudás handed out the assignments to the staff. There was no problem with the financial and technical support, but rather with the lack of journalists; Dudás was almost forced to pick reporters off the street. There were enough, however, to issue a paper of one or two pages.

THE *FÜGGETLENSÉG*

The newspaper, entitled *Függetlenség* [Independence], was published in about fifty thousand copies, disseminated by the criers immediately.

This publication, relevant to the history of the revolution as well as to the fate of Dudás, was supposed to be the paper of the Hungarian National Revolutionary Committee. The headline of the first issue created a tremendous stir, the biggest possible: "We Do Not Recognize the Present Government." This was far more provocative than the twenty-five-point program. All of a sudden Dudás appeared on the scene as a dangerous rival to Imre Nagy. Even those who criticized Nagy for being a "wimp" were made to feel uneasy by this headline. There was widespread concern that the head of the government might fall, about the potential for extreme radicalization, about the spread of the extreme right, but most of all about the danger of destabilization.[24]

Under the headline came the "Twenty-Five-Point Program" and the "Appeal" of Dudás[25]—the reason Dudás had gone there in the first place—and the Kossuth coat of arms that was the people's choice to replace the discarded Communist emblem.[26] In addition there was an article by Iván Witt, "In Preparation for the United Nations Debate" which also lashed out at the Imre Nagy government. On the flip side, "The Hungarian People Will Not Produce as Long as They Don't Know for Whom" also written by Iván Witt, the thesis of which was "We want to produce for ourselves, and raise the quality of the products to the same high level as before, but for the benefit of the nation." The articles and the unsigned news items are indicative of the editors' main concerns.[27]

The second issue came out on the afternoon of the same day, likewise two pages, printed in fifty thousand to one hundred thousand copies. The change of the headline is most obvious: "We Will Not Accept the Coalition Government Either," which was a belated reaction to the change of government of October 28.[28] The "Twenty-Five-Point Program," and the "Appeal" were reprinted, whereas the headline on the flip side stated: "Farmers! The Struggle is Also in Your Interest." This page was designed to appeal to the rural areas and the articles probably reflect the concept of Dudás. "The Appeal of the People of the Villages!" without a by-line, argued "We want neither this [the agricultural policies of the Communists], nor the rule of the landlords." In the article "What the Farming Population of Hungary Wants?" a likewise anonymous author demands the appointment of the Smallholder leader Béla Kovács as minister, an end to the system of requisitions, the dissolution of collectives created under duress, the reprivatization of the land.

One result of launching the paper was that several of his former fellow inmates at Recsk, including the writer Zoltán Benkő and the economist Tibor Zimányi, came to call on Dudás.

DUDÁS AND THE REVOLUTIONARY COMMITTEE OF INTELLECTUALS

In just twenty-four hours Dudás rose to become a significant entity in the eyes of the political leaders. On October 29 he had not been received by Nagy because he appeared to be just another leader of the many revolutionary organizations. The next day, when the *Függetlenség* appeared on the streets with a program, and lambasted the government in much sharper, rawer terms than any other paper, the conditions had changed. Now the government became cognizant of the leader of the committee who had an independent paper, who could be assumed to have a political and military base, was considered an important player and one of the main adversaries, with whom one must negotiate. To become acquainted with the stand of revolutionary organizations at the same time, the secretariat of Nagy asked Dudás to invite other committees to the meeting.[29] The chairman of the committee asked Nagy for a safe-conduct, because he had heard that the Soviet troops and the ÁVH might arrest him at the Parliament.[30]

Dudás contacted the Writers' Association and the university students. He found György Ádám, Pál Jónás, László Kardos, Péter Kuczka, István Márkus—i.e. the members of the Magyar Értelmiségi Forradalmi Bizottság [Hungarian Intellectual Revolutionary Committee]— at the Law School of the Eötvös Loránd University of Budapest, and informed them that Nagy had extended an invitation to all of them. Having read the *Függetlenség* they were already familiar with the program of Dudás and, "after their initial shock, they resolved to try to integrate this 'new force' which asserted itself, or at least consolidate with it."[31] In order to achieve this they tried to win over the fellow inmates of Dudás from the prison and the forced labor camp, beginning with the economist Pál Jónás, and György Egri, the journalist, who paid a visit to the university. They asked him to assist in the editing of *Függetlenség*, because "cooler heads were needed there."[32]

The group awaited State Secretary Géza Losonczy and a member of the Nagy circle, Ferenc Donáth. "I got the impression that they had come with a mission from Imre Nagy to sound us out regarding our opinion on the matter."[33] Dudás regarded them as "true communists," that is, not Muscovites nor fellow travelers, but the kind he could accept.[34]

In the name of the committee, Dudás presented the principal demands: the formation of a new provisional government, with the inclusion of coalition members and leaders of the insurrection, and the complete withdrawal of Soviet troops, by a specific, early date. A debate ensued: according to Losonczy's testimony, the goals of Dudás were not accepted without reservation even by his former acquaintances, the ones from the camp at Recsk.[35] Dudás also mentioned a nationwide congress of the Hungarian National Revolutionary Committee. He made it sound as if he were the political and military leader of the insurrection.[36] Losonczy and Donáth sketched their own version of the consolidation, according to which the Imre Nagy government would continue to lead. According to Balázs Nagy, they were vehemently opposed to calling in United Nations troops,[37] but they were also at odds on other issues. Losonczy: "My opinion of Dudás was that, though well-intentioned, he was politically muddled, somewhat of a maverick."[38] Péter Kuczka: "Dudás debated with Donáth and Losonczy in a threatening, demanding tone, whereas they rejected him."[39] One of his followers—probably Pál Jónás—remembered as follows: "...the creation of a joint national guard was unsuccessful, because Losonczy and his friends were adamant. They were thinking in terms of Communist leadership and the disarming of the insurgents. Dudás and his friends, on the other hand, argued that as long as the Soviets remained in the country, we must not lay down a single weapon."[40]

After Losonczy and Donáth left, Dudás offered the committee of intellectuals his armed support, provided the insurgents recognized him as their overall leader. They were unwilling to go that far.[41] He tried aggressively to make them commit themselves, but this led to no outcome. No consensus was reached, except to call on Imre Nagy that afternoon, on the 30th.

Thus we can see that our protagonist was unable to win over his hosts at the university. Gábor Tánczos and István Márkus recalled: "He made a very poor impression on us, we thought of him as an adventurer...."[42] "Indeed he projected the image of a little Mussolini, even by his physical appearance and in his demeanor, and it was the impression of us all—even Laci Kardos—that he was half mad, a man with an excessive opinion of his own importance."[43]

TALKS WITH IMRE NAGY

Besides Dudás, the delegation was made up of Mrs. Dudás, escorted by four armed men, Benkő, Egri, Árpád Göncz, Jónás, Kuczka, Márkus, Balázs Nagy, and Zimányi.

They ran into Zoltán Tildy in the hallway; Tildy approached Dudás with a friendly greeting, as an old acquaintance. Dudás, however, paid no heed, since he was convinced that Tildy had sold out the Small-holder Party to the Communists.[44] Inside the meeting room Dudás told József Bognár, the minister of commerce, to leave, without mincing words. Indeed, he had even less regard for the "fellow travelers" than he did for the Stalinists, because of their lack of principles and their unbridled ambition (as he explained to the prime minister during the discussions).[45] Dudás did not demand that Imre Nagy leave, although he has been accused of doing just that. His program and his statements make it clear that he regarded Nagy as the key personality of the transition period. He was of the opinion, however, that in free elections, Nagy's party would receive no more than 5 or 6 percent of the votes.

After the greetings Imre Nagy declared that the revolution was triumphant, democratization and consolidation were under way, the Soviet forces had withdrawn from the city. The most important tasks, he felt, was to maintain order and preserve the purity of the revolution. All of this is endangered by any factor of destabilization, for instance, by the fact that the committee does not recognize the government. Those demands which rub Moscow the wrong way unnecessarily are likewise dangerous—for Hungary is exposed to its powerful eastern neighbor. He expressed his pleasure at having the opportunity to clear up the differences of opinion.

In response, Dudás objected to the composition of the government, given the fact that, in spite of the victory of the revolution, a number of Rákosi's followers remained, and almost all the others were fellow-travelers. Dudás stressed that among the Communist politicians the committee accept Imre Nagy, Losonczy and Kádár in leading roles, but the others would have to leave. Let the representatives of the democratic parties be given parity.

The prime minister expressed his disapproval that "some" place all controversial issues in front of the masses, for the favorable developments may break down as a result of renewed disagreements, if the calm of public opinion is stirred up needlessly. He saw the need for focusing on launching new reforms, and making it possible to prevent further bloodshed.

The discussions continued in an atmosphere of tension. Dudás kept criticizing the government for its indecision, for lagging behind the events, and urged timely action, especially withdrawal from the Warsaw Pact and the declaration of neutrality. He assured Imre Nagy that the masses do not blame him for the intervention of Soviet troops, but the leadership must also have trust in the people of the country, who had demonstrated their political maturity. All of a sudden he choked on his emotional words and broke into tears, probably because of his fatigue. Several other members of the delegation began to wipe their eyes under the impact.[46]

Finally, one of those present suggested, that in order to overcome mutual distrust, Dudás should be given a cabinet post, preferably the ministry of the interior. Dudás protested that he was not driven to represent the interests of the insurgents by personal ambition; according to eyewitnesses, however, his facial expression betrayed his words, he seemed to favor the idea. Nagy skirted the issue by saying he could not make a decision without the consent of the entire cabinet, and he assured the delegation that he will inform the government regarding the topics discussed.[47] Then he agreed with the suggestion of István Márkus, that a bulletin be issued regarding the meeting over the radio and in the press.

Imre Nagy referred to every member of the delegation as "comrade," whereas Dudás and the other veterans from the camp at Recsk called him Mr. Prime Minister.[48] Márkus summarized the discussion as follows: "Dudás had maximum demands, while adopting a jovial, gentlemanly demeanor toward Imre Nagy. He called him Uncle Imre, and practically licked his ass, but did not compromise with the '48 [a proverbial reference to the revolutionary demands of 1848]."[49] Géza Losonczy recalled: "While I was in there Imre Nagy made serious reproaches to Dudás and company, that the insurgency interfered with the country's political and economic order...."[50]

Ferenc Donáth remembered the encounter as follows: "On this occasion Dudás began with the demand that the government recognize him as the leader of all insurgent groups. Thereupon he demanded that the government entrust the maintenance of order to his armed groups, acting in concert with the military and the police. In a sharp and lively debate Imre Nagy rejected the notion of recognizing Dudás as the leader of all insurgents."[51]

It became clear during the discussions that the delegation was divided into two groups, for those from Recsk were divided into "militants" and "analysts," depending on whether they backed Dudás or the "intellectuals."[52] Márkus, however, seems to recall that all of them participated as neutrals, but Dudás wanted to "give the impression that we were behind him, backing him. We were forced to interrupt occasionally that this was not what we had agreed upon, that it is not so, we have a third, or a fourth point of view."[53]

The prime minister left the meeting room and arranged a meeting for high-ranking police officers to meet with Dudás. Collaboration was desirable, if for no other reason because the police, mostly as a result of the tragedy on Köztársaság Square, felt completely demoralized. There was talk about the ÁVH agents held prisoner by the group under András Kovács, at the headquarters of the *Szabad Nép*. Dudás too was not unhappy about getting rid of them; like some of the other revolutionary leaders he would have preferred if, after the consolidation, the criminals of the Rákosi regime would be tried in an independent court; therefore he easily agreed to have the existing and future prisoners transferred to national police headquarters, on Mari Jászai Square.[54]

According to Dudás's recollection they also agreed that he would publish an article in his paper urging all members of the ÁVH to report to the police, where they would be placed in custody, and he promised, in the name of the insurgents, that it was their duty to direct them to the head of the national police.[55]

Thereafter Dudás and company sought out Pál Maléter and Zoltán Vas. They talked about the activities of the insurgents and the regular armed units, the setting up of joint patrols to preserve law and order. While Dudás spoke to the colonel in a pleasant tone, Maléter responded coldly, using a superior tone.[56] The parties could only agree on one thing: to continue the discussion the following day, with the participation of others, at the Kilian barracks.

Around 8 P.M. the following announcement was read over the radio, twice: "Today, on the afternoon of October 30, 1956, Imre Nagy, the chairman of the Council of Ministers, and the representatives of the freedom fighters, as well as the representatives of revolutionary intellectuals and university students, met for negotiations. On the basis of the proposal submitted by József Dudás, the chairman of the National Revolutionary Committee spoke for the freedom fighting insurgents in a positive atmosphere, and the proposals will be presented to the cabinet by Imre Nagy, chairman of the Council of Ministers."[57]

Next Dudás held an international press conference in the building of the *Szabad Nép*, reporting on his talks with Imre Nagy. On the basis of what he head learnt, the American journalist Barett McGurn presented the chairman of the committee as a rival of Imre Nagy.[58] The political career of Dudás had reached its zenith at this time. He was in charge of an independent newspaper, he had an armed unit at his disposal, and had negotiated at the Parliament with the head of government Imre Nagy—the only one among the civilian commanders or revolutionary leaders to do so;[59] this was broadcast over the radio and communicated in several papers. Within a few days his name had become a houshold word, and elicited interest even among the foreign press.

There are sources which would place Dudás in a different light, if they could be verified: as lacking in character, uninhibited and unprincipled. According to these, Dudás resorted to underhanded maneuvers to discredit Imre Nagy in his struggle for power.

Lieutenant General Evgeny I. Malashenko, the chief of staff of the Special Army Corps of occupation, was an eyewitness to the events of 1956. According to him Dudás asked to be received by the Soviet commander in chief; he was disappointed when he was received not by Lieutenant General Piotr Lashchenko, the commander of the Special Forces in Hungary, but by his deputy, Malashenko.[60] "Dudás announced that he was the president of the National Revolutionary Committee, and the commander of all armed groups. He was acting against the Imre Nagy government, and he requested that we recognize the committee as Hungary's highest authority....The commander of every significant armed group was directed by him, including János Szabó and Iván Kovács [the commander of the Corvin group]. At that time he really did hold political and military power." He spoke of his antifascist record and his negotiations in Moscow; nevertheless, he gave the Soviet officer the impression of "being a political adventurer."[61] Thus Dudás tried to evoke a common nostalgia for the World War, and win over the sympathy of the occupation force to establish a foundation for his eventual power, behind the backs of the Hungarian political leaders.[62] The totality of the sources do not corroborate this degree of depravity in Dudás; I will not regard this source as authentic, unless supported by further evidence.

The other, more serious "charge" against Dudás, was that he was attempting to form an alternative government at Győr, on November 1. We do have a contemporary source about this, namely "The appeal of the Transdanubian National Council to the National Councils of the Nation," broadcast by Radio Győr at 6:25 P.M., on November 3, 1956.[63]

The program of Imre Nagy expresses the universal wishes of the nation....On November 1, the representative of some news bulletin, a journalist named József Dudás, made a proposal to the National Council for an alternative government. The people of Győr and of Transdanubia reject such proposals without hesitation. The National Council of Transdanubia declared the divisive forces to be traitors....

Although similar charges were raised against Dudás even after the defeat, I cannot accept such statements as factual. Anyone could have presented himself or herself as an agent of Dudás, without incurring any risks; or the eyewitnesses were mistaken about the name.[64]

HUNGARIAN INDEPENDENCE

After the evening of October 30 increasing numbers of old acquaintances came forth to meet Dudás and offer their assistance. He was able to raise the standard of his publication with their help. Rudolf Janesch had been a cell mate of Dudás in the early 50s for two weeks; he reported for duty, upon reading the paper. Janesch took over the technical aspects of publishing the newspaper, and many considered him the associate of Dudás. Another one who joined the staff after the paper was launched was the poet László Nyugati, who became the literary editor. Dudás found the writer József Kopré thanks to the secretary of the Eighth District Council; Dudás called by phone, asking for an "intelligent person, who could write."[65] Kopré was entrusted with the redaction of the cultural column but Dudás informed him, at the same time, that he could not leave the building without special permission. Two or three days later Kopré escaped.[66] György Gábori, an acquaintance from the internment camp, described his decision to join:

...I woke up when someone was banging at the door....Two young men were standing on the threshold, armed to the hilt...."We belong to the group of József Dudás," said the taller of the two. "We will take you to him" explained the shorter one....I tried to recall Jóska Dudás... the last I saw of him was in a cell at the internment camp. Even when beaten half to death he had enough energy to lead ten revolutions, and I had to realize that, even though I vowed not to get mixed up in the insurgency, I could not resist a request from Dudás.[67]

Egri and Gábori, the two regular journalists and editors, consulted with Dudás regarding the lead articles, raised the quality of the paper significantly, and functioned as political advisors.

On the night of October 30 Dudás held a briefing in order to win over those at headquarters—Sándor Fekete, Tibor Gellért, Pál Lőcsei, Vilmos Tóth. He did not succeed. Lőcsei belonged to a minority who were basically in agreement with Dudás, and offered to help in the typesetting of the first issue, but felt that his political views were too extreme. He did, however, warn Dudás that there had been a government paper with the title *Függetlenség* [Independence] in the Horthy era, and it is not a good idea if a revolutionary paper appears under the same title.[68] Dudás took the advice; after the next day the title appeared as *Magyar Függetlenség* [Hungarian Independence].

The writer Sándor Fekete has a much less favorable opinion, and agreed even less with his political ideas. According to him, Dudás insisted on—in addition to the already named three government members—including six members of the committee who would represent clearly revolutionary views. He wanted the key posts—defense and foreign affairs—to be awarded to two members of the committee.[69]

Dudás was most concerned with the editorials and the preservation of the committee's line. Between October 31 and November 3 the paper was printed in varying number of copies, between fifty and one hundred thousand.[70] It was the only daily which did not refrain from criticizing the government, especially its composition and its indecisiveness. Yet Dudás helped other papers edited in the building he controlled. ("There will be freedom, every party will have its place.")[71] He spent ten thousand forints of his savings on his paper.[72] The sums collected from the sale of the issues were locked in a safe, or were guarded by armed guards.

Two issues were printed on October 31[73] and both editorials were signed by Dudás. "The Armed Stage of the Revolutionary Struggle Ended in Victory"; he once again urged the transformation of the government, in such a manner that next to Imre Nagy, Béla Kovács, and János Kádár, a member of each of the democratic parties be included. "These persons would have to be from among those who had not lost the trust of the rank and file....Without wishing to interfere in the internal affairs of the parties, in our view Anna Kéthly, on the part of the Social Democrats, and on the part of the Smallholders Béla Kovács and Sándor Kiss, stand clean before the people of the country....The representatives of the insurgent freedom fighters must be the creative members of the government as guarantors of the achievement of the revolution."

The insurgent groups—whom Dudás wanted to represent—by that time did not sympathize with his partisanship because they saw in it a sign of divisiveness.

In his article "For Whom Is the Restoration of Order Not Urgent?" he again attacked the government, or to be more precise, some of its members: Münnich, Ferenc Erdei, and József Bognár. In the two-page issue there was repeated mention of the organization of the committee, the situation in the provinces, the international press reaction to the revolution, and the comments of Hungarian and Soviet leaders. The paper criticized the looters, and those who took the law into their own hands. It called for lawful justice, and expressed its wishes of remaining in good neighborly relations with the Soviet Union. It rejected the presence of foreign troops in the country. This declaration, in fact, contradicted a paragraph of the twenty-five point program, which called for the presence of UN troops.

Unfortunately the article remembered the most often is Richard Velvart's "Open Letter to László Benjamin," in which the author equates the followers of Imre Nagy with the Stalinists. This idea also appeared in the November 1 issue. This kind of criticism offended many, as they saw the change of direction by the reform Communist as a sincere act on their part.[74]

Dudás in this four-page issue wrote a lead article "Divide et Impera!" in which, much as earlier, he pressed for personnel changes in the government in the name of the "tumultuous crowd." It may be that it is in this writing that he contrasts most sharply the "retarding forces" with the "honorable and well meaning" Imre Nagy, who "supported by the Hungarian people and with the help of international law assures for the Hungarian nation freedom and independence, and the road of honorable socialism, which leads to progress." There is a mention of the preservation of the socialist economic system. "We do not return land, we fight against the monopoly capitalist restoration with the same force that knocked Rákosi and Gerő out of power."[75] The sources on Dudás's thoughts about private ownership are contradictory.[76]

On November 1, in the name of the Hungarian National Revolutionary Council, he launched a new daily, *Paraszt Függetlenség* [Peasant Independence]. This intended to support the reorganization of the Peasant Alliance [Parasztszövetség].[77]

In the editorial to the two-page November 2 morning issue of *Magyar Függetlenség*[78] Dudás listed the twenty-five points once again, as "reward for the fighters of the revolution," then summoned them to a new struggle, to return to work." Although "we may work with but one hand, for the other is still grasping the weapon," for news had arrived about the Soviet troop movements. A short item underneath informed the reader about the deployment of Soviet units, leading to the conclusion: "We may conclude from the battle array…that they have no intention of attacking." At the bottom Nagy's declaration of neutrality over the radio was printed. There was a report printed on the second page, with the caption, "Imre Nagy's Important Communication to Ambassador Andropov"; the prime minister protests the infiltration of Soviet units, demanding their immediate withdrawal. Moreover he announced that the country is withdrawing from the Warsaw Pact and requests the United Nations and four Great Powers to help defend its neutrality.

The noon and the evening issues were published with identical content. Dudás's name did not appear in subsequent issues as author, and we do not know whether he had a hand in the preparation of editorials but, considering his mounting problems, it is possible that he had but little time to devote to writing. The editorial "Do Not Harm the Hungarian!" [Ne bántsd a magyart!] stressed self-control, an end to the strike, while praising the government for the latest developments, noting that while the negative forces were still hanging around, they were not the ones taking decisions. He noted triumphantly: "the demands of the Hungarian National Revolutionary Committee, set in twenty-five points, has become the program of the government. We have concluded our struggle, we have won." The idea underlying the editorial on November 3 "This is justice and the truth!" [Ez az igazság!][79] was to clear the name of our protagonist from the charge of fascism, of belonging to the extreme right. Although such an assumption is clearly at odds with Dudás's life history, nevertheless several revolutionary leaders entertained quite negative opinions about him. This article presented a completely antitotalitarian position. If our analysis were limited to the *Magyar Függetlenség*, there is nothing there to suggest that Dudás was facing problems, even though he was less and less able to cope with them.

THE ARMED GROUP IN THE BUILDING OF THE *SZABAD NÉP*

Dudás always presented himself primarily as a leader of the freedom fighters, as a representative of their interests, and he tried his very best to be recognized as the commander in chief of the insurgents of Budapest; this objective, however, had no basis in fact. He did not even enjoy unchallenged control over his own armed group, for András Kovács and others told him, from the outset, that they would brook no interference in their work. They told the chairman of the National Revolutionary Committee: "Dear Dudás, you worry about politics, we take care of restoring order!"[80] At the beginning, however, their collaboration was effective, if not without friction. Dudás could not deliver commands, but did entrust the armed group with specific tasks which they would then execute on their own. Our protagonist became well-known to the public, but those on the outside knew nothing about the internal relations; moreover, the identity cards of the insurgents were all signed by Dudás. They used the designation "Dudás group" throughout. It may been more appropriate to refer to them as the group from the *Szabad Nép*, as Péter A. Baló recommends.[81]

The occupation of the paper's headquarters elicited resentment among some; in fact, some armed groups were preparing to attack. One journalist turned for help to Lieutenant Colonel János Solymosi, who dispatched two armored vehicles and twenty-five infantrymen, to "reconnoiter." The next day Solymosi was visited by the same journalist who argued that although order was restored in the building, Dudás should be arrested nevertheless. The Ministry of Defense did not endorse the action, and there was no concerted attack.[82]

Sándor Kopácsi, the head of the Budapest Department of the Ministry of the Interior, set off to "liberate" the building on October 30, probably on instructions from the Minister of the Interior Ferenc Münnich. Colonel Kopácsi wanted to avoid a confrontation, therefore he arranged for a fake skirmish.[83] The National Guard of the Alliance of University and College Student Unions [Magyar Egyetemi és Főiskolai Egyesületek Szövetsége [MEFESZ] was also preparing to attack. As their leader recalls, "we were already on the bridge, when they called off the mission."[84]

We also have indications that soldiers were getting ready to recapture the building on the night of November 1 and 2, with Imre Nagy's consent.[85] The leaders of the All-National Committee [Országos Nemzeti Bizottság] were planning to blow up the electric cables leading to the *Szabad Nép* building.[86] The defenders of the building, however, were able to avert the dangers coming from the outside.[87]

There were between 120 and 150 armed fighters in the building. The nucleus of the group had come over from Széna Square on October 29, and were joined by others along the way, whereas yet others had been active in the building or its vicinity all along. The core group numbered about 80 to 100, the others were in and out. Their leader all along was András (alias "Bandi") Kovács, there was no debate about that. He had a confident demeanor, energy, toughness that went along with his military experience, going back to the siege of Budapest in 1945 when, as a thirteen-year old, he fought against the Red Army. These qualities were obvious from the beginning, as discipline soon prevailed, under his direction. There were others who assisted in the leadership.[88]

Having organized guard duty, they began to ferret out and charge the members of the ÁVH, and party officials. This activity took place in spite of Dudás's protests, and more consistently than happened in the case of other groups. In fact, there was more than one "special section" within the building to conduct this operation. Several of their members had been recently released, or were just released from incarceration at

Tiszaplakony. The best known among them was the brigade referred to as "Head-hunters," [Fejvadászok] led by the fifty-three-year old stoker Ferenc Pálházi (alias "Feri bácsi"—Uncle Feri). It is said that Pálházi and András Kovács fought in the same battalion in 1945.[89]

This squad proved itself more relentless than any other in the city. The reason may be that the members of the Headhunters were bitter people who had been severely tortured by the ÁVH.[90] Among them three had served in the French Foreign Legion.[91] The brigade may have numbered between twenty-five to thirty members. On November 2, on orders from András Kovács, they installed themselves in the Corvin Department Store, and their task included maintaining order within that building.[92] The Headhunters worked separately from all other units, and secretively.

Another squad, far less well known, was called the "Little Lambs" [Báránykák], made up of twenty to thirty persons. They were directly under the command of the commander in chief, actually his bodyguard, inasmuch as Bandi felt they were the most reliable. They scoured the city together.[93] It was generally believed in the city that ÁVH agents were detained at the *Szabad Nép* building, for strangers would often come to deliver prisoners they deemed suspicious. Hence there were some organized as prison guards.

The sources agree that in the unbridled anti-ÁVH atmosphere, the tone was rude, the detained were threatened. Few of our sources, however, mention that they were physically harmed. Dudás paid a visit to the detained on two occasions, and tried to insist on moderation.[94] Later, until November 3, they were transferred to police headquarters on Deák Square, or to the National Police Headquarters [Országos Főkapitányság] (ORK) building on Mari Jászai Square. The measure was proposed by Dudás, while Kovács and his troops went along.[95] Several members of the group participated in the siege of Party headquarters on Köztarsaság Square, but we have no detailed evidence.

On November 1 further officers from the Zrínyi Military Academy came over: Captains Jenő Kiss and László Kovács, and Lieutenant Szilárd Székfy. Sergeant Gyula Andrásy assigned each of them to head a squad, and placed Lieutenant of the Engineers Sándor Rónyai in charge of the entire detachment. Their task was the preservation of order in the streets. András Kovács objected that they should not be appointed platoon commanders, since the personnel already present might take umbrage. On November 3 he asked them to supervise the military preparedness of the platoons, the commanders, and help with training, in the proper use of arms. At the same time he made it clear that they did not have the right to give orders, only the right to make comments, in his presence.

In the meantime Dudás's relations with Kovács was deteriorating. He did not approve of the group's main activity, headhunting, but more than likely he was not happy about his diminishing control over the armed group.[96] According to András Kovács Dudás had no inkling about military affairs and, in any case, his trust had been shaken, since he felt Dudás was switching allies rather often, or may even be a turncoat, who did not have the aims of the revolution consistently at heart.[97] On his part Dudás felt: "...I can say with full responsibility, that he is a rather dangerous man, because every one of his actions is driven by considerations of personal vengeance....As regards his character he is a rabid anarchic type, an anarchist who was able to get hold of weapons, and use them at his discretion. He took advantage of the confusion to carry out vendettas."[98]

On October 31 Dudás asked Captain Pál Arnóczki, an officer from the Zrínyi Military Academy, to use his men to disarm Kovács and the main spokespersons, and take over their assignments. Indeed, the captain showed up the next day with ten officers, but did not confront Kovács, because the latter made it quite clear that he was not about to hand over command to the officers without a fight.[99]

In spite of all this there was no open rift between Dudás and Kovács, their collaboration continued.[100] Their rivalry became acute only from November 2 on, but the insurgents from "the outside" were at odds with Dudás already earlier.

AT THE CONFERENCE OF THE REVOLU-TIONARY MILITARY COMMITTEE

The revolutionaries at the *Szabad Nép* building—the journalists, workers and armed personnel there—were personified almost exclusively by József Dudás to the outside world, in an increasingly negative light.

The first negative manifestations became apparent at the conference of the Revolutionary Military Committee held within the Kilián
barracks. The participants resented the fact that Dudás did not appear in
person and were even more incensed by the statement of his representative, Tibor Zimányi, that those of the national committee had no
desire to join the united National Guard, then being formed. Thereupon
Pál Maléter argued in favor of ostracism, and after the meeting he was
the one who had the most negative assessment of Dudás.[101] Just about
all of the commanders of insurgents in Pest were severely critical.[102]
They felt that Dudás was suffering from megalomania, having named
himself chairman of the Revolutionary National Committee. Only the
group from Széna Square remained loyal to him.[103]

The isolation of Dudás and his armed group at the *Szabad Nép*
building continued in the following days; he continued not to recognize
the authority of the National Guard, ignoring its prescriptions. He continued to distribute identification cards with his own signature, even to
the insurgents on the other side of the city, at Széna Square. He rejected the groups of insurgents and their leaders operating in his immediate vicinity. He felt they owed him obedience, for he was far older than
they and had a wealth of political experience.[104]

Dudás thus refused to cooperate with the insurgents to any extent,
even though he acted in their name. Such tactics were awkward, since
they revealed that he was intent on personal gratification. Even his
loyal followers admitted as much. Relying on documentary sources, we
may even add: the fact that Dudás became the inflexible spokesperson
of the insurgents and of the "people" only after October 26 raises
issues, although his caution may be explained by his vicissitudes in the
past. The insurgents, however, never attacked him for not having taken
part in the armed resistance, they probably never even knew, and they
probably never knew that a day earlier he tried to present himself as the
commander in chief of the insurgents to the Committee of Intellectuals
and to Imre Nagy—further evidence of his megalomania. No one else
had such ambitions during the revolution.

At the same time the government deemed his activities increasingly
embarassing, and reached a crushing decision in his regard on November
1: "The Council of Ministers deems it necessary to liquidate the Dudás
group, therefore Imre Nagy will talk to Dudás and, should such talks

bear no fruit, will authorize Pal Maléter, the first deputy of the minister of defense, to arrest Dudás and continue the talks with one of his lieutenants."[105] Dudás, however, never lost his self-confidence.

THE PREDICAMENT OF THE HUNGA-RIAN REVOLUTIONARY NATIONAL COMMITTEE

In addition to the interests of the insurgents, Dudás often referred to the Hungarian Revolutionary National Committee, of which he was the chairman. He called his newspaper the explicit organ of this organization. The committee had been established on October 29 in the second district and, as we have already mentioned, Dudás attempted to place it on a wider foundation once he reached the building of the *Szabad Nép*. At his request, Rudolf Janesch read his proclamation to all the district councils over the telephone, between October 30 and 31:

> I call upon the revolutionary committees working with the district councils, to establish contact with the district police. The police received similar instructions from the Police Headquarters of Budapest (BRFK), that they should form mixed night patrols with the armed men of the committees. All those disturbing the peace, the shooters, drunks, and looters should be disarmed and brought over to the Police Headquarters of Budapest.[106]

The task of József Kopré was to distribute the twenty-five-point program in the Council building of the eighth district and to establish the local branch of the Hungarian Revolutionary National Committee.[107] Indeed, on October 30 and 31 Dudás announced a congress to be held with the participation of all revolutionary and freedom fighting organization at the Sports Hall, albeit in the November 1 issue he printed a proclamation according to which the meeting would be indefinitely postponed, for security reasons "because the Soviet forces around Budapest are…making it most difficult to participate." Nevertheless, by then delegations had come from the local committees in twenty towns across the country; from the Council building in the second district, they were redirected to the building of the *Szabad Nép*.[108] Thanks to the *Magyar Függetlenség* Dudás had a following in the country, even though he did not have enough energy left to turn it into a truly nationwide organization. Thus the Hungarian Revolutionary National Committee never existed as a truly national committee; Dudás merely used it as a bluff, to disguise the fact that there was no real power backing him.[109] The organization only prospered in a single district, the one where it was launched; Dudás was not very successful in exploiting his initial success.

On October 29, after Dudás left the meeting on Leó Frankel Street, establishing the committee, he was in contact with his followers in Buda infrequently, by phone; they in turn realized they would have to do without the presence of their charismatic leader. The direction of the organization was assumed by the attorney Tamás Pásztor, former Smallholder Party MP and by the apprentice Zoltán Kovács, formerly a financial expert.[110] The next day they were joined by the civil servant Tibor Seifert, who took care of the military affairs in the second district and earned the respect of all. Therefore First Secretary Zoltán Kovács awarded Seifert the rank of lieutenant colonel for his "merits earned during the revolution"—which was to result in serious complications. Until then Seifert had been merely corporal in the reserves, but he did everything possible to earn a promotion and become the supervisor of the officers around him, even officially.[111] Zoltán Kovács appreciated his work and intervened on his behalf. There is some disagreement among witnesses as to the manner in which he intervened, although this became an important issue during the revolution, as well as during the reprisals. Kovács had always claimed that he had consulted with Dudás before the appointment, and the latter gave instructions to that effect.[112] Seifert also claimed that Dudás had agreed to the promotion, and it was reported in the press.[113] Dudás himself, however, denied this, saying he gave orders merely to maintain law and order, that is, he ordered Kovács to appoint military commanders to head each armed group.[114] Probably, since Dudás had neither the time nor the means to verify what was happening on Leó Frankel Street, he trusted Pásztor and Kovács sufficiently to make it possible for them to promote Seifert, thus contributing to his appointment.[115]

On the morning of November 2 Dudás intended to hold a review of the forces on Széna Square, in the company of General Béla Király, the commander of the National Guard, with the participation of the military, the police and the National Guardsmen.[116] Dudás enjoyed considerable prestige in the district. Pásztor, Kovács, and Seifert were in agreement that Dudás's expectations must be met at the highest level.[117] They organized the review very thoroughly, down to the last detail.[118] But they waited in vain for, as it turned out after an hour and a half, Dudás was involved in an activity he deemed more important.

FOREIGN JOURNALISTS CALL ON DUDÁS

At the time scheduled for the review Dudás was on the phone with Stockholm. Then he received a visit from the reporters of the Italian illustrated magazine *Epoca*, Massimo Monicelli[119] and Mario de Biasi. By then Dudás presented himself not only as the leader of the insurgents, but also of the civilian revolutionary forces, who had control over university students, intellectuals and soldiers not assigned to units. According to the published report he was in constant contact with Imre Nagy, and he represented the interests and demands of civilian revolutionaries. His assessment of conditions had not changed in days: "The government tries to stay on top. At this moment it enjoys rather little power. Order in Budapest is assured by the insurgents and groups of revolutionaries." He explained his two principal demands: the withdrawal of the Soviets and the transformation of the government. Nevertheless the report presented Dudás as an experienced, careful politician, who considered both the domestic and foreign implications of events, and was far from representing extreme radical views.[120]

The same undaunted confidence is reflected in an interview with the Polish journalists, Hanka Adamiecka, Marian Beilecki and Wiktor Woroszylski, on November 1. The latter devoted a whole chapter of his book to this interview, under the title "The Leader of the Band."[121] It appears from this and from Adamiecka's report[122] that the Polish journalists were far less impressed by Dudás than the Italians had been.

He is tall, with broad shoulders, his hair is dark brown, his face large, with somewhat prominent cheekbones; expressive, but rather repulsive....A pistol concealed in his belt, black galoshes. He steps into the room like a courtier....

We ask Dudás to define the movement he represents....He blurts out four attributes: national, revolutionary, democratic, socialist...."The government must be complemented by representatives from the traditional democratic parties. But we must not tolerate right-wing or fascist groupings...."

His statements remain at the level of generalities, that we must owe respect for the political astuteness of our conversation partner. We try to corner him, asking him how he relates to the existing political parties, or does he intend to form a new one?

"For the time being it is a matter of consolidating the achievements of the revolution so far. Later, if the situation continues to improve, I will probably join a party that conforms to the above-mentioned goals."

Which party appeals to you most?

"None of them have a clear economic program. All democratic parties are agreed on the basic political issues, so they are equally appealing to me."

Do you support the present government?

"Only in part. I could completely support a coalition government only if it were to include Imre Nagy, János Kádár, Béla Kovács, Anna Kéthly, Sándor Kiss, and the representative of the [Hungarian] National Revolutionary Committee."

It is not hard to guess who he has in mind. During the conversation it becomes increasingly clear that József Dudás, quite apart from his program, is driven by personal ambition. This becomes obvious at the end of our conversation.

"Our next tasks are to form a coalition government, reach an agreement with the Russians regarding the schedule for their withdrawal from Hungary, announce the date for free, universal and secret elections, create order and peace in the country.

In order to resolve all these issues I got in touch with Moscow and recommended joint measures to restore order. I also proposed a government such as the one I described to you."

I don't know if what I now hear is just an ordinary bluff, or has some basis in reality. In any case, the aspirations of Dudás are not very modest. But who is this man, leader of the [Hungarian] National Revolutionary Committee, who publishes his own paper, surrounds himself with the paraphernalia of a Cossack ataman, brags about "his contacts with Moscow" and declares in an interview with Polish journalists that he wants to participate in the Hungarian government? Is he really a fascist?[123] What would be the indication? Or is he merely the leader of a band, an adventurer, a "strongman" who strives for personal popularity and power? If that is the case, does Dudás constitute a danger to the revolution of the people? And how many other Dudás are there in this country?

The Polish journalists, who enjoyed the hospitality of the headquarters for days on end, do not appear to have preconceptions. They emphasized also that Dudás did not prevent others from publishing papers, not even the staff of the *Szabad Nép* who are now publishing the *Népszabadság*.[124] They found the young freedom fighters who were staying there, the loyal followers of Dudás, very likable.[125]

INCIDENT AT THE MINISTRY OF FOREIGN AFFAIRS[126]

Two SOS messages came from the Ministry of Foreign Affairs in the afternoon of November 2 to the effect that there were a hundred members of the ÁVH hiding in the building of the ministry.[127] Seifert decided that he will investigate, but there is no evidence indicating that he had consulted with anyone. He called the base of the Széna Square group on Maros Street—where the majority of the insurgents and their commanders were stationed—but, since he could not reach commander János Szabó, he instructed the person who picked up the phone to send out two squads under the leadership of competent officers to the Ministry of Foreign Affairs, and arrest the ÁVH members; if they were to attempt to break out, they must be targeted. Seifert turned to the insurgents for want of anything better, since he felt they were lacking in discipline. There was no one else to whom he could entrust the mission. In fact, he ordered the commander of the Bem barracks not to interfere in the combing through of the ministry building.[128]

In accordance with the orders, about fifty insurgents surrounded the building under the command of First Lieutenant Mészáros. Mészáros proceeded to the entrance with twenty men, placing the rest of his troops in firing position. He warned them that a counterattack of the ÁVH group could be expected both from the top floor and the attic. He instructed them that, if they heard three shots, that would be a signal to launch an assault immediately.

"All of sudden the gate opened and about twenty armed men poured in. They were shouting threats at the top of their lungs," the ministry employees recalled. They were forced to raise their hands and stand against the wall. Mészáros informed them that he had come with an open command, their mission was to search the building, capture the ÁVH members in hiding, and he began to conduct a body search. If a weapon was found, that person was told to stand apart, to be charged. The guards were disarmed. Having body-searched the personnel he led his men to scour the building. One employee guided the insurgents through the offices; then they searched the basement and the attic. Since they did not have the key to the iron grill barring entrance to the personnel department, they fired three shots to bust the lock open. The insurgents on the outside took that as the agreed-upon signal and started firing at the building, blowing out the windows. Those on the inside assumed their comrades were under fire, and joined in on the shooting. No one got hurt, but there was some damage.[129]

In the meantime the personnel in the ministry notified the Ministry of Defense, and Colonel László Zólomy was instructed to intervene. The people at the Széna Square command and the Second District Council were also notified about the shooting, but by the time one of the deputy commanders of the insurgents and Seifert—in the uniform of a lieutenant colonel—had reached, the shooting had stopped, and everyone realized there were no members of the ÁVH hiding in the building. Zólomy asked to see the identification of some of the insurgents and blamed the damages on them.[130]

Finally General Béla Király arrived. He also blamed the insurgents, and ordered Mészáros to lead his unit back to his district. Then Király turned to Seifert. Noting the uniform, he inquired about the unit to which Seifert was assigned. "I informed him that I was the military commander of the second district, I had been appointed as lieutenant colonel by the National Committee of the district, and I presented my orders. Király declared that they were not valid, and said something along the lines that Dudás was always in his way. Király instructed his officers to have me arrested."[131] Király confiscated his pistol personally.

At the Ministry of Defense, Király asked Seifert about the whereabouts of Dudás, and wanted to know who Dr. Zoltán Kovács was, what gave him the right to issue documents promoting people. Within an hour or two the "lieutenant colonel" was made to confront Dudás, who was summoned by Béla Király and company, then was arrested upon arrival.[132] They did not know one another. Thus Király held Zoltán Kovács and Seifert responsible not only for the action against the ministry, but for the illegal promotion as well.[133] Once the misunderstanding had been cleared a more cordial relationship evolved between the general and Dudás.

Our protagonist made a promise that he would attend the conference of the National Guard on Deák Square the following day and join the body.[134] Then he used the moment to his advantage to get rid of András Kovács with the help of the general, and secure the allegiance of the armed people in the *Szabad Nép* building.[135] Kovács was enticed according to a plan by Béla Király; he was arrested in the building of the Military Court of Budapest on Fő Street, after Mrs. Dudás[136] sent the message that he should bring over one of the ÁVH prisoners.[137] The next morning, however, he was released upon orders from the government.

Dudás was released that very evening by Király, even though he had received orders to the contrary from the office of the prime minister.[138]   The incident at the Ministry of Foreign Affairs, however, was the final blow to the prestige and good name of Dudás,[139] a process that became irreversible.

RUNNING THE GAUNTLET ON NOVEMBER 3

The events at the Ministry of Foreign Affairs were reported in the *Magyar Honvéd* [Hungarian Soldier] on the morrow. Also on November 3 Dudás became involved in a dubious banking affair. A call came from the National Bank to István Benedek, in charge of the Szikra Publishers operating in the same building, that, as successors to the *Szabad Nép* they were entitled to collect 500,000 forints earmarked for the Party newspaper. Dudás sent two of his men to collect the funds, but the bank refused to disburse the sum, since the deputy finance minister had not signed off. Albeit he failed, it is obvious that Dudás was intent on securing the money, if not for his personal gain, nevertheless without being entitled to it. The attack on the Ministry of Foreign Affairs, the bank affair, the occupation of the building of the *Szabad Nép*, his destabilizing activities prompted the decision of the political and military leaders to finally remove Dudás from his position, and to deal with one of his deputies instead.[140]

András Kovács was singled out as the negotiating partner; he would leave for Deák Square, for the headquarters of the National Guard, but not without the escort of his armed men.[141] Here he was received by Sándor Kopácsi. "I informed him that the Dudás group did not meet the standards to join the National Guard. Kovács said we should give him a bit of time to find a way of getting rid of Dudás, because there are many in the group who trust in him. He is willing to recognize the program of the government and subject himself to the command and rules of the National Guard. He promised to abstain from all arbitrary acts. I told him if it was more than just a promise, but the promise is validated by the removal of Dudás, then we can continue our discussion....Indeed, Kovács made it clear that he did not identify with Dudás and was willing to subject his group to the authority of the Revolutionary Military Committee."[142] Dudás remained unaware of all this.

The conference of the National Guard was soon to start at police headquarters—attended, in addition to ranking military and police officials, by the commanders of most of the significant groups of insurgents in the capital. Under the impression that Kovács had been arrested, Dudás showed up at Deák Square and tried to promote one of his men to fill an important position and be accepted as a delegate to the conference.[143] It is difficult to understand how he could have failed to realize how unpopular he had become among those in attendance.

The first speaker was a member of the *Szabad Nép* group, the university student Sándor Varga, who attacked Béla Király for the arrest of András Kovács, and declared that he and his group will boycott collaboration until Kovács is released.[144] Király informed him that this has already happened. Then Dudás and company became the target of attacks. They were blamed for their oft criticized behavior; moreover they were scolded on the basis of all the rumors floating around, warranted or not. The barbs were so poisonous that, according to some, physical confrontation was imminent. Király, however, intervened to state that he had given his word of honor that, should Dudás come to the conference and explain his objectives, he would not be harmed.

Almost all the representatives of the civilians groups ostracized Dudás, even more so than before. No one was willing to collaborate with Dudás except for the delegates of the insurgents of Széna Square. They even passed a resolution that those carrying identification cards issued by the Hungarian Revolutionary National Committee will have their weapons confiscated. At this point, however, the armed men accompanying Dudás took matters in their own hands and dismissed both Dudás and György Márton. One of the deputy commanders of the group from Szabad Nép promised that his group would subject themselves to the leadership of the National Guard. György Márton and Sergeant Andrásy intervened to say that they would recognize only András Kovács as their commander, they would consider no one else.[145]

Dudás, however, refused to give up. He asked for support from the Zrínyi Military Academy to "teach his mutineering deputy commanders a lesson."[146] Commander Colonel András Márton promised military assistance, provided he changed the tone of his newspaper, the *Magyar Függetlenség*.[147]

András Márton, who had been appointed commander of the defense forces of Budapest by that time, was summoned to the Parliament, where he was ordered by Minister of Defense Maléter to arrest Dudás, for reasons already mentioned.[148] Lieutenant Colonel Lajos Teleki arrested Dudás, in the name of the chairman of the Council of Ministers, in the building of the Zrínyi Military Academy, but András Márton released him soon thereafter, probably because he felt the arrest was unjustified. The military leaders—Király and Márton—had no desire to function as police; they were probably concerned that the arrest of Dudás would destabilize the situation. (Presumably Márton was unaware of the loss of prestige by Dudás.)

Dudás requested help from András Márton against the "mutineers" a second time. He believed that once Kovács and György Márton were removed, the others would rally to him again. In exchange he promised the colonel that he would make the facilities in the building available for a new government daily. Márton, however, did not wish to commit the military academy in the affair of the *Szabad Nép* building. He only gave Dudás a revolver, offered him a place of refuge, and had him escorted back by two officers. Back in the building Dudás supervised the galleys for the next issue—the mutineers did not stop him.

SOVIET INTERVENTION

On November 4 the armed personnel in the building heard alarming noises from the street. "We heard the loud rumble of tanks rolling in from the direction of the boulevard. On somebody's orders the lights were extinguished along the corridor leading to the boulevard....From the dark room we could observe the Soviet tanks roll by."[149]

Dudás arrived soon after. Motivated by Imre Nagy's appeal over the radio, he summoned the civilian and military commanders, giving them instructions: we must build barricades with the help of the civilian population, acquire weapons, prepare bottles of fuel. He appointed personnel responsible for carrying out each of these tasks.

The commanders of the squads got to work; evidently, at this stage, the Soviet tanks were not attacking, merely passing through. Dudás and Kovács continued their discussion in an office, over a map.[150] The guard at the gates were given orders not to allow anyone out of the building without orders.

Then Dudás got in touch with the headquarters of the National Guard—Colonel Kopácsi in person; the latter objected to armed resistance, given the overwhelming military superiority of the Soviets, and even suggested that the barricades be taken down. Our protagonist fully accepted the recommendation, and was about to issue orders countermanding his previous orders. Consequently he got into an argument with András Kovács far more intense than their earlier disagreements and, since he got the lower end in the confrontation, he withdrew with five of his followers to "sulk" in a distant cellar.[151]

In the meantime the confrontations with the Soviets had already begun. During the fighting György Márton had Dudás returned as a prisoner. András Kovács confronted him because of his latest orders calling for the dismantling of the barricades and halting all resistance, and even informed him that he was under arrest for the betrayal of the cause of the revolution. Then he declared that Dudás may continue as editor of the paper, but only under watch and, should he resist, he could expect "the worst." Thus our protagonist was arrested for the third time in two days.

The fighting became intense during the night, and the *Szabad Nép* building suffered serious damage from the projectiles fired by the Soviet tanks. Dudás was hurt by the blast and his wife fell ill also. Finally they were able to escape to the Rókus hospital with the help of Lt. Sándor Rónyai, where they were admitted as patients.[152] The fighters at headquarters killed all their captives at night, including the prosecutor István Sarkadi, ÁVH First Lieutenant Pál Fodor, and probably even a Soviet soldier, more than likely with the authorization of András Kovács; this caused no measure of harm to their reputation, and to the reputation of Dudás, who had nothing to do with it.

The vulnerability of the building became increasingly obvious, therefore the group transferred to the nearby food market, and continued to resist, in dwindling numbers, until the late hours of November 7. Then it dispersed.

DUDÁS UNDER ARREST

The Dudás couple remained in the Rókus hospital until November 8; then, because of the poor conditions there, transferred to the MÁV [Hungarian Railways] hospital. Dudás was still suffering from the blast and from a wound in the leg, and had to wait ten days to recover and leave. His wife went out into the city; while observing the rules of conspiracy, met with her husband's follower, György Gábori, who recommended escape abroad, since the security police of the puppet Kádár government was on the tracks of her husband. He offered to help with the escape. Dudás would not hear of it, even though his "banditism" was the subject of conversation all over town.[153]

In the November 15 issue of *Népszabadság*, in connection with his negotiations with the Budapest Workers' Council delegates, János Kádár was forced to manufacture legends wholesale. Here we only stress that he attributed his own betrayal of the revolutionary government to the role played by "Dudás and his kind": "They robbed and looted while pretending to be the representatives of a patriotic uprising. They visited the government to negotiate. Then I realized that there could never be democracy built on such foundations, nor independence, give them another week and they would have cut Imre Nagy out of the coalition. Then I resolved to resign from the cabinet."

We must agree with the assessment of Péter A. Baló: "Kádár on the defensive, because he was relying on the exclusive support of Soviet arms, in his cornered situation pointed the finger at Dudás, who because of his paper was the best known revolutionary leader, with the excesses of bandits that was for Kádár the 'patriotic uprising.'[154] In the dictionary of the new regime the name of Dudás, whose reputation was not so good even during the revolution, became synonymous with reactionary."[155]

Dudás became aware of the contents of this article only on November 18, but he was still hoping in some kind of a turnaround. He wrote a letter to Kádár:

> To Mr. Prime Minister János Kádár!
> We speak and write only the truth. We are obligated to the as yet unburied masses of heroes who gave their life for freedom and independence, who confronted the delusions and pack of lies, even as they took up arms for democracy, for human freedom and socialism.
> Therefore I am asking for correction, but even the start of peaceful construction would demand such objectivity; I regret that the *Népszabadság* would revive calumnies against me, more fitting for the Rákosi era, and allow Mr. Prime Minister to make statements on the basis of false information.
> For the sake of truth, about myself I will only say that I spent six years in the jails of the fascists, and eight more in Rákosi's jail. I did not collect any funds from the National Bank, I did not break into department stores in order to distribute the goods and enhance my popularity. As the chairman of the [Hungarian] Revolutionary National Committee I was of assistance in publishing the *Nép-*

szabadság, the paper of the Hungarian Socialist Workers' Party. I call upon editor in chief Szántó who, in my opinion, has the duty to speak up on my behalf in this matter. My politics are reflected in the editorials and appeals printed in the *Magyar Függetlenség* under my by-line. On several occasions I urged the initiation of socialist life on the broadest, most democratic and constitutional base. There were no right-wing or fascist slogans whatsoever in our program; to the contrary, we definitely rejected all thought of returning the plants and large estates into private ownership.

The withdrawal of Soviet troops, the defense of socialism, the resumption of work is suffering major setbacks; the road to development is outlined in the recommendations of the workers' councils, the revolutionary youth, the intellectuals; we only wish to add, on behalf of the national committee, that the workers' councils, the university youth, the Writers' Association, etc. should participate in the work of restoring order.

Such a declaration by the Soviet government would go a long way to consolidate trust and friendship. It would clarify the issue on the international stage as well, strengthen world peace and, at the same time, deliver a blow to the warmongering groups. It would provide protection against nefarious rumors, promote peaceful evolution and the start off production.

An unequivocal statement of the government in favor of a multiparty system—of course, we only need progressive democratic parties, and not counterrevolutionary or reactionary groups—would make it impossible for backward forces to create further disturbances.

As of November 5 severe wounds have hampered me in my work. Since that time I have had no discussions with anyone, and it is only now that I find out about the attacks, untrue, without foundation. I desire to serve socialism and democracy, within the framework of Hungarian independence, with all my might. I did not covet recognition or position for myself. I am willing to make every effort for the sake of preserving the achievements of the revolution and start the work of construction.

It has come to my attention that there are posters with the imprimatur of the [Hungarian Revolutionary] National Committee, produced by unauthorized persons who have no right to it. I disapprove of these and reject them.[156]

Thus Dudás had in mind collaboration with Kádár on a compromise basis, referring to what they had in common: their antifascist past and the jails of Rákosi. Starting from what was possible, he gave up one of the two most basic points of his program, the withdrawal of Soviets, but continued to advocate a multiparty system. He trusted in the leader of the Hungarian Socialist Workers' Party (MSZMP), probably assuming that with his rule over the entire country the process of destalinization would continue, even if by other than revolutionary means.

It is hard to understand how Dudás, with his wealth of political experience, could have been naive enough to believe that constructive collaboration with Kádár and company was possible. Although there were others who elaborated plans for consolidation in those days, and because in the period of "dual power," the new leaders, given the minimal support they received, were indeed forced to negotiate with other political factors, Dudás should have known that he would never qualify as a negotiating partner, to the contrary. Apparently he could not overcome the delusion of playing the role of a "revolutionary leader"— although this time he made it clear that he was not driven by personal ambition. He should have realized by then that, apart from his wife, there was no one on his side. (Almost all his closest friends and followers had left the country by then.)

Upon leaving the hospital, Dudás spent a few days with relatives of his wife. That is where he heard that Kádár was preparing to have a discussion with the leaders of the workers' councils and national committees in two days, in the Parliament building, and he too was expected to attend. "On November 20 I said that the next day I would look up Kádár and contribute to the resumption of work."[157] By then he was dogged by feelings of insecurity. He told his wife that should he not return within two hours, she should notify the Writers' Association that he had been arrested. Then he voluntarily walked into the trap: upon entering the building of the Parliament, he was arrested by Soviet counterintelligence.

CAPTIVITY, TRIAL, DEATH

Upon instructions from a Soviet general, the day after his arrest Dudás composed an appeal "to the Hungarian people" to return to work immediately.[158] The Soviet leaders—Mikhail Suslov, Averky Aristov, and Serov, led by Georgy Malenkov—held discussions with Kádár, as well as Münnich, and "agreed" that six to eight dangerous "counterrevolutionaries" should be court-martialed immediately, for that body had the authority to bring about death sentences rapidly in the name of "socialist justice." "The court-martial—as the Hungarian comrades say—is a rather prestigious judicial court in the eyes of the people which, if passing a death sentence by hanging or firing squad, would have the right impact on the country. The Hungarian comrades, thanks to Serov" designated Dudás among others.[159] They only needed an excuse to place him in front of a military court, but that was not difficult, for Dudás held command over the unit dispatched to the building of the *Szabad Nép*, and tried to propagandize them to back his committee.[160] Once in captivity Dudás composed his opinion regarding the revolution and his own role, as follows:

The cause of the revolution were the mistaken policies of the Rákosi and Gerő clique. It broke out spontaneously, the various committees multiplied like mushrooms and the government failed to restore order and maintain revolutionary virtues at the same time in this confusion; nor could others, such as myself, achieve success along those lines. All this took place in just five days, the events overlapped in rapid succession, huge masses of humanity, not attached to any unit, moved around with weapons in their hands....It was at this point that I intervened in the events, sure enough, with limited results I must admit, but with good intentions; from the many good intentions, one became reality. Between October 28 and November 3 the National Guard was established, there was no looting, the revolutionary forces overcame the reactionary forces and I can say, with a clear conscience, that I was progressing on the side of the revolutionary forces: I published the paper and acted against those who would hold us back. During those five days, as during my entire life, as a true son of my people, I fought for the continued achievements of democracy and socialism, with what little talent was available to me.[161]

We have no reason to doubt the sincerity of this confession. Dudás must have realized by then that he had committed numerous mistakes during the revolution.

He faced the Special Tribunal of the Military College of the Supreme Court, along with János Szabó, the commander of the insurgents at Széna Square. The chairman of the tribunal was Judge Advocate Ferenc Ledényi. Although the death sentence was passed on Soviet "advice," on January 8, 1957, even before the proceedings began, they wanted to preserve the semblance of legality. This is indicated by the participation of several witnesses for the defense. Attorney Emil Zarubay did everything possible on behalf of his "client." He argued well, he was able to prove that no act of violence could be tied to Dudás's participation, that, in fact, he did his best to restrain others. He referred to the declaration of amnesty, still in effect.

During the trial and in his petitions Dudás denied the charges, often distorting the facts, sometimes even resorting to tactics. In his final statement he chose to be more defiant: "my conscience was clear," he argued,

I could have escaped to the West, or gone into hiding....I did not aspire to power. If I must die, I will die for the cause of Hungarian freedom, if what I had done was more counterrevolutionary than revolutionary. I did not relinquish an iota from the achievements of socialism. The international situation evolved in such a way, in the case of Suez, that Hungary's position could hardly have been different. I have faith in the will to live, the determination of the Hungarian people. My condemnation means that the counterrevolution gets off scot-free. At the same time it rebukes the reputation of the proletarian society of honorable workers.[162]

On January 14 the tribunal announced the death sentence. The justification did not demean his role in the worker's movement and it was mentioned, as an extenuating circumstance, that he had not indulged in acts of cruelty, in fact tried to prevent such acts; he allowed the publication of the *Népszabadság*, and provided identification cards for its staff. It was admitted that many of his articles had socialist overtones, calling for the resumption of work, for the cessation of arbitrary acts, of looting, speaking in favor of public ownership. What is perhaps most surprising—there was not one word about the attack on the Ministry of Foreign Affairs, nor even about the illegal promotion. All this, however, proved insufficient, because the writings in his paper were deemed unqualified rabble-rousing. He gave instructions to state authorities, he undertook decisions within the purview of state authorities, bypassing the government: turning to the United Nations, and abrogating the Warsaw Pact. His demands for the armed elements served to promote anarchy. He was also indirectly responsible for the activities of András Kovács and company. He procured weapons for them. Originally, he was the one who gave the commands; if he could not handle them, why did he not leave the premises? Thus his rule was aggravated by "Kovács and his band." He was accused at length of misleading people by referring to a non-existent national committee: "...all of this was done deliberately, and he saw this as the only road to convert the Hungarian Revolutionary National Committee, which had no real base, into a truly national political factor, which would have assured a political career for him." (In our opinion, this statement is almost undeniable). According to the conclusion: in the long run, Dudás served the interests of the counterrevolutionary forces.

The tribunal opted for the most severe punishment because they felt the accused was "one of the most important persons among those who brought about the tragic events. József Dudás was primarily an intellectual guide of the revolution [at that time it was still called a 'revolution'], and he is directly responsible for the actions of the misled masses, for the strikes, for the lynchings, for the killings and looting by armed bands."[163]

His appeal for mercy was rejected the same day, by majority voice vote.[164] There was no possibility of an appeal.

On January 16 the Chinese Premier Chou En Lai, in Budapest for talks, argued that the "principal culprits" (meaning József Dudás who, according to the Hungarian leaders was "in touch with Imre Nagy, and carried out the latter's instructions") should be left alive, "because it is better if you have a living proof in your hands." Moreover, if they are executed the enemy will make martyrs out of them. Kádár, however, disregarded the Chinese suggestion: "Unless the leaders are punished, the masses will not realize that this government is serious about dealing with the counterrevolution."[165] Two days later chief prosecutor Géza Szénási, and József Domokos, the president of the Supreme Court, also argued in favor of an execution, and the Presidential Council went along.

The sentence was carried out on January 19. (János Szabó was also hanged on that day.) This signaled the start of Kádár's reprisal mechanism. In 1993 the Hungarian Supreme Court declared the sentence of 1957 null and void on a petition filed by Mrs. Dudás.[166]

DUDÁS LEGENDS, AND HIS AFTERLIFE

The personality of Dudás and the political role he played proved most conducive to creating the most diverse legends based only on flights of fancy, misunderstandings, and deliberate distortions. Some of these have been mentioned in the study above—the ones that played an important role in the formation of events.

Many of his followers and admirers perceived Dudás as a Knight of St. George. According to them he took part in the uprising and fighting already on October 23. The author of an article in *Neues Österreich* was told that on October 23 he was among the first to procure weapons from the armories, then fought on Széna Square. "He was an excellent strategist. He obtained tractors and had several railway carriages dragged there."[167]

Another unknown author reported that on October 23, 1956, he [Dudás] obtained weapons at the radio station. On October 24 he took a group to Buda and started fighting on Széna Square. Since he was an outstanding organizer, he was able to muster about eight hundred men in a short period. During the establishment of the committee in the second district, he was introduced as follows: "Here is József Dudás, the hero of the revolution, one of the liberators of Budapest."[168] The foundations for such improbable events, that he was an armed freedom fighter, were probably laid by himself.[169] In any case, this legend has taken hold since the change of regime,[170] even though there is nothing to back it up in the documents from the Kádár regime.

According to others, Dudás confronted the troops of intervention in November with the same indomitable spirit. "On November 4 he was able to get back to Buda, and take up the struggle on Széna Square, along Margit [Mártírok] Boulevard. He received his wound there."[171]

"On November 4 he had enough left of his superhuman energy to confront the Soviet tanks breaking into the capital....Already wounded, Dudás accompanied his comrades all the way to the country's borders, providing them with armed defense....At the border he bid them good-bye. He turned around. The heroic resisters at Csepel and Dunapentele were awaiting him."[172]

There were some who imagined that an enormous armed might rallied around him during the revolution. On November 3, if it is at all possible to talk about centralized power during those days, "the greatest power was under the control of Dudás."[173] "...he had the largest armed group at his disposal."[174] "He had more armed troops under his control than Maléter."[175] "Dudás and company took over the telephone central in downtown Budapest."[176] (The latter legend was adopted by the pro-Kádár authors.) The might of Dudás was overestimated even by François Fejtö, who writes that he was the adversary of Maléter in the struggle for power, and his fall was due to the fact that Imre Nagy backed the colonel.[177] Maléter did not regard Dudás as a rival, but disliked him, viewing him as a "reactionary," and also because he appeared to be a divisive force who was striving to build an independent power base for himself.

In connection with Imre Nagy's negotiation with Dudás, two rather interesting legends of unknown origins surfaced.

[Dudás] became the trusted spokesperson of the revolution....In the first moments it looked as if they were going to hand power over to him right then and there. But Dudás himself rejected the assignment. He said the Russians were not likely to accept him, a man who chased them out, as a conversation partner. He added, it would be better to give Imre Nagy a vote of confidence because, while he is a heretic, he nevertheless belongs within the

Marxist family; in fact, he should be appointed minister of foreign affairs. Finally, his argument was accepted."[178] "In the course of the revolution [Dudás] probably joined in at the express wish of Imre Nagy.[179]

As we have seen, the incident at the Ministry of Foreign Affairs was blamed on him already at that time, and this myth became so entrenched that it is mentioned in scholarly publications.[180] The incident is related in several variants. "When Dudás tried to conduct foreign affairs on his own initiative and had the building of the ministry occupied, Maléter simply arrested his rival."[181] "One group loyal to Dudás took over the Ministry of Foreign Affairs, and proclaimed their 'own leader' as Minister of Foreign Affairs."[182] György Gábori, the loyal follower of Dudás, accepted responsibility for the action against the ministry, but proudly claims the legend on behalf of both. "...If we retain our positions, it would be important to take the post of foreign affairs...."[183]

The testimony of Colonel Tibor Piszker is undoubtedly the most imaginative: "Dudás gave orders, through Seifert, to a company of insurgents from Széna Square to carry out the action. At the same time Dudás must have commissioned a smaller group with the mission of having them fire at the insurgents from Széna Square. Dudás must have done this with the goal of putting the army and its leaders in a bad light, I suppose, for the sake of his personal interests."[184]

In dealing with the testimony, the demonization of Dudás knows no bounds. There was no longer a trace of restraint, however absurd, in the justification for the death sentence, or even the charge-sheet. The pro-Kádár authors, with access to the archival records that others could not access, deliberately falsified the record.

Thus Dudás is described as "an agent for the Siguranca," "a police spy," "who managed to worm his way into the antifascist resistance movement," "one of the most despicable figures of the counterrevolution," "the leader of the band of killers" responsible for the lynchings on Köztársaság Square, for the murder of prosecutor Sarkadi and of Pál Fodor of the ÁVH, for the harassment of other members of the ÁVH and Party officials, for the looting of department stores, for the appropriation of Red Cross donations, for the occupation of the telephone central.

Thus Ferenc A. Szabó is correct in saying that during the Kádár era [Dudás] was saddled with all kinds of crimes[185] but he fails to mention that the assessment of Dudás was not much better among the participants in 1956, even at the time of the revolution.

We have already read the opinions expressed by the Revolutionary Committee of Intellectuals. Let us consider how he was viewed by intellectuals around Nagy who did not meet him personally.

György Fazekas: "I believe it was our unanimous assessment... that it would have been better if we had not allowed the proto-fascist forces, such as Dudás and his group, to function."[186]

József Szilágyi, at his trial included the following in his last statement "I had the worst opinion of Dudás, from the very beginning. He evolved into a sorry figure...."[187]

Tamás Aczél: "Dudás was merely a little mercenary leader....He carried out terrible executions."

Pál Ignotus: "He was executed as a fascist, and that is what he was."[188]

The martyred Miklós Gimes refused to work in the building occupied by Dudás and company.[189]

Tibor Méray assumes, on the basis of reports by eye-witnesses, that Dudás had good intentions, but was basically a maverick.[190]

Jenő Széll had the definite impression that Dudás was not a right-winger, but a dreamer, whose ambitions exceeded his intellect by far, with the fixed idea "of attaining an important role, skipping the intermediary steps, by a double flip, during a state of confusion."[191]

György Litván: "We viewed him as rather dangerous. Before the arrival of [Cardinal] Mindszenty on the scene, he was the only new figure who might have competed with the coalition and progressive leadership around Imre Nagy. We considered him a maverick politician. Indeed, we thought he had political talent."[192]

Pál Szalai: "I would not rank Dudás among the right-wingers. His methods may have been most unappealing, even to myself; I think he was not a particularly intelligent person. But we must not forget one thing, that he was among the heart and soul of the anti-German resistance in 1944...."[193]

Thus we may note that some of the intellectuals who had an impact on public opinion felt Dudás was one of the dangerous public enemies,

and describe him in far more unfavorable terms then the judges who
sentenced him to death. (They did not refer to him as a fascist, or as a
cruel murderer.) Apparently, it was from the moment of publication of his paper
that he became disliked; his attack against the poet László Benjamin,
in particular, made him irrevocably obnoxious to the intelligentsia.
According to László Gyurkó: "What was really provocative…was
the headline in inch-long font…." ['We Do Not Recognize the Present
Government.'] What is unusual, exacerbating, irritating and repulsive
in his twenty-five points was the tone, its tone of superiority, its
Napoleonic pretense and phantasmagoria. His sin was that he had trans-
gressed the unspoken established norms."[194]

To the question, "how could a politician with a leftist, national, and
democratic program be accused of fascism?" Péter A. Baló wrote:

> Dudás appeared all of a sudden as a "populist leader." Through
> him, the masses, the "street" announced their expectation of hav-
> ing an impact on the higher spheres politics. The revisionists have
> gotten used to making politics "as a vanguard for the people, but
> without the people"; therefore they could not and would not accept
> as partner, probably a subordinate role, that they were offered
> when the revolution broke out. They were outraged by the fact that
> for Dudás Imre Nagy was not a "holy man," but rather an impor-
> tant player in politics who will fulfill a less important role once his
> mission is accomplished. Many knew about Dudás's past in the
> Communist underground, they knew something about his contacts
> wit the Demény faction and the Smallholders as well. The Com-
> munist movement expected strict commitment and discipline of its
> members. A person who was seeking his way in different directions
> at the same time could not be authentic. His "confused past," "his
> curlicues," "his adventurism" elicited distrust: "he is not our man."
> …Dudás's national propaganda caused misunderstandings. He was
> a democrat, his nationalism was not ostracizing, yet his slogans
> seemed aggressive, his mixed metaphors elicited the most unfa-
> vorable association of ideas.
>
> Dudás was not a Renaissance man, he was not always able to
> express his ideas ad lib, in free form, in strict logic; moreover, he

was inclined to gesticulate, he resorted to exaggerated rhetorical devices, often resulting in creating an adverse impression on his interlocutor.

His physical appearance also created a negative impression.[195] ...The diverse attitude of his conversation partners was a further factor. The revisionists had difficulty dealing with the doctrinaire way of thinking of the movement, the events overtook them. They must have found the spontaneity, dynamism, pragmatism exhibited by Dudás rather irritating.

...The evolving mood must have contributed greatly to the fact that his adversaries accepted the horror stories attributed to Dudás uncritically. The attribute Fascist seemed most appropriate to describe his politics. After 1945 this term....became increasingly used to lump together all the adversaries of the Communists.

...In no way did Dudás deserve it. His adversaries were guided by old reflexes, prompting them to use the terminology of their political environment....The many misunderstandings concerning Dudás are more illustrative of his contemporaries than they are of himself."[196]

Baló's view is correct, but one-sided. His research took him too emotionally close to his subject, and he is unaware of the shortcomings. At least he should have investigated the reasons why it was not only the intellectuals, but also the insurgents who had almost totally ostracized him.[197]

Both of us appreciate Paul E. Zinner's summary: "His program essentially expressed the demands of the people. But as an individual seeking a voice in the affairs of the state on the basis of incipient, new institutional frame (his national council), he failed." Zinner gives as reason the reorganization of the parties because, in his opinion, under the circumstances, it was only the old, accustomed institutional channels that made it possible for the individual to rise politically. On October 30–31 he reached the apex of his success; he had nothing to show thereafter. He was a one-man national committee, his fighters turned against him, abused the documents he had issued to them, he was unable to take advantage of the events.[198]

For a few years after the regime change in 1989–90 Dudás became the main hero of the Smallholders, and not merely because he was connected to the party at a certain stage in his life, and continued to have quite a few Smallholder friends. They appreciated his rhetoric regarding "commitment to the nation." They tried to alter his political ideology and role increasingly in a rightist direction. They wanted to pretend that Dudás was not intent on reforming the shortcomings of the people's democracy, but rather to topple it,[199] even if his program and articles show otherwise.

NOTES

1. In the early 1990s Péter A. Baló, coworker of the 1956 Institute, studied the Dudás issue in depth, but interrupted his work after drafting a few essays. He gave his collection and notes to me in 1995, I owe him a debt of gratitude to this day, and I am utilizing his material in this study.
2. His father was a factory worker and a stoker, his mother a housewife. József was the oldest of four children. When he obtained his high school diploma he was also certified as a locksmith. Finished technical school in Bucharest in 1932. Institute of Political History (hereafter PIL), Dudás's self-defense, 290/62, 1956. XII. 21., pp. 242–244.
3. Ibid.
4. Communist Youth Association [Kommunista Ifjúmunkás Szövetség].
5. In connection with his participation in the Romanian Youth movement, Dudás provided the following details in his confession in PIL, 290/62, p. 242. In 1927 he joined the United Labor Union and participated in the congress of labor unions in Timişoara [Temesvár] as a delegate of the young workers. In the meantime a labor union leader died in captivity at Doftana, and the angry congress organized a protest, which was met by soldiers and gendarmes. He was involved in the fighting, was arrested for the first time, spent a few months in jail. In 1932, in the name of the central committee of the youth organization, he was appointed by Andor Bernát secretary to the local leadership in Braşov [Brassó]. He received his instructions from Sándor Mogyorósi (according to one of his confessions he reorganized the youth movement on the instructions from Mogyorósi. HL, 00115/57, tárgy., 1957. I. 8. He joined the Communist Party thanks to District Secretary Ferenc David. The Party entrusted him with organizing the demonstration of the unemployed, leading to his arrest, along with others; he was charged, but the trial was postponed, and he was released. The Party sent him to Cluj

[Kolozsvár] in January 1933. Here he organized a national railway strike. Half a years later he was assigned to Timişoara, because the political police had arrested and killed the district secretary there, the branch had been liquidated, and needed to be replaced. "I carried out my assignment well....The Fifth Party Congress and the thirteenth plenary meeting of the Comintern provided the proper ideological framework for the struggle...." The local branch published many underground papers and illegal leaflets. His arrest was due in part to the role played by Richard Wurbrandt, who graduated from the party school in Moscow, and who was dispatched to Timişoara, to back the "ideological work." After nine months under investigation "I was taken to court martial as the principal accused among sixty-five defendants, where I exposed the preparations for a fascist takeover, Wurbrand, the antiworker and antipeasant policies of Romanian capitalism. I was sentenced to nine years in jail, whereas Wurbrand was found innocent." The nine-year sentence was eventually reduced to five and a half. At Doftana he got in touch with "comrade" Gheorghiu-Dej, who praised him for his courageous stand. The politician Zoltán Pfeiffer wrote as follows:

> In 1937, in connection with the proceedings against the conspiracy in Transylvania, it turned out that Dudás recruited a young Hungarian nucleus in Temesvár and Kolozsvár. He was arrested, interrogated; in order to keep them from extorting the names of his companions, he knocked out the Siguranca official conducting the interrogation with his manacled hands. Few young men would have been able to survive the vengeance of Romanian chauvinism. Dudás was taken to the hospital of Dobrudja covered in blood, unconscious. By the time he recovered, a more lenient Romanian government gave extradited him as part of an exchange of prisoners.

See Pfeiffer, "Egy vérbeli forradalmár" [A true revolutionary], *Magyar Élet* 11, Nov. 13, 1965. Pfeiffer probably did not have reliable sources at his disposal, his story smacks of legend and is inaccurate. Dudás was imprisoned from 1934, and he was not exchanged.

6. "I took the initiative in creating a movement against fascism, under the name Freedom Association of Hungarian Patriots" In HL, Dudás jkv., 1956. XII. 29; and István Pintér, *A Magyar Front és az ellenállás* [The Hungarian Front and Resistance] (Budapest: Kossuth, 1970), pp. 119–120.

7. Pál Demény, *"A párt foglya voltam. Demény Pál élete"* ["I Was a Prisoner of the Party." The Life of Pál Demény], ed. József Kiss (Budapest: ELTE-MKKE, 1988), pp. 131, and 173.

8. Péter A. Baló wrote about this program in his study. "Dudás József—
arcképvázlat" [Sketch for a portrait of József Dudás], manuscript, 1956
Institute, notes, p. 1. He refers to document TH, V–2000–9/A.
9. Baló wrote that Dudás applied for membership in the Hungarian Communist Party, but was turned down. See ibid., p. 3. According to the
confession by Dudás he remained a member until 1944. HL, Dudás
tárgy., 1957. I. 8.
10. According to Baló, Dudás joined the Independent Smallholder Party in
January 1946. Dudás mentioned on several occasions that he belonged
to the left wing of that party, but was not a card-carrying member. HL,
Dudás jkv. 1956. XI. 29; and HL, Dudás tárgy., 1957. I. 8.
11. Dudás's contacts with the faction were not appreciated by the leaders
of the Smallholders, and he was excluded from the Administrative
Committee. See István Vida, *Az FKgP politikája 1944–1947* [The Politics of the Independent Smallholders] (Budapest; Akadémiai Kiadó,
1976), p. 253.
12. HL, Dudás tárgy., 1957. I. 8.
13. TH, V–2000/27/A.
14. "Is that not your husband over there?" a friend asked Mrs. Dudás, who
was astounded to discover her husband was the speaker. Communication by Mrs. Dudás, in documentary film by Tibor Puszt, *Akit a vihar
felkapott...*[Carried by the Storm], Filmex, 1995.
15. Open Society Archives (hereafter OSA), Item No. 733/57.
16. According to one of his confessions, he based his demands on the six-
teen point program of the university students and the resolution of the
Writers' Association. HL, Dudás önv., 1957. I. 1; see also Appendix,
pp. 187–189.
17. Baló, "The completely 'regime-changing' program includes demands
regarding Hungary's status as a nation and the future political system,
as well as about topical issues....The text implies that until the issue of
leadership is settled in accordance with the program, the committee and
the leadership of the uprising represent the Hungarian Revolution to the
outside world" (Baló, "Dudás," p. 9).
18. Lajos Izsák, József Szabó, and Róbert Szabó, eds., *1956 plakátjai és
röplapjai* [Posters and Leaflets from 1956] (Budapest: Zrínyi, 1991), p.
133.
19. "Who had thought of decorating those who lost their lives in the fighting with the award for freedom, and to succor their dependents? Who
before him thought of providing the participants with identification
cards, recognition, and even representation in government? It also
occurred to Dudás that the extant and future revolutionary formations,
distrusting the government, were waiting for solidarity and guidance,

as were the councils embracing various strata of society and the resurg-
ing labor unions. A democratic society cannot be imagined without representation of interests; therefore, in his program, Dudás wrote about
the importance of freedom of organization for political parties, but
without overemphasis, reflecting his political savvy under the circumstances," wrote Éva Standeisky, "A Magyar Nemzeti Forradalmi
Bizottmány" [The Hungarian National Revolutionary Committee],
manuscript, 2003, p. 1.
20. Baló, "Dudás," p. 15.
21. HL, Dudás jkv., 1956. XI. 26.
22. The building of the *Szabad Nép* became a focus of activities already on
October 23. The demonstrators broke into the building, threw out and
burnt papers and books. The authorities, however, felt it was most
important to preserve it, and entrusted its defense to the Zrínyi Military
Academy. The one hundred or so troops from the academy occupied
the building without a fight. They were replaced by another unit on
October 28.
23. The armed civilians were made up in part of the group from Széna
Square, while others joined spontaneously. See Oral History Archives,
1956-os Intézet [1956 Institute] (hereafter OHA), "András Kovács," p.
25.
24. Specifically the excuse the Soviets might use to intervene again. Verbal
communication by István Eörsi, 2003.
25. Lajos Izsák and József Szabó, eds., *1956 a sajtó tükrében* [1956 as
Reflected in the Press] (Budapest: Kossuth, 1989), p. 157. The appeal
was reprinted on the back page.
26. The seal appeared in other papers as well.
27. Baló, "Dudás," p. 34.

The impression on the newspaper reader must have been that
this was not a run-of-the-mill product of the press, for programs
and appeals are 'genres for leaflets,' yet they are presented here as
front page editorials. The other items in the paper were not classi-
fied by topic or edited stylistically. (Of course, one cannot expect
a revolutionary paper to conform in every respect to the rules of
journalism; but there were many other newspapers appearing on
the 30th that were better edited, in comparison to which *Függetlenség* did not hit the mark.)

28. In his memorandum of January 4, 1957, Dudás claimed that he stopped
the presses and the distribution of this issue.
29. HL, Dudás jkv., 1956. XI. 26.

30. HL, Dudás tárgy., 1957. I. 9; HL, János Vida tk., 1956. XII. 28; OSA, "The Dudás Story," News and Information Service Radio Free Europe, Hungary, January 21, 1957.

31. Communication by Zoltán Benkő and Pál Jónás to Péter A. Baló in Baló, "Dudás," p. 38.

32. Communication by György Egri to Péter A. Baló, ibid., p. 39.

33. HL, Dudás jkv., 1956. XI. 26.

34. Communication by Mrs. Dudás to Péter A. Baló in Baló, "Dudás," p. 42.

35. Hungarian State Archives (hereafter MOL), XX–5–h 1/1, Géza Losonczy jkv., 1957. IV. 17.

36. Ibid.

37. Balázs Nagy, Az igazság a Nagy Imre ügyben [The Truth in the Imre Nagy Affair] (Budapest: Századvég, 1989), p. 66.

38. MOL, XX–5–h 1/1, Losonczy jkv., 1957. IV. 17. Donáth described him as a demagogue. See MOL, XX–5–h 15/13, Ferenc Donáth jkv., 1957. VI. 18.

39. MOL, XX–5–h (Tibor Déry and fellow defendants) 69/5, Péter Kuczka jkv., 1957. VI. 27.

40. OSA, News and Information Service, RFE Hungary, "The Dudás Story," January 21, 1957.

41. Interview with István Márkus, by László Kardos, 1898, OHA, no. 217, p. 370. According to Balázs Nagy it was not much later that Dudás asked Imre Nagy to recognize him as the commander in chief of the insurgents. See Balázs, Az igazság a Nagy Imre ügyben, p. 66; same in Bill Lomax, Magyarország 1956-ban [Hungary in 1956], (Paris: Magyar Füzetek, 1982), p. 124. Donáth had similar views, see MOL, XX–5–h 15/13, Donáth jkv., 1957. VI.18. It is likely that Dudás raised the issue at both meetings.

42. Quoted in László Gyurkó, 1956 (Budapest: Szabad Tér, 1996), p. 289.

43. OHA, "István Márkus," p. 395. It is noteworthy that Jenő Széll and Per Olaf Csongovai were also reminded of the Duce. See András B. Hegedűs, ed., Ötvenhatról nyolcvanhatban [About '56 in '86] (Budapest: Századvég, 1992), p. 180.

44. Zoltán Benkő, Történelmi keresztutak [Historic Crossroads] (Miskolc: Felső-magyarország Kiadó, 1996), p. 169.

45. Ibid. Márkus also recalls that Dudás entertained the same negative feeling toward another "fellow-traveler," Ferenc Erdei. See OHA, "Márkus," p. 371.

46. Pál Jónás, "An Eyewitness Account, by Pál Jónás: Josef Dudas," East-Europe, no. 9 (1957); Adrienne Molnár, "Interjú Abod Lászlóval, 1988–1989" [Interview with László Abod], in Szuronyok hegyén nem

lehet dolgozni [One Cannot Work on the Tip of Bayonets], ed. Gyula
Kozák and Adrienne Molnár (Budapest: Századvég, 1993), p. 125.
Abod adds: "The image I formed on the basis of all this was that he was
emotionally unstable, passionate and obstinate. He negotiated very
insistently, everyone else was more inclined to compromise. He was a
strange man."

47. Jónás, "An Eyewitness Account"
48. Communication by Pál Jónás....
49. OHA, "Márkus," p. 391.
50. MOL, XX–5–h 1/1, Jkv., 1957, IV. 17. Imre Nagy remembered the
     whole discussion incorrectly: "Dudás raised the following issues in a
     rather impertinent, defiant manner. Our disagreement was about his
     group laying down their arms and joining the forces of law and order.
     If I remember correctly, his idea was that his group should enter the
     National Guard as a unit. I was opposed to that, and I told Dudás, first
     you must lay down your arms, and join one by one, but not as a group."
     In MOL, XX–5–h 12/1, Jkv., 1957. VI. 20. As we shall see, Dudás had
     no intention of joining the National Guard.
51. MOL, XX–5–h 15/13, Jkv., 1957. VI. 18.
52. Pál Jónás's communication to Baló, in Baló, "Dudás," p. 44).
53. OHA, "Márkus," p. 371.
54. Sándor Kelemen, a leader of the Peasant Party, was an eye-witness:
     "Dudás, as far as I could see, argued soberly and responsibly. He gave
     the impression of a self-confident person. He has something of a ten-
     dency to dominate. He conducts the meeting well. If he were the Min-
     ister of the Interior, he would be a strong broom in the hands of the new
     regime." See Kelemen, "Mindenki munkát kért, szerettek volna vala-
     mit csinálni" [Everyone was asking for work, wanted something to do],
     in *Pártok 1956* [Parties of 1956], ed. Zsuzsanna Kőrösi, Péter Pál Tóth
     (Budapest: 1956-os Intézet, 1997), p. 117.
55. HL, Dudás jkv., 1956. XI. 26.
56. Benkő, *Történelmi keresztutak*, p. 170, and personal communication by
     Benkő, 1992. Benkő's assumption that Maléter's unfriendly disposition
     was due to the rivalry is mistaken. Maléter's hard feelings, which grew
     only worse as the days passed, was due to his belief that Dudás was
     divisive, had inordinate ambition, and right-wing tendencies.
57. János Kenedi, ed., *A forradalom hangja* [The Voice of the Revolution]
     (Budapest: Századvég-Nyilvánosság Klub, 1989), p. 236. The declara-
     tion was published as a news item the next day in the *Magyar Nemzet*,
     Népszava, and the morning edition of *Magyar Függetlenség*. See Izsák
     and Szabó, ed., *1956 a sajtó tükrében*, pp. 165, 170, 182.
58. *New York Herald Tribune* (Paris), November 2, 1956. Baló, "Dudás,"

p. 53. McGurn saw little chance for consolidation. According to him it would be difficult to take even the weapons back from those not entitled, but the widespread anti-Communism and pro-American feelings may marginalize even Dudás.

59. If we disregard the few minutes Imre Nagy spent at the armistice negotiations on October 29 with the delegates of the insurgents.

60. The precise date of this meeting is not known, but it could not have occurred before October 30. The author mentions "without a doubt" October 26 or 27.

61. Malashenko, "The Special Corps Under Fire in Budapest—Memoirs of an Eyewitness," in *Soviet Military Intervention*, ed. Györkei and Horváth, pp. 238–239.

62. See also Attila Szakolczai, "Az ismeretlen szovjet-magyar háború" [The unknown war between Soviet Union and Hungary], in *1956-os Intézet évkönyve 1998* [The Yearbook of the 1956 Institute 1998], ed. György Litván (Budapest: 1956-os Intézet, 1998), p. 356. "The description by Malashenko is supported only by an interview with Mrs. Dudás in 1989, who had very serious reservations."

63. József Bana, *Győr, 1956* (Győr: Polgármesteri Hivatal, 1996), p. 190.

64. The same occurred with others, for instance according to Malashenko, in the case of György Fancsik, the last commander of the Corvin group, and according to the confessions of István Marián, repeatedly with Gergely Pongrátz.

65. "The writer who, according to his passive self-description, did always what he was told, responded to the call." Baló, "Dudás," p. 30.

66. József Kopré, *Lőporfüstben '56-ban* [In the Smoke of Gunpowder, in 1956] (Budapest: FSP Literator, 1993), pp. 122–162. Also, interview with Kopré by Péter Baló, OHA, No. 493, pp. 112–116.

67. George Gábori, *When Evils Were Most Free* (Toronto: Denean, 1981), pp. 266–67.

68. Personal communication by Pál Lőcsei, 2003.

69. HL, Sándor Fekete tk., 1956 XII. 28. Fekete described him as "a man pretending to be a hero, inclined to give orders and lead, yearning for power....Almost obsessed with the desire for power."

70. According to the confessions of Dudás.

71. According to the recollections of the journalist Lőrinc Szabó, Dudás said this when his Communist fellow prisoner from Doftana sought him out, on a mission from János Kádár, on November 1, and asked for permission to print the *Népszabadság*. In Judit Csáki and Dezső Kovács, *Rejtőzködő legendárium* [Collection of Hidden Legends] Budapest: Szépirodalmi, 1990), pp. 90–93. Péter A. Baló, "Dudás József élete és tevékenysége. Kronológiai vázlat" [The life of József Dudás and his

activities], in *1956-os Intézet évkönyve, 1993*, ed. János Bak, et al. (Budapest: 1956-os Intézet, 1993), p. 225. Pál Lőcsei has always emphasized that Dudás assisted other editorial offices. On the other hand, Rudolf Janesch claimed: "Those present were generally not so enthusiastic about the paper of Dudás. What characterized the situation was that they felt indebted to Dudás. If they refuse something, then maybe Dudás would no longer let them print their paper." In BFL, 3272/57, Jkv., 1957. II. 8. In my opinion, however, Janesch is very prejudiced against Dudás. The same applies to Tivadar Pártay who goes so far as to assert that Dudás, during their incarceration in the fifties, was an agent. According to his recollection he rejected point blank Dudás's offer to collaborate in 1956, when he came to visit at the offices of the *Magyar Nemzet*. His account , however, has inaccuracies, and there is no corroboration from any other source. István Hegedűs and Sándor Révész, eds., "1956-ban a Kisgazda Párt nem készített pártprogramot, nem volt időnk erre" [In 1956 the Smallholders Party did not prepare a platform, there was no time], in *Pártok 1956*, ed. Kőrösi and Tóth, pp. 32–33.

72.   Dudás enjoyed an income far above the average. He was paid over 2,000 forints per month at the refrigerator manufacturing company as a locksmith, and 1,500 forints as an expert at the plant for light industry equipment, and the same for being an expert of precision machinery.

73.   Izsák and Szabó, eds., *1956 a sajtó tükrében*, pp. 182–85.

74.   The consequences will be discussed further.

75.   Izsák and Szabó, eds., *1956 a sajtó tükrében*, p. 217.

76.   According to János Szabó, from the Széna Square group, Dudás advocated the return of private property; the small enterprises and farms under fifty acres should be returned immediately to the former owners, whereas the fate of the remainder to be decided later; maybe the state would compensate them in cash. In HL, Dudás jkv., 1956, XI. 26. According to Sándor Fekete the platform makes it clear that Dudás meant to restore private property (HL, Fekete tk. 1956. XII. 28. HL). We don't know what platform Fekete was referring to, since the twenty-five-point program contains nothing of the sort.

77.   Standeisky, "A Magyar Nemzeti Forradalmi Bizottmány," p. 6.

78.   Izsák and Szabó, eds., *1956 a sajtó tükrében*, p. 267.

79.   Ibid., p. 349.

80.   Letter from György Márton to Baló, 1993. "Akit a vihar felkapott...."

81.   The ones from the *Szabad Nép*, manuscript, 1993, p. 13.

82.   TH, V–150005/7, Solymosi önv., 1958. III. 11.

83.   See Eörsi, *Ferencváros 1956*, pp. 63–64

84.   Tibor Erdélyi, university student in 1956, interview by András Domány, *168 óra* [168 hours], June 13, 1989.

85. TH, V–150005/14, Károly Csémi tk., 1957 III. 5.
86. Gyurkó, 1956, p. 190. The All-National Committee was founded primarily by writers belonging to the opposition within the party, first of all Péter Kuczka. Their goal was similar to that Dudás, with the idea of providing leadership to other spontaneously formed organizations. Their plans were crossed primarily by the committee of Dudás. See Éva Standeisky, *Írók és hatalom* [Writers and Power] (Budapest: 1956-os Intézet, 1996), pp. 55–57.
87. During the first two days of occupation of the building, according to András Kovács, even a weak attack would have proved disastrous for the occupants, given their lack of organization. Personal communication, 1999.
88. TH, V–145629, Gyula Andrásy, jkv. 1957. V. 22; and HL, 674/57.
89. András Kovács introduced Pálházi to Dudás as a reliable former officer. Our subject told him that Communism is finished in Hungary, the elections will determine what sort of regime will come next. He offered Pálházi an assignment as secretary. He told Pálházi, confidentially, that he should keep an eye on Kovács, because he is impulsive. MOL, 5004/57, Ferenc Pálházi jkv., 1957. I. 9. Among the Headhunters Pálházi and Zoltán Preisz were executed in 1957. Pálházi, as is convincingly demonstrated by Tamás Kende, remained an amoral figure to the end. See *Beszélő*, nos. 7–8 (2003): 114.
90. OHA, "András Kovács," p. 31.
91. MOL, 5004/57, Rezső Varga jkv., 1956. XII. 28.
92. MOL, 5004/57, Ferenc Pálházi jkv. 1957. I. 9.
93. OHA, "András Kovács," p. 31. "The little lambs became lambs, because they were wolves dressed in lambskin. They were all wolves, but in lambskin."
94. Mrs. Jenő Szemes: Indeed Dudás asked every prisoner if he had been mistreated, "but only as long as Kovács was not in the room." See HL, Jenő Szemes tvall., 1957. I. 10.
95. According to Kovács the prisoners had to be transferred out, because it was not possible to hold them in the long run.
96. According to Kovács, Dudás had no influence over the group, although he tried several times, he was always chased away. György Márton had the same impression. All the records, however, contradict this interpretation; for instance, HL, Tibor Spielmann jkv., 1956. XII. 20., 23. HL; Ferenc Pálházi jkv. 1957. I. 9; MOL, 5004/57, Gyula Andrásy jkv. 1957. V. 22, and 1957. VIII. 21; TH V 145629, Tibor Haraszti-Andrásy szemb, 1957. VIII. 3. According to Andrásy, Dudás held "a briefing, regarding the arrangements within the building, the setup of the watch, the guard of the arms supply."

97. OHA, p. 26., letters to the author. OHA, "György Márton," p. 24. Márton also criticized Dudás's politics.
98. HL, Dudás jkv., 1956 XI. 29. HL.
99. HL, Dudás jkv. 1956. XI. 26, HL, Dudás önv. 1957. I. 1.
100. According to Tibor Spielmann, Dudás and Kovács held a secret discussion on November 1, in the presence of Mrs. Dudás and a police captain, about acquiring weapons from the police. See HL, Tibor Spielmann jkv., 1956. XII. 20.
101. MOL, XX–5–h 16/17. "Only pro-democracy persons may be admitted into the National Guard. We will not talk to good-for-nothings like Dudás." Someone interrupted, how dare you refer to Dudás as a good-for-nothing? Then the majority intoned: "Maléter is right. Dudás is a hoodlum." The colonel stuck by his words, and even provided evidence: "Whoever wants to take the land, the factory, the power away from the people, is our enemy." There was applause by those present. Dudás once revealed (HL. Dudás jkv. 1956. XI. 26.) that he did not like Maléter, because he had been an officer under Horthy, then Tildy's follower—commander of Tildy's bodyguard until 1948—and used his aura as revolutionary also to bolster Tildy's position. Therefore, he backed not Maléter, but Kopácsi, for the post of Minister of Defense. Dudás's confession, however, does not support this interpretation.
102. See, for instance, Lászó Eörsi, ed., *Angyal István sajátkezű vallomása* [The Confession of István Angyal in His Own Hand] (Budapest: Pesti Szalon, 1991). Sándor Fekete shares the views of the insurgents: "He wanted to Square the national committee, as his organization, in control, which was probably the reason why he would not allow his armed followers to submit to the joint command." See HL, Sándor Fekete Tk., 1956. XII. 28.
103. A clear example of this is the appeal in that day's *Magyar Függetlenség*, inserted by István Szőnyi, the insurgent at Széna Square: "Freedom fighters of Buda!...For the sake of unity, an absolute necessity, we have to join the Hungarian National Revolutionary Committee led by Dudás."
104. Dudás was to claim: "I did not succeed in extending my authority over the commanders of the insurgents: over András Kovács, János Szabó, or the Pongrátz brothers, because they adamantly rejected my attempt to limit their power." See HL, Dudás jkv., 1956. XI. 29. We don't know when and how did Dudás try to extend his influence to those of the Corvin group, the sources are lacking. He had no chance of achieving this anyway, if only because both László Iván Kovács and Gergely Pongrátz, the two commanders, attacked him. In fact, there was even talk of taking over the *Szabad Nép* building, with the assistance of the

military. But Dudás was able to preserve his prestige among the group from Széna Square.

105. TH, V–150005, Minutes of the third cabinet meeting of November 1, 1956. There are no sources to indicate that another meeting between Imre Nagy and Dudás was in the offing.

106. Budapest Főváros Levéltára [Archives of the Capital City of Budapest] (Hereafter BFL), 3272–57, Rudolf Janesch tárgy., 1957. VIII. 30.

107. Kopré, *Lőporfüstben*, pp. 133–34; OHA, "József Kopré," p. 113.

108. HL, Zoltán Kovács jkv., 1956 XII. 28. .

109. According to the imprimatur of the *Magyar Függetlenség*, it was the paper of the Statewide Chairmanship of the Hungarian National Revolutionary Committee. Such chairmanship, however, did not exist. It also has assertions such as "The Hungarian National Revolutionary Committees are formed by the heroes of the armed struggle in each district, their central bulletin is the *Magyar Függetlenség*....Rubber stamps may only be issued by our chairman József Dudás, no one may even use the name of the committee without his permission." See "Bizottmány és bizottság" [Committees and trust], *Magyar Függetlenség*, November 1, 1956. An unknown follower understood the situation well: "Dudás proved to be an organizer of genius. He formed the leadership of the revolutionary committees in each district, which consisted of himself." See OSA, no. 733/57.

110. Regarding the Hungarian National Revolutionary Committee in the second district, see the essay by the author in *1956-os Intézet évkönyve 2003* [The Yearbook of the 1956 Institute 2003] (Budapest: 1956-os Intézet, 2003).

111. Seifert insisted on the rank of colonel, at least, to avoid subordination to the head of the Reserves Command. His deputy, major József Szmetana, warned him he could not be promoted to colonel because he would need the endorsement of the Ministerial Council for that, so he had to settle for lieutenant colonel. This was signed and sealed by Kovács, who asked him not to mention the circumstances of the appointment to anyone. See TH, V–141833, Szmetana jkv., 1957.I. 8; HL, Zoltán Kovács jkv., 1956. XII.15. 28; HL, Seifert jkv., 1956. XII. 12.,19., 27., 29.

112. HL, Zoltán Kovács jkv., 1956. XII. 15., and 28; HL Zoltán Kovács tárgy, 1957. I. 9.

113. HL, Seifert jkv., 1956. XII. 27., and 29; HL, Seifert tárgy., 1957. I. 9; "Mi történt tegnap a Fő utcában" [What happened yesterday on Fő Street], *Magyar Honvéd*, November 3, 1956.

114. TH V–76898/2, Dudás jkv., 1956. XII. 22., and 29.

115. We have reason to believe that Dudás made no issue of ranks. Several

sources indicate that he also appointed János Szabó as lieutenant colonel; András Kovács wrote to me: "When Dudás named me commander of the *Szabad Nép*...he promoted me to major, but I never used that rank...." The reason is the same as in the case of Seifert: "...because as a mere platoon commander...I would not have the right to give orders or instructions to soldiers whose rank was above mine."

116. HL, Dudás jkv., 1956. XII. 22; HL, tárgy. 1957. I. 8.

117. It was mentioned at the meeting on October 31 that there should be permanent liaison with the national committee, i.e. the building of the *Szabad Nép*, and "that is our only head organization, others may not give instructions." Complete loyalty to Dudás is also shown by the fact that the *Függetlenség* or the *Magyar Függetlenség* was disseminated in a huge number of copies in the district.

118. Zoltán Kovács was expected to greet Dudás thus: "National commander in chief, sir, as the secretary of the National Revolutionary Committee of the second district, I report to you. We are ready for the review." Seifert would follow thereafter (he had procured a lieutenant colonel's uniform at dawn), to report regarding the armed formations in the district, their emplacement, their effectives (about 2,500), their order of battle.

119. His pen name as a journalist: Mauri.

120. *Epoca*, November 11, 1956. Special issue dealing with the Hungarian Revolution of 1956, p. 53; Baló, "Dudás," pp. 51–53.

121. Wiktor Woroszylski, *Magyarországi Napló* [Diary from Hungary] (Budapest: Századvég, 1994), pp. 31–33.

122. Hanka Adamiecka, "Láttam Magyarországot" [I saw Hungary], *Életünk*, nos. 3–4 (1992): 268–69.

123. Before the inteview Bielecki warned his colleagues that he had heard many negative things about Dudás.

124. Woroszylski, *Magyarországi napló*, p. 35.

125. Adamiecka summarized what she saw as follows: "We must distinguish those hundreds who are ready for self-sacrifice, have principles, are ready for any struggle and to die at any moment who make up the Dudás detachment from Dudás himself, the typical ambitious gang leader." In Adamiecka, *Láttam Magyarországot*, p. 269. This probably did not refer to the group under András Kovács, and the numbers are highly exaggerated. Bill Lomax also heard from the emigrants that Dudás had loyal followers. See Lomax, *Magyarország 1956-ban*, p. 123.

126. The episode discussed here is off the subject, if the subject is the activities of Dudás during the revolution. But the event has given rise to the most virulent myths, from the day after to our own days, that Dudás had planned and carried out the occupation of the Ministry of Foreign

Affairs. It is important to see exactly what happened, to debunk, the myth.

127. HL, Seifert jkv., 1956. XII, 29; HL Zoltán Kovács jkv., 1956. XII. 28.

128. Ibid. Later on Seifert would defend his actions by claiming that he had forbidden the use of weapons under any circumstance. Moreover, about four times as many participated than instructed; He did not send soldiers because he received no detachment for the Bem barracks. See TH, V–145715, Seifert jkv., 1958. V. 22.

129. János Druzdik (department head), Jenő Lipsz (foreign department head), István Varga and Pál Kun (internal affairs administrators), HL, tk., 1956. XII. 29; HL, tk., 1956. XII. 29; TH, V–145715/1, Varga tk., 1958. VI. 2.

130. HL, László Zólomy jkv., 1956. XII. 28; HL, tk., 1958. VI. 14;. Zólomy's account of the events corresponds to the information in the records: "Én is ezredes voltam a vezérkarnál" [I too was colonel of the general staff], *1956-os Intézet Évkönyve 1992* [Yearbook of the 1956 Institute] (Budapest: 1956-os Intézet, 1992), pp. 184–86; Béla Király, "Mi történt a Külügyminisztériumban?" [What happened at the Ministry of Foreign Affairs?], *Irodalmi Újság* [Paris], October 23, 1961, p. 5. This recollection is much less objective and accurate than that of Zólomy.

131. HL, Seifert jkv., 1956. XII. 19.

132. As mentioned, the arrest of Dudás was contemplated in a government directive already on November 1, but we cannot know whether the arrest would have been carried out had there been no incident. Allegedly Béla Király received instructions from the ministry that he may even use tanks to carry out the arrest. Király carried out the arrest with the help of Emánuel Butkovszky, and the teacher János Virág. See TH, V–150006/1, János Virág jkv., 1957. IV. 9.

133. Both were incarcerated at the prison on Fő Street, and not released until November 5.

134. TH, V–150006/1, Virág jkv., 1957 IV. 15.

135. "...It would have been in my interest if András Kovács had been removed for at least one day, enabling me to appoint someone else in his place, and bring some officers from the Zrínyi Academy, thus bolstering the discipline among the group" In HL, Dudás jkv., 1956. XI. 29., and XII. 1.

136. Mrs. József Dudás, née Aranka Horváth, accompanied her husband everywhere, to the end. Sometimes she had to interpret for him, for our protagonist became hoarse, losing his voice almost completely.

137. HL, Dudás jkv., 1956. XI. 29., and XII. 1. HL, Dudás önv., 1957. I., 1., HL, Dudás tárgy., 1957. I. 8–14.

138. According to Király's account, he reported to Imre Nagy that Dudás had nothing to do with the attack at the ministry, and that it may have

been a provocation. See István Stefka, "'56 arcai—Király Béla a Nemzetőrség főparancsnoka" [Faces from 1956—Béla Király the commander in chief of the National Guard], *Magyar Nemzet*, June 4, 2003. It would appear from the articles in 1961 and 2003 that Király liked Dudás, but the eye-witnesses saw it otherwise.

139. Dudás was not responsible for this at all.

140. "Imre Nagy declared that he had had talks with Dudás, he did not know that Dudás was such a fraud, let us show him up for what he is, separate him from his group." In MOL, XX–5–h 20/28, Kopácsi, jkv., 1957. VII. 24.

141. MOL, XX–5–h 19/26, János Virág jkv., 1957. IV. 15; also in TH, V–150006/1.

142. MOL, XX–5–H 20/28, Kopácsi önv., no date; and Kopácsi jkv., 1957. VII. 24. Kopácsi felt that Dudás was aiming at becoming prime minister and was acting against the interests of the Imre Nagy government. See MOL, XX–5–H 20/27, Kopácsi jkv., 1957. II. 28.

143. HL, Dudás jkv., 1956. XII. 1.

144. TH, V–1503388/3, Sándor Varga jkv., 1957. IV. 10.

145. HL, Dudás jkv. 1956. XII. 1; MOL, XX–5–h 19/26, Virág jkv., 1957. IV. 15; also in TH, V–150006/1.

146. HL, 1.d. 1.e., 352 ff., Report from the Miklós Zrínyi Military Academy (ZMKA), 1956 documents. According to another military source, Captain Pál Arnóczki, and Lieutenant László Erdős were instructed to invite Dudás to the academy, then place him under arrest. According to this version the optimism of our protagonist was still undaunted: "You see, boys, whether Münnich likes it or not, now it seems I am the minister of the interior, and not he"—he told the officers. In TH, V–150005/1, László Erdős, jel., 1957. II. 19.

147. TH, V–150005/2, Márton jkv., 1957. IV. 11.

148. "Maléter mentioned that Dudás, that good-for-nothing, should be arrested. That was when I informed Maléter that Dudás was staying at the Zrínyi Academy. Maléter then told me, by way of instructions, that József Dudás must be arrested on orders from Prime Minister Imre Nagy....If I did not execute, I must suffer the consequences." In ibid. Because Béla Király did not carry out the orders, Maléter was thinking about taking Király into custody as well, maybe he had even reached that decision. He was more lenient toward Kopácsi, although the latter likewise did not execute the order. "On November 3, around 8 pm, two workers came to find Maléter in the ante-room of Zoltán Vas, to ask, who was this Dudás, who is preventing them from doing their job. Maléter looked at his watch and declared that Dudás is a fascist bandit, already under arrest." In HL, 031/58, János Mecséri jkv., 1957. VIII. 8.

149.   HL, Jenő Kiss jkv., 1957. III. 10., and V. 25; HL, önv., III. 28; HL, 674/57 ü., 1957. VIII. 17.

150.   Jenő Kiss HL, önv., 1957. III, 28; HL, ü., 1957. VIII. 10; TH, V–145629, and HL 674/57, Székfy, jkv., 1957. V. 25., and 27., ü. VIII. 17. András Kovács and György Márton do not mention this in their communications; in fact, they exclude the possibility of having consulted Dudás on such specialized military matters.

151.   Communication by György Márton, 1999.

152.   HL, Dudás jkv., 1956. XI. 26., and XII. 12; PIL 290., f. 62. ö.e., önv., 1956. XII, 22; TH, V–159033/1. Rónyai jkv., 1971. VIII. 16; TH, V–159033/2, 1971. IX. 9.

153.   HL, Dudás jkv. 1956. XII. 29; verbal communication by Mrs. Dudás and Gábori to Baló, "Dudás, p. 79.

154.   Let us repeat that the Hungarian Revolution of 1956 was not characterized by banditry.

155.   Baló, "Dudás," p.80.

156.   TH, V–150002/9. In Baló, "Dudás," pp. 80–81.

157.   HL, Dudás jkv., 1956. XII. 10.

158.   HL, Dudás, önv., 1957. I. 1.

159.   Vyacheslav Sereda and Alexandr Stikalin, eds. *Hiányzó lapok 1956 történetéből* [Missing Pages from the History of 1956] (Budapest: Móra, 1993), p. 182.

160.   HL, Indictment (Chief Prosecutor Géza Szénási), 1956. XII. 29., p. 3.

161.   HL, Memorandum by Dudás to the Military Tribunal of the Supreme Court, 1957. I. 4.

162.   HL, 1957. I. 10. Several witnesses testified for the defense, including Pál Lőcsei.

163.   It is interesting that this document described the Imre Nagy government as the "legitimate government"; this formula was omitted on later occasions.

164.   Colonel Ferenc Ledényi, chair of the council, and Lieutenant Colonel János Szimler, sentencing judge (since Prosecutor Lieutenant Colonel István Kovács continued to argue in favor of execution, then left the chambers, as prescribed), declared: "We do not recommend József Dudás for mercy, because he was a leading figure of the counterrevolutionary events. His activities contributed greatly to the fact that our country suffered so much loss in lives and economic materiel." Lieutenant Colonel Sándor Nagy, the sentencing judge opined:

        I recommend József Dudás for mercy. The reason being that, although he engaged in widespread counterrevolutionary activities, he tried to prevent acts of violence and cruelty. In addition to articles urging action...his newspaper also published many articles with the right message. The issue of November 3, 1956, especially, contains articles which were conducive to calming the excited spirits of the masses.

165. János M. Rainer, *Nagy Imre* (Budapest: 1956-os Intézet, 1999), vol. 2, p. 378.
166. BFL, 2902/57. Mrs. Dudás was sentenced to three years confinement in 1958.
167. PIL, 290. f 99. ö. e., 1956. XII. 16., pp. 4-5.
168. OSA, "The Dudás story."
169. At least this was discussed in Woroszylski, *Magyarországi napló*, p. 3
170. Ildikó Hankó, "Mikor halt meg Dudás József?" [When did Joseph Dudás die?], *Magyar Nemzet*, November 18, 1991.
171. OSA, "The Dudás Story."
172. Pfeiffer, "Egy vérbeli forradalmár," p. 9.
173. OSA, "The Dudás story."
174. OSA, no. 338/57, "Communication by a young Hungarian economist."
175. Communication by Benkő in *Akit a vihar felkapott*....
176. MOL, XX–5-h 19/26, Vilmos Oláh tk., 1957. III. 27.
177. François Fejtö, *Behind the Rape of Hungary* (New York: D. McKay, 1957), pp. 225–26; Baló, "Arcképvázlat," p. 14.
178. Indro Montanelli, *1956 Budapest* (Budapest: Püski, 1989).
179. Gábor Jobbágyi, *"Ez itt a vértanuk vére"* [This Here Is the Blood of the Martyrs] (Budapest: Kairosz, 1998) p. 51.
180. Karola Némethné Vágyi and Károly Urbán, eds., *A Magyar Szocialista Munkáspárt ideiglenes vezető testületeinek jegyzőkönyvei* [The Minutes of the Provisional Leading Bodies of the Hungarian Socialist Workers' Party], vol. 2, *1957. január 25–1957. április 2* (Budapest: Intera, 1993), p. 233.
181. PIL, 290. f. 99 ö. e., *Neues Österreich*, December 16, 1956, pp. 4–5.
182. Adamiecka, *Láttam Magyarországot*, pp. 268–69.
183. *Akit a vihar felkapott*....
184. TH, V–150005/17, 1957. IV. 29.
185. "Az én fiam egy fanatikus magyar...." [My son is a fanatical Hungarian], *Magyar Nemzet*, October 20, 2001.
186. András B. Hegedűs, ed., *Forró ősz* [Hot Autumn] (Budapest: Magyar Hírlap Könyvek, 1989), p. 142.
187. István Javorniczky, *"Eljő az a nagy szép idő...."* ["The Beautiful Great Day Will Come...."] (Budapest: Héttorony, 1990), p. 161.
188. Tamás Aczél and Pál Ignotus are quoted in Gyurkó, *1956*, p. 289.

189. Sándor Révész, *Egyetlen élet* [The Only Life] (Budapest: Sik, 1999).
190. Tibor Méray, *Thirteen Days that Shook the Kremlin* (New York: Praeger, 1959), p. 228.
191. Hegedűs, ed., *Ötvenhatról nyolcvanhatban*, p. 180.
192. Litván added that Pál Jónás, whose opinion should be taken seriously, spoke positively about Dudás.
193. Hegedűs, *Ötvenhatról nyolcvanhatban*, p. 167.
194. Gyurkó, *1956*, p. 191.
195. See Woroszylski, *Magyarországi napló*.
196. Baló, "Arcképvázlat," pp. 6–15.
197. According to the essay by Tibor Beck and Pál Germuska, Dudás was not well liked at the university. See *Forradalom a bölcsészkaron* [Revolution at the Faculty of Humanities] (Budapest: 1956-os Intézet, 1997), p. 100.
198. Paul E. Zinner, *Revolution in Hungary* (New York: Columbia University Press, 1962), pp. 290–92.
199. According to Sándor Fekete as well. See HL, Fekete tk., 1956. XII. 28.

ILONA TÓTH

Ilona	Miklós	Ferenc	József	József	Gyula
Tóth	Gyöngyösi	Gönczi	Gáli	Molnár	Obersovszky
			with glasses		

"Ilona Tóth and fellow defendants in court"

POLITICAL RESISTANCE AT THE
HOSPITAL ON SÁNDOR PÉTERFY STREET

The hospital on Sándor Péterfy Street was one of the most important revolutionary foci in 1956 at the time of armed conflict, and became even more important during the political resistance that followed Soviet intervention. Large numbers of insurgents, especially those from Boráros Square, found a hiding place here; although many kept their weapon, they converted to nonviolent resistance and joined the hospital staff, the volunteer nurses, the students and workers who found refuge there. After November 8 their principal activity was to draft, duplicate and distribute leaflets, under the leadership of István Angyal, the legendary commander of the insurgents of Tűzoltó Street. Some engaged in brining in food supplies from the countryside. One group was active in preparing the flight abroad of the revolutionaries. Many used the hospital merely as a place of refuge; because their apartment had been destroyed, were afraid to go home, or lived in the village and were simply awaiting an opportunity to travel home. There were some who, from the beginning of the revolution, slept in the basement, commuting to their place of employment.

The area bordered by Thököly Avenue, György Dózsa Road, Rottenbiller Street, and Damjanich Street were part of the hospital's sphere of influence, but there were contacts with resistance groups in more distant districts. During the fighting the hospital was filled; for those not severely wounded an annex was established on András Cházár (formerly and better known as Domonkos) Street, number 3 in the fourteenth district, some two or three hundred meters away. In the night of November 4 to 5, when the administration at the main hospital was seeking volunteers for the position of interim leader of the annex, the medical graduate and intern Ilona Tóth accepted this post, without pay.

Before the revolution Tóth was doing her internship in internal medicine at the Sándor Péterfy hospital. She was at the demonstration on October 23. From October 25 she became a member of the Volunteer Rescue Service.[1] Along with her companions she transported the wounded, provided bandages and food for the fighters. She performed these duties on November 4 as well, although she was ill. What more: "On one occasion, on Üllői Road, I removed my red cross armband, went up to an apartment in one of the buildings—having asked a teenage girl for her hand grenade, threw the grenade at a Soviet tank. I don't know if it hit the mark."[2]

The number of wounded in bed at Domonkos Street oscillated between twenty and thirty, the walkabout patients were somewhat fewer. Medicine and groceries were brought over from the main hospital, but they were able to cook on site. Insurgents found a hiding place in this annex as well. Tóth listed quite a few of them as hospitalized. She raised the number of food rations from fifty to seventy. She also took care of a wounded Soviet soldier, ensuring his safety, then had him transferred to Pestújhely, the Soviet military hospital.

She read István Angyal's leaflets at the Péterfy Street location. "Angyal said we have to fight in two directions, because so many hooligans have infiltrated our ranks and they are bandits. We saw that there are problems and our bitterness only increased....Our leaflets served the purpose of saving what could still be saved from the achievements of the revolution. We attacked the government for that reason, we demanded the immediate withdrawal of Soviet troops, and we tried to force that issue by calling upon the workers to go on strike."[3] Angyal insisted that only the leaflets drafted there should be printed and distributed. "He warned (to use his own expression) that if we see any kind of 'fascist nonsense' posted, let us tear it down....He expressed that the object of the leaflets is only to defend our independence, keep the fourteen points, but not to attack socialism."[4]

The two of them shared the same ideas on many subjects. By socialism they meant the same principles, they did not feel that help from the West would be beneficial, they disapproved of those who fled abroad. On all these issues they probably represented a minority among all the freedom fighters, by then. Perhaps the main difference was in their estimation of Imre Nagy. Tóth had confidence, whereas Angyal thought he was an opportunist.[5] Both were adamant, enthusiastic, even foolhardy revolutionaries, who were more afraid of being deported by the Soviets than of being arrested by the police. At their meeting Angyal warned her to be careful. He thought he was already being sought, and that spies had infiltrated into the movement. He would not allow even Tóth inside the mimeograph workshop.

"There was a stencil machine in the annex on Domonkos Street, and there was plenty of ink and paper at their disposal. There were many willing to help, especially Ferenc Maráczi and Béla Gráczi. My understanding with my 'boys'—fifteen and and sixteen-year-old youngsters—who assisted with the distribution was that, if they ever got captured by the ÁVH men, let them not beat you to a pulp, but blame me for everything."[6] They organized the local watch patrol. Between November 10 and 16 under the leadership of Tóth, they distributed almost eight hundred leaflets of Angyal and about four hundred other illegal items reproduced by mimeograph. The twenty-five-year old Ferenc Gönczi joined them on November 12 or 14, to organize the dissemination of flyers. Tóth developed the closest work relationship with him, since they took food to the country together in October. Gönczi was an officer in the military and a member of the Party, but had become disabused by the regime years earlier. During the revolution he was transporting the wounded, food, and copies of the *Igazság* [Truth], to the very end. The twenty-seven-year old Miklós Gyöngyösi joined shortly after; he was known to most as "Piros" [Red] or "Piri." He was also in touch with Angyal and became a leader of the insurgents from Baross Square who eventually found refuge in Jenő Landler Street. Gyöngyösi was brought up in an orphanage. Although he had been sentenced eight times for common crimes, of which his companions were unaware, in October and November he defended the purity of the revolution tooth and nail. He wanted to participate in the distribution of leaflets because he too felt that the armed struggle had become hopeless. He was accompanied by the seventeen-year-old József Molnár, who belonged to the same armed group.

In addition to her underground activities, Ilona Tóth did her utmost to maintain order within the hospital: "The bottle of wine was thrown out with its owner. There were three things I could not abide. Weapons, cursing, and drinking."[7] She did allow for an exception. "After I met

Gyöngyösi, it once happened that he held a fully loaded pistol under my nose, saying he was this district's commander. I told him the next time he should leave the weapon at the entrance, because I will not tolerate it. He told me he had spent time [at the erstwhile headquarters of state security] at 60 Andrássy Avenue, where he was beaten half to death. He made it clear that he would never give up his gun, he will hold on to it to his death, and I began to respect him for his fanaticism."[8] The personnel of the hospital, as the members of the resistance, accepted Tóth's leadership; she had a confrontation only with Mrs. József Turcsányi, the superintendent. Indeed, Mrs. Turcsányi resented the fact that Tóth overlooked the rules of the hospital by admitting people who were quite healthy, by receiving strangers, by granting them lodging. Mrs. Turcsányi also noted the illegal printing activity; hence she was suspected of being in touch with the police.

THE DEATH OF ISTVÁN KOLLÁR

On November 16 the movement suffered a very serious blow. Their center, the hospital at Sándor Péterfy Street, was occupied by the police. Almost eighty distributors of leaflets were arrested, including their leader, István Angyal. The stencil machine was sequestered. The mood at both hospitals became tense. "Gönczi informed us that Angyal is missing. We were in despair, we were afraid we would never get to see him again."[9] In hindsight it seems almost unbelievable that there were still some who agreed to carry on underground activities in face of the enormous risks. The group on Domonkos Street felt that their struggle might force the government to make the Soviets leave the country,[10] furthermore, persuade the government to do more on behalf of the workers, to make it "truly a workers' state."[11]

Tóth decided to take over Angyal's functions. Under her leadership the leaflets were run off at the Domonkos Street site, from 8 A.M. to 8 P.M. To use her own expression, she became a typist, and the presentation—as seen from Angyal's confession, entailed a great deal of minute work: "Since the machine was small and primitive, one had to struggle all day long to print eight hundred or one thousand copies. At time the cylinder was too close to the drum, at times the drum would get clogged, or the handle did not operate smoothly. A thousand problems, I had never experienced in previous life, yet had to deal with them, overcome them."[12] At the same time Tóth took care of the sick, dealt with personnel issues, and paid daily visits to the hospital on Sándor Péterfy Street. She was able to accomplish all this by drinking or shooting up five or six ampoules of caffeine. Her companions, Gönczi and Gyöngyösi, also tried to cope with their waking hours by means of caffeine injections.

After November 16 the campaign to locate the internal enemy became feverish. The news spread that Angyal had been denounced by an insider in the hospital. The suspicion was warranted although no one was able to come up with proof.

The anxiety of those at Domonkos Street was made worse by the fact that the dispatcher Gyula Fuchs (alias "Pipás") showed up again on Péterfy Street; back in October, it was assumed that he was in the pay of the ÁVH, and consequently was beaten up by Gönczi and company. (More than likely the suspicion was warranted.)

The insurgents from the former Baross Square group joined in the work of distributing leaflets, mainly with the help of Gyöngyösi; they were now housed at one of the women's hostels on Jenő Landler Street or Murányi Street. Some of the girls from the hostels helped with the work as well. The feelings of distrust had spread among these fighters during the conflict, and there was already one victim.[13]

The very day of the big raid, on November 16, Gyöngyösi and his former comrades-in-arms escorted the sixteen-year old Erzsébet Petruska to the hospital at Domonkos Street. She had been captured and released by the Soviets earlier. Her escorts accused her of betraying Angyal. Ilona Tóth was conducting the interrogation. Gyöngyösi threatened her with a weapon, Gönczi with beating, if she did not reveal what she had told the Soviets. The young József Molnár, who intervened to defend the suspect, was sent away. They continued the following day, Tóth even took minutes of the interrogation. Eventually they found no proof that she had played any role in the arrest of Angyal and company, but she was excluded from the work as being unreliable.[14]

On November 18 they accused an insurgent named "Colos" of being a spy, because he did not show up for a planned action at the appointed time, but the cops did. Once they became convinced of his innocence they let him go, and even gave him provisions. "Then I told the boys not ever to bring anyone here, because we are full of traitors."[15] Mrs. Turcsányi, the superintendent, was believed to be a spy, for far more tangible reasons. There was talk of doing her in.[16] The tensions were exacerbated by various rumors. It was mostly Gyöngyösi who was inclined to suspect others. He trusted no one and kept many, including Ilona Tóth, under surveillance. On her part she was convinced that her phone was bugged. She even asserted that she had noticed, on several occasions, that her belongings had been searched, the lining of her coat inspected. In the evening of November 18 the former comrades-in-arms of Gyöngyösi arrested the stockroom clerk István Kollár, in the name of the "revolutionary youth," at the hostel where he was visiting his fiancée Erzsébet Polgár. They were just getting ready to distribute leaflets and, for some reason, almost all of them found Kollár suspicious.[17] Their leader had him escorted to the hospital on Domonkos Street, saying that he was an agent of the ÁVH who was investigating the illegal printshop. Gyöngyösi took him to an office on the third floor.

An hour or two earlier, as previously arranged, József Gáli, Gyula Obersovszky and two others had arrived to draft the first issue of *Élünk* [We Are Alive]. Some members of the group were conversing with the writers, in Ilona Tóth's office, also on the third floor, when Gyöngyösi called out the doctor and Gönczi. "I was most afraid, I was nervous, I was afraid for the editors; I even called down to the entrance at the very beginning of the conversation, to keep an eye out."[18]

Tóth remained with the writers for a while, while the two men were interrogating the prisoner. Kollár claimed to be a stock clerk—as, indeed, he was—and kept insisting that he was no traitor. After they searched him they refused to believe him, and beat him up for trying to mislead them. Indeed, they had found a picture on which Kollár was wearing the uniform of an agent of the ÁVH. He also had his book of military service which indicated that its owner served with the secret service.

The photo was taken in August 1956, Kollár was wearing my clothing....I warned my brother-in-law that it is not advisable to carry such a picture on him, as indeed I hid my own, confessed the husband of Kollár's younger sister, András Vári, who served in the ÁVH as a driver, in the rank of sergeant major. István Kollár, on the other hand, had only functioned as a rank and file soldier with the outfit, and there was not a single item of proof that he was ever a spy....The photo, much as in some Greek tragedy of fate, fulfilled the fate of all of us.[19] My way of thinking was, that after the identification, once I am convinced that it was a mistake, and he is not a member of ÁVH, we would let Kollár go. When Gönczi convinced me that Kollár had not told the truth, and we found among his documents a picture of him in the uniform of a staff member of ÁVH, we realized we had no alternative but to do away with him, to protect ourselves and our companions.[20]

Thus both Gönczi and Gyöngyösi found their theory confirmed, that they had a spy on their hands who would denounce the movement, and Ilona Tóth shared their opinion:

...I saw that there was big trouble, which was why they had captured the ÁVH man, because he was spying on us; I also came to this conclusion because during the preceding days we were already worried that the police was on our tracks, on account of the distribution of illegal leaflets.

...My conviction at that time was that this man must be killed right away, because if we did not, the state security agents will swoop down on us.[21]

By the way, Tóth had misunderstood Gyöngyösi; she thought "Piros" had recognized in Kollár the man who had tortured him at ÁVH headquarters.

"...We decided on the killing within minutes, and carried it out quickly, because we feared that the personnel of the hospital would notice."[22] Gyöngyösi pulled out his revolver, but Gönczi rebuked him, saying using a firearm within the hospital would entail automatic firing. They sent József Molnár out to stand guard with two others, and Ilona Tóth got ready to put the man to sleep. By then Kollár was sitting half unconscious on a chair. In order to finish him off the sooner—not to have to undress him—Tóth tried to inject the contents of a chloroform ampoule into the vein of his neck, but in her nervous state of mind, she missed in several attempts. (According to medical opinions in 1957, this would not have been an easy task even for an experienced physician). By then the ampoule was empty, then Tóth tried to pressure air into the area of the heart, but the injection needle broke in her hands. Gyöngyösi then offered his pocketknife, but she would not take it. By then all of them began to feel dizzy from the large volume of anesthetic they inhaled; they opened the windows, laid Kollár on the ground, and left the office space. According to the medical opinions from 1957 by then the wounded man had wounds that could cure in twenty days. Tóth was called into the kitchen, where she had yet another argument with Mrs. Turcsányi, whereas Gyöngyösi went over to the writers and, upon an inquiry from József Gáli, told him that an ÁVH man who had been sent after them had been put to sleep, and later they would let him go. Tóth made the same declaration later on. The writer insisted that it is not proper to arrest persons.[23]

Kollár began to gasp for air, thereupon Gönczi stood on his neck for about half a minute. According to some medical opinions this was the cause of death. But the victim moved even after that, and Gyöngyösi reached for his revolver once again. Then Tóth ordered him to stop, examined Kollár and determined that he was no longer breathing. They could not leave the victim in the office, they carried him into a toilet. As they let him down, they noticed a jerking of the head. Then Gyöngyösi placed the pen-knife in her hands, and she stabbed Kollár in the heart. According to some medical opinions, this was the cause of death, although he could not have survived the previous wounds either.[24]

The corpse was buried in the yard of the church on Domonkos Street with the help of spades and shovels borrowed from the stoker at night. (They were afraid to take the body further, for fear of the Hungarian-Soviet patrols. Tóth declared during the trial that they had agreed on complete secrecy during the burial. Nevertheless, it is obvious that the medical intern told the story to the male nurse István Veszprémi on the following day, who basically belonged to the group, and who asked them what had become of their AVH prisoner.[25]

Tóth had a tendency to disclose secrets: "My mother would visit me. My mother was there on the afternoon of the November 19. I did not mention the Kollár affair to her. Indeed, I could not have, for we were not alone."[26] Furthermore, there were sources to indicate that, in addition to the two guards, there were two women distributing leaflets—Edina Drucker and Éva Török—as well as Ferenc Maráczi, who may have been eyewitnesses,[27] or at least could suspect something from the sounds he heard.

In the meantime, the writers had installed themselves in the basement to edit the paper, and went to rest, while Tóth was typing another leaflet. At dawn it turned out that József Gáli already knew about the tragic event. How he found out, we do not know for sure, the sources do not agree; in my opinion he was told by Veszprémi, with the proviso that he should not reveal the information.[28] Gáli accused Gyöngyösi and Tóth; he did not know about Gönczi's participation. "I seem to remember that I told Gyöngyösi that we fight for human life, and that is why we write. I asked [Ilona Tóth] how could she do such a thing as a doctor, had she not taken the Hypocratic oath? She answered, not yet."[29] Ilona Tóth: "When I went down to where the writers were, I was in a bad state. Gáli asked: 'Ica, what have you all done?'...All I said was that I did it for the first and last time." Gáli: "Gyöngyösi said he was a member of ÁVH, he was spying on them. But whoever he was, it is not permissible to kill a human being. I cannot reconcile that with my principles.[30] When I asked Obersovszky whether he knew what was going on in the building, he said all he had heard is that they put a man to sleep. I said, I know more, because they killed him."[31] Then they agreed with Obersovszky that they would leave the hospital and break relations with Gyöngyösi and Tóth.

When the insurgents escorted Kollár from the dormitory on Jenő Landler street, his fiancée, Erzsébet Polgár, quarreled with them, and threatened to denounce them. "I told them, if they take Pista away, there would be dire consequences, many would get arrested."[32] Since the insurgents were afraid of being denounced or getting in trouble, they lured Polgár to the hospital on Domonkos Street, to "take care of her" over there. Gyöngyösi, however, refused, and Polgár managed to escape.

Already on the night of November 18 a resident notified Ilona Tóth that the group had been denounced for possessing a mimeograph machine. Then, with the help of Maráczi, they destroyed the leaflets and the drafts. There was not enough time to hide the machine in a safe place. The police appeared late in the next evening. They found the mimeograph and other incriminating objects suggesting a print shop, so they arrested Tóth and eight others, including József Molnár and Maráczi, and took them to police headquarters.

"Ilona Gizella Tóth revealed in the course of conversation that she had fought from the very beginning of the revolution, and will continue to fight until the Soviet soldiers leave Hungarian territory. She said that she had been preparing leaflets as late as last week, distributed by young men from the hospital and by herself," reported Police Captain István Garami.[33] Gyöngyösi was registered as a patient, but Gönczi escaped, and was the first to tell Gáli and Obersovszky about the raid. Gönczi continued to be active in the printing and distribution of *Élünk*. Gyöngyösi did likewise after November 24, having left the hospital at that time. Both, along with two others charged later, were arrested by the Soviets on December 5. (Just as they were trying to place a stencil machine into a safe hiding.) They were soon transferred into Hungarian custody.

ILONA TÓTH AND FELLOW DEFENDANTS

On November 19 the police raided both the hospital on Domonkos Street and the worker's hostel on Jenő Landler Street. This was occasioned by Erzsébet Polgár's report that her fiancé, István Kollár, had been dragged away and killed. By then it was common knowledge. The police did not take minutes, but suggested she report it to police headquarters. Indeed, Polgár made a statement to the police on November 22, where she was taken by the late Kollár's brother-in-law, András Vári. By then there were all kinds of rumors circulating about the hospital on Domonkos Street—that there were heaps of corpses stabbed or killed by lethal injection lying in the basement. The news of the murder of Kollár had also spread within the hospital.[34]

Thus the authorities had knowledge of the affair by November 22, although the Police Headquarters of Budapest still knew nothing about it for another ten days. This is hardly surprising, since the authorities were not functioning as efficiently as they would just six months later.

Tóth remembered the first day in jail as follows: "The police came to the hospital during the raid, looking for the stencil machine, the weapon, the leaflet. When they took me in, I was interrogated on account of these objects. The killing was weighing on my conscience. I was confronted with Gráczi, when I told the person in charge of the interrogation, that I would not denounce my comrades, because of my word of honor. I sent a message to Gyöngyösi and Gönczi from the police station, via First Lieutenant Kárpáti, if I remember correctly, telling them to escape."[35]

According to the documents available to us it was on December 4 that Tóth made a confession about the Kollár case for the first time. The detectives were inquiring about Gyöngyösi the day before. There was also a denunciation according to which about ten members of Gyöngyösi's armed group from Jenő Landler Street, had raped the wife of an ÁVH officer. "When I found out about the Salamon case, it was then that I realized who Gyöngyösi really was; that day, however, I made no confession, and the following night I reviewed my entire life, and the following day I asked to be heard, and I related the happenings."[36] (It is almost for certain that the charge about the sexual assault was false and, indeed, no one was charged with it.) "...I was asked whether I knew about the execution of Piri; I said yes, and that 'I took a very active part in it.' I was never forced to make a confession. It was only when I found out about Gyöngyösi's past that I told about the murder of Kollár."[37] Gönczi was of the same opinion: "Had we known that he had a criminal past, with eight convictions, we would not even have talked to Piri."[38] It should be noted, however, that this is not quite fair; for Gyöngyösi, just as the two of them, was defending the purity of the revolution with all his heart. It was also on December 4 that József Molnár confessed, as did Gönczi and Gyöngyösi a few days later.

They all felt they were guilty of the murder of Kollár. There were other charges in the case of Gönczi and Gyöngyösi—distributing leaflets, preparing and distributing an underground newspaper, concealing weapons. Regarding the illegal newspaper Tóth had this to say: "...I know it was against the law, but I do not feel guilty."[39] During the investigation she recalled the tragic evening as follows:

...We were afraid that the police were after us for distributing illegal leaflets....Gyöngyösi only said that this one was spying on us and; when they seized him, he claimed to be a stockman, although it turned out that he was a master sergeant in the ÁVH....I attribute our deed to the fact that in the days preceding November 18 I was so exhausted from working day and night, that I was only able to maintain my strength by dint of injecting caffeine. My nerves were especially wrought by the fact that in the last days we were constantly on edge, that sooner or later we will get caught. Our fear was only increased a few days earlier, when there had been a raid at the hospital, and my companions felt that the commander of the police unit in charge of the raid had also been a member of the ÁVH. Thus when Kollár was brought to the hospital after being captured, I asked no questions, because I took it for granted that he was a member of the ÁVH tracking our group; I and my companions could only avoid the danger of arrest if we got rid of him fast. Under the quick succession of events not only was I unable to assess my action, I did not even have time for thought. Only later did it strike me that, being a doctor, I had committed the greatest sin in misusing medical methods.[40]

Throughout her incarceration Tóth was eaten by remorse; moreover she was disappointed by the lack of purity of the revolution—probably because of the accounts she heard in jail, for instance, about the lynchings on Köztársaság Square. During the period of the trial, from February 18, 1957, she also felt guilty about inciting to revolt. Gönczi went through the opposite process, for he only felt guilt about the murder of Kollár. It is typical of Tóth's confession that she insisted on the truth, whereas Gönczi was accusing the government and the regime, and he was reprimanded several times by the presiding judge, Matild B. Tóth.

Their attitude differed also with regard to the main charge. Ilona Tóth argued: "I killed a person, it did not matter whether or not he belonged to the ÁVH."[41] Gönczi: "If Kollár was indeed a stock clerk and innocent, then it is shameful [brief pause], but if he was a member of ÁVH, it is still shameful, because we killed a human being."[42] (The tone of voice is decisive here, because this confession, as we shall see, engraved itself into the memory of the court.)

Gyöngyösi behaved much more like accused persons usually do. He defended himself to the maximum extent: "My fellow defendants, who have far more education, certainly more than two years of prima-

ry school, also did not take the path of virtue and justice; how could I
have realized the unforeseen consequences of my act?"[43]

The prosecutor György Molnár passed a strict sentence on Ilona
Tóth, the strictest in the cases of Gyöngyösi and Gönczi. All three
lawyers challenged the charge of murder, by arguing there was no premeditation. In other words, "the killing of a human being was decided
on the spur of the moment, and this excludes the crime of murder." Had
the court accepted this argument then the most severe sentence would
have been 18 years in jail. János Kardos, the lawyer assigned to Ilona
Tóth, even added: "She was not in full control of her faculties at the time
of execution, as is expected if murder is the case....Moreover, we should
credit her with her way of life, she made a full, honest confession...."
Below are the quotes from the last statements of the three defendants:

I hesitated for a long time whether I should speak, whether I
had the right to say anything. I came to the conclusion that I must
speak, provide explanations to some of the questions....In the years
1945–47, when the people's democracy was evolving, I experienced some surprises. Among others, two of my relatives had been
taken to internment camps, although they were rehabilitated later.
It remained a bitter memory. I enjoyed reading the works of Lenin
most. I examined how our way of life corresponds to it in practice.
I became aware of the personality cult, the Soviet cult....On October 23, we were at the climax of the burning brush fire, both
domestically and internationally. We viewed the fourteen points as
the highest achievement of our evolution. We felt that people were
once again turning into Hungarians. Unlike my classmates at the
university I took no part in the armed struggle. I saw the idealistic
side of the revolution. I went to the country for provisions, I only
saw heroes, I did not see what went on behind their back. At the
Petőfi Circle, a victim of the Rajk trials, a woman doctor told us
how she had been treated. Until then it never occurred to us that
such things could happen. What I heard then contributed to the fact
that I believed everything negative about the ÁVH, and none of the
positive ...I did not notice that behind our backs people were getting lynched, we did not want to lynch. A copy of Dudás's paper
fell into my hands, and I read about what happened on Köztársaság

Square....Then came November 4. Imre Nagy's cry for help at dawn, "The revolution is in danger!" I could not understand how the Soviet Union, who functioned as a friend until then, could come at us with weapons in hand. Likewise I did not understand János Kádár, who had suffered so much under Rákosi....There was talk about getting out of the country. I said, I was going to stay, leaving was not an option. Angyal and Gáli were of the same opinion. Whoever escapes is a traitor, those who fight cannot see what is happening around them. I heard horror tales from all sides, and I believed them. Before he got arrested, Angyal said, we are fighting a two-front war, because so many hooligans had infiltrated our ranks and they are thieving. We saw that there was trouble, and it only exacerbated our bitterness....It was a big mistake to place me at the head of a hospital. There is a limit to human endurance, but I refused to believe that. When I realized what I had done, the man was already dead. I cannot face myself since that moment, I take responsibility for what I had done, and now it's all over....

Miklós Gyöngyösi stated:

Let the court consider that I was raised without father or mother....That I now stand in front of a court of justice, and that my life was such until now, is because of those ignoble parents, who threw away their child, did not care for him, where he would sleep at night, or if he even had a place....I never made any attempts on people's lives, we did not carry Kollár upstairs with the intention of killing him, but rather of checking him out and letting him go. I know I am guilty of a crime, I have committed a crime, but let the court consider what were the conditions in Hungary in those days.

Ferenc Gönczi said:

I know that the charges against me are serious. It is not my intention to deny my culpability. I am guilty because I took part in a senseless, brutal crime that deserves condemnation by far when viewed by reasonable standards. We took someone's life, and we must answer for it, but not I alone. The prosecutor's office has examined the case, what took place, one-sidedly, as if on purpose. In those days the events were not everyday events in this country. It did not even mention the atmosphere of confusion, the anarchy, the chaos, which characterized the days of October and November. It is not permissible to examine and understand these events in springtime, in fair weather, with rose-colored glasses, not even from the prosecution's point of view....On a quiet day in the fall I knocked on the door of the Party, from where warmth and light were spreading, and some bright looks beckoned me. I entered as if I had been visiting dear parents or siblings....I followed the Party, but I was disappointed in it, I was disappointed in the army. What they told me was different from reality. Lenin was an exception; he not only taught, but showed the way. I strove to follow him in every way. I resigned from the ranks of people who assent to everything, who are always ready to compromise—I spoke out on behalf of the true principles, of justice, against all high-sounding slogans. Against the servile imitation of Soviet socialism.

Not much later the prosecutor interrupted: "It is not permissible that the defendant should be allowed to deal with the social and other problems of the past twelve years, this is completely unnecessary. It sounds strange that a murderer dares criticize the state and the army."

Then it was the turn of Gönczi's defense lawyer: "You cannot deprive the defendant of his right to a final statement."

The prosecutor: "I represent the state, which is why I spoke out."

Then the presiding judge warned Gönczi that he should talk about what led him to kill a human being.

In the Soviets I saw friends, and this was shown by the Soviet officers stationed here and who refused to fight as well. [Those] who replaced the Soviet units stationed here were misled people. I was convinced that they too are decent working people, much as I am. They were looking for the Suez canal and the like in our country, in 1956....I took in two wounded Soviet soldiers and a wounded ÁVO guard to the hospital....The court should consider that my judgment was at its clearest, I had taken a lot of caffeine pills, and had inhaled the chloroform. Who is responsible for the dead per-

son? First of all us, who are standing here in front of the court, but
we must also look at the honest youth, what brought them to this
point. Society is responsible as well, who did not temper the steel
well, who taught us to be suspicious. The Hungarian people were
merely fighting for a better life, the traitors became martyrs, Rajk,
etc.

On April 8 the court in the first instance condemned all three of them
to death; József Molnár received eight months. All appealed for mercy.[44]
At the mercy hearing the prosecutor, György Molnár, did not recommend any of them for mercy. In the case of Gönczi he even mentioned that "what bothered him the most during the trial, was whether
Kollár was indeed a state security agent, or not." The members of the
court agreed on rejecting the appeal for mercy and its justification,
except for the presiding judge Matild B. Tóth, who intended to com-
mute the death sentence of Ilona Tóth to a life sentence.
On June 9, Ilona Tóth turned to the Presidential Council of the
Hungarian People's Republic for clemency.

My father was an apprentice cabinet maker, then a factory
worker; my mother is a teacher. My parents had divorced in 1934,
I was raised by my mother amidst difficult circumstances. She was
unemployed until 1945; she was able to provide for us only by giving private lessons and with the help of my grandparents....I wanted to become a doctor, because I loved life and people, I wanted to
fight against suffering and death.
Although the war was hard on us too (our apartment was
destroyed, we are living in a sublet ever since), we nevertheless
started the new life with confidence. We realized that the teachers
were no longer "the nation's sharecroppers," we will enjoy a more
humane existence! My mother soon joined the MKP, then the
MDP. We read the works of Lenin together, we studied and we
worked. We had faith in the future. My mother became a decorated teacher, and I devoted all my strength to my studies to become
a good doctor. (I attained the rank of outstanding student both in
secondary school and the university.) ...I was active in the DISZ
[Democratic Youth Association]. I became study leader at the

Blanka Teleki High School, class president, then secretary of the
DISZ for the entire school in 1949–50. In the meantime, however,
I experienced bitter disappointments. Thus my two uncles were
interned unjustly in 1947–48. (One of them was severely harmed.
Both were rehabilitated later.) I also recall a slap in the face from a
political agent, in front of the entire camp. I knew, however, that
this was not at all a feature of socialism, but only of some people
who did not deserve to be referred to as true socialists.

I love justice, purity, I hate hypocrisy. Even in the DISZ I was
among those who dared to make critical remarks. The result was
that, in spite of the protests of the students, I had to resign the post
of secretary of the DISZ. This made me feel bitter, yet I did not
withdraw from the organization....

Keeping track of political events I noted with satisfaction how,
since the last Party congresses, those "excesses" which repel every
decent human being, and which hampered the evolution of our
people's democracy, whether Party member of not, were being
worn away. I was interested in the Petőfi Circle, in the courageous,
fresh voices I heard there. I was especially pleased to note that
there was greater interest in our national particularities....We
greeted the fourteen points with satisfaction....but we heard terrible
things from the lips of some of the defendants in the Rajk trial
regarding the ÁVH, and how medical instruments and medical
devices had been abused....

In the evening of November 4....I was assigned to the emergency hospital on Domonkos Street (because no one was willing to
transfer on account of all the shooting). I worked here alone until
November 10. It was hard. I did everything possible for my
patients and for the wounded....I admitted eight young fighters
(without their weapons!), because I feared that otherwise they
might get deported or shot. From about this time on I began to distribute illegal leaflets I received from István Angyal, with the task
of duplicating them....I was completely disheartened. I felt we had
lost the revolution, we had lost Hungary. I regarded the Soviet
Army as our enemy, the ÁVH also (I did not believe it was disbanded), and the new government. Unfortunately, there was no one
to tell me, "You are heading in the wrong direction!"....Those who

lived at the Academy of Councils,[45] as it turned out during the trial, only dared to speak behind my back, while they were flattering me up front, and tried to impress me with a flood of rumors to stop the production of leaflets. What they achieved is that I was more and more afraid. My mother also asked me to quit the illegal activities, it will end up badly. I, however, felt it would be dishonorable and cowardly to run away. At night I did illegal work, in the daytime, hospital work. Instead of sleeping I lived on caffeine. I felt my strength diminishing, but I kept hoping: perhaps everything will be resolved through diplomacy. Then came the arrest of Angyal (on November 16), then came the awful November 18, when, forgetting about my duties as a doctor and as a human being, I killed a person....

I am very guilty. But I do not feel that I am a murderer. What I had done was not cold-blooded, base premeditation, but the result of sudden collapse, a panic-like escape. By the time I realized what I had done, it was too late....I also insist that I was not and I am not an enemy of socialism....I just happen to mention, that until I have committed this serious crime, I had never taken a step in my life that I would be ashamed of in front of my mother...I could hardly wait for the time to come when I would be living and working for her, when I could make her happy. Now, as I am asking for mercy, I am thinking primarily not of myself, but of her. Perhaps I do not deserve a pardon, but she does. Therefore, I am asking the Honorable Presidential Council, to grant me mercy.[46]

During the trial on appeals Ilona Radó, the representative of the chief prosecutor, supported the death sentences; the defense lawyers used arguments very similar to the ones they had used during the original trial. Then Ilona Tóth spoke as follows during her final speech:

I would like to use a few words to complement those that I had used in my last speech during the original trial. I stand by all my confessions; except for some minor details, they correspond to reality. I want to speak not to the court, but to human beings. I have never tried to shirk responsibility, I will not unburden myself of the weight of the crime. What is hurtful for me is that when I implicated myself with my confessions, the court in the first instance would not accept what I had said in my defense. My politics, my intentions do not excuse me, but what I had done, I did it with good intentions. I could not see what was happening inside the Parliament, I did not know what was happening on Köztársaság Square. It is a grave thing, that I acted in this way, in spite of my duties as physician. But imagine all the circumstances that have brought me to this state of mind. I love my calling. It is not true that there is so much evil in me, that it could have been my premeditated design to kill all those who have betrayed. I knew I could not avoid the responsibility and the punishment, if we execute all of them. Mrs. Turcsányi was right next to me, it was obvious that she was a traitor, yet it did not occur to us to advocate her execution. During the transportation of the wounded I made no distinction between one human and another and that, indeed, was what my duty told me. Anyone could be admitted to my hospital and feel secure, I would have hurt no one. I committed this act because I was acting under stress. What I had done is alien to my personality. Perhaps I am not as lowly as the documents indicate. I regretted my act, not in front of the court, but in front of my own conscience. It is not likely that I would ever commit another crime. I accept the responsibility, I am prepared to die, but one can achieve a lot by willpower, and the crimes can be mended. My mother is present at this trial, and I have heard that her employment is at risk because of my case. This hurts me considerably, because it is not just that an innocent should suffer for the guilty. I only want to add that, during these proceedings, my father is closer to me, I just found out how much he means to me, and that makes me very happy.

The Council of the People's Court, under the chairmanship of Zoltán Radó, endorsed the three death sentences meted out in the Kollár case on June 20. The sentence of Molnár was increased to three years in jail. Here is an excerpt from the justification:

Indeed [Ilona Tóth] undertook her act of killing in a state of confusion, limiting her ability to think....According Article 10 of the criminal code, third paragraph, if a state of confusion in self-awareness limits the culprit in recognizing the antisocial dangers of her act, or in behavior in accordance with that will, the punishment can indeed be reduced indefinitely. But paragraph four of the same article of the law states the provision cannot be applied to the person who caused her own confusion for the purpose of committing the crime. Since Ilona Tóth, according to the above, caused her own state of stress, in order to continue her counterrevolutionary criminal acts, the state of confusion noted by the medical experts cannot be taken into consideration as a mitigating factor.

Once again, all three requested mercy. Neither the prosecutor nor the Council of Mercy favored granting mercy in their case. The people's judges were of the opinion that, "insofar as one may speak of mercy at all, it would behoove Ilona Tóth best."

Thus the sentence was carried out. Gönczi and Gyöngyösi were executed on June 26, Ilona Tóth the following day.

THE BIRTH OF LEGENDS

Even during the trial, the view in Hungary and abroad was that Ilona Tóth was sentenced on the basis of fake evidence, much as in the case of the classic show trials of the previous regime. This is quite understandable; Ilona's fellow students and friends held her in high esteem for her exceptional talents, her outstanding scholastic achievements, her qualities as a human being, and simply could not believe that her hands were stained with blood. We also cannot be surprised that foreign journalists suspected Stalinist fake show trials similar to the one in the case of László Rajk.

The Ilona Tóth legend spread even before the proceedings. As mentioned, it was rumored that there were "heaps of corpses" in the hospital on Domonkos Street. If indeed the state had engineered a show trial, it could have added this as evidence.[47]

In 1957 the trial became the focus of international attention. The overwhelming majority of foreign papers considered the trial as fake from beginning to end. The authors of the articles took their share in manufacturing the legend—as one may see from the anthology by Sándor Polgáry. For instance: "There were numerous reports that Ilona Tóth was pregnant at the time of her arrest. It is easy to assume that she lost her child as a result of the harm inflicted on her."[48] Polgáry compares the reports in Hungary with the foreign ones. For instance, an important excerpt of her confession was quoted at cross-purposes: "I consider myself very guilty in the crime of murder" (*Népszabadság*). "Whatever I have done, I do not consider myself a murderer" (*Morgen Tidning*). Polgáry resolves the contradiction: "This [last] data originates with a Western daily, and we have reason to give it more credence than we would to data printed in Hungarian Communist papers." This formula works in other cases as well: the *Manchester Guardian* referred to the fact that the judge Matild B. Tóth[49] interrupted Gönczi when he asserted that the Soviets harmed him severely. Of course, this was omitted from the Hungarian reports.[50]

The Swedish writer Paul Karlsson deserves special mention: after several years of dedicated research, somewhat overblown and containing contradictions, he nevertheless published a worthy volume on Ilona Tóth.[51] Karlsson makes several interesting observations. For instance:

> The similarity between the case of Ilona Tóth and the trials of those who resisted the Nazis in the occupied territories is obvious. The Hungarian Communist court is quite similar to the Nazi "People's Court." There is no difference between Ilona Tóth and those patriots who were killed by the Nazis for being involved in the underground movement. Had Ilona been of age during the times of Hitler, she also would have fought against the Germans. And Hitler would also have referred to her and her companions as bandits, much as the Communists did in 1957!...Ilona and her friends fought and died for a just cause. They were not criminals, and no one has the right to despise them. Ilona and Zoya sacrificed their life for the same cause, freedom.[52]

Given the ÁVH picture it was Karlsson's conviction that Ilona Tóth and the others killed the dangerous member of the secret police in self-defense. "It is unbelievable that he was innocent; it is impossible just as if we were to argue that a Pole from Warsaw during World War II would have let himself be photographed in German SS or SA uniform, to impress people!" In our opinion, it is far more unbelievable that a real secret agent would walk around with such a photo in those days.

Karlsson often makes the reader believe it was a show trial, by referring to the "directors of the trial," and to "brainwashing." Finally, he reaches the right conclusion: "Every war and revolution has its innocent victims. That the authorities invented the murder from scratch is hardly believable. They had no reason to do so, moreover the international press was invited. István Kollár probably really did exist, and died by and large as described to the court and asserted in the Hungarian press."

Beginning with the change of regime variants of the Ilona Tóth legend, sometimes mutually exclusive, found wings to soar. Since 1998, thanks to the so-called "bourgeois nationals," these have received political overtones.

The legends support the view that the trial was a show trial, that Tóth did not participate in liquidating Kollár, but was forced to make a totally false confession by means of cruel tortures, drugs, hypnosis. This view is shared by all those participating in the Tóth cult.

First let us take a look at some folk-tale elements:

> János Kardos, [the lawyer assigned to Ilona Tóth] soon acquired a loyal companion who tried equally desperately to save Ilona, but lacked the power and influence: it was János Kádár, who was then a prisoner still. It is natural also that they could not save Ilona's life because in Hungary the ruler of the administration of justice was no less a person than the sometimes hangman, sometimes savage minister of foreign affairs, the Stalinist bloodhound from the thirties, Vishinsky. And he decided that Ilona Tóth must perish....[53]

"Münnich offered Moscow seventy thousand dead bodies to help consolidate their rule, and the first martyrs delivered were Ilonka Tóth and her innocent companions."[54]

"According to the recollection of her fellow inmates, her child was ripped out of her body without the use of any anesthetic, and then public opinion was led to believe that the death sentence was carried out after the delivery."[55]

Others claim to remember that she said on the gallows "I am a virgin; I was raped by prison informants. They scraped my body out without anesthetic."[56]

"Nothing is more typical of those in charge of restoring 'law and order' than that Ilona Tóth was arrested already on November 19, on Lenin Boulevard, picked out from the crowd of pedestrians, as the eyewitnesses say: they kicked her around, then threw her on top of an all-terrain vehicle."[57]

There are others who emphasize Kollár's evil deeds, and feel it was all right to liquidate him. For instance, he handed over to the Soviets two carloads of sick patients.[58]

In most of the writings published since the regime change in 1989, Ilona Tóth is described as a practicing Catholic. That does not sound likely. There is no reference to this in the voluminous documentation about her case, except for the fact that she would not put up with cursing on the premises of the hospital. If she was indeed a believer, this would have come out in the records.[59]

It is noteworthy that the majority of fabricators of legends defend Tóth's reputation in contrast to Miklós Gyöngyösi and Ferenc Gönczi,[60] who were also executed, and who do not even have relatives who could apply for their rehabilitation.

FACTORS THAT CANNOT BE RECONSTRUCTED

Several aspects of the trial are not clear. Undoubtedly, the authorities in charge of punishment were so overconfident that they left many details unanswered. In order to resolve these, several historians and journalists are engaged in retroactive detective work but, of course, there is no hope of correcting what was overlooked in 1956–57. For many, the incomplete data, the confusion of some the documentation is proof enough in itself that the whole affair was made up.[61] More recently, the fog has settled, in the guise of "it could not have happened then, there, under those circumstances." The insignificant questions of detail thus serve to obscure the essential.

Those asserting "show trial" base their argument most often on expert medical opinion. These, however, are so contradictory, that the historians knows not what to make out of them. Sometimes even the doctors are at a loss. To cite just one example: according to Professor Gábor Jobbágyi of the Faculty of Medicine, "in 1989 Vilmos Földes, the physician specializing in autopsies insisted he felt that Ilona Tóth was completely innocent."[62] But in his expert opinion of 1957 Vilmos Földes wrote as follows, along with Endre Kelemen, the expert in forensics:

...the immediate cause of death was the stab wound at the heart, as a consequence of which the heart lining filled up with blood and death occurred as a result of the so-called obstruction of the heart....The stab caused the blood to spill into the envelope to the point of bursting, then through the walls of the envelope at the point of the wound the blood flowed into the left chest cavity; thus we found 480 grams of blood in that cavity. The immediate cause of death was this stab at the heart. The fact that the stab occurred when the victim was still alive is demonstrated conclusively by the fact that there was bleeding also along the stab wound, underneath the inner membrane of the heart.[63]

Which Dr. Földes should we believe?

There is an unresolved contradiction even in regard to the contents of the syringes. Several, sometimes even Ilona Tóth herself, spoke of an injection of gasoline, there was mention of ethyl chloride, and of the use of ether; but, according to the report on the autopsy prepared by the National Judicial Chemical Institute the analysis of these chemical proved negative, whereas in the case of ethyl alcohol it was definitely positive.[64] Once again this is an area in which this author has no expertise, but perhaps neither do my debaters. We don't know what compounds and what quantities of those compounds got into Kollár's body that could have made a difference. In other words, we have no hard data whatever regarding the contents of the syringe. Even the accused were uncertain, hence their confessions are contradictory in this regard.

The same goes for the negative laboratory examination of the knife. I have no idea whether after two months of exposure to water traces of blood can still be detected. But it is possible, for instance, that

Ilona Tóth cleaned the knife after the stabbing, put it away, and decided to throw it into the toilet only half a minute later.

We have no sources regarding these details. Nevertheless, the conscientious defense never raised these issues. On the other hand, it would be hard to understand why those who devised the alleged show trial would have insisted on various medical and chemical analyses which had an outcome unfavorable for them, and why would they have left the key evidence to posterity, in such an easy to obtain manner.

The argument brought up most often to prove Ilona Tóth's innocence is that the victim, according to several medical experts, was dead already when she stabbed him. The likelihood of this interpretation is enhanced by the fact that Tóth also felt this was the case. ("I thought nothing of stabbing a dead person.")[65] But she did not mean to avoid the charges by saying so, because she felt that the action had been carried out by the three of them.[66] None of them denied it, not even their lawyers, who did everything possible on behalf of their clients.[67]

Several have claimed that Ilona Tóth was subjected to some form of torture, forcing her to testify against herself. A medical examination dated from 1957 got into the hands of Gábor Jobbágyi, according to which the sole of Ilona was "insensitive" on both feet; in other words, the reflexes in her sole were not working. He concluded from this that she had been terribly beaten.[68] On the other hand, I was informed by neurologists that there is a completely different explanation of the "mute sole" phenomenon.[69] The social historian Pál Gyenes, who also believes the trial was a show trial, does not believe it is likely that she was beaten on her soles during the trial, or beaten at all.[70] Others, including Jobbágyi and the historian Sándor M. Kiss suspect the use of drugs, of psychological manipulation, of brainwashing.; according to Mária Rozgics, the accused were being hypnotized even during the trial, from the bench.[71] But there is no evidence to this effect.

All four of the accused emphasized, during the interrogation, that their confessions are voluntary, under no pressure, and they never changed their testimony in this regard. In fact, József Molnár confirmed this in his interview.[72] (Gönczi did mention that he was harmed during his capture by the Soviets, but that had nothing to do with forcing a confession.) Their defense lawyers would have known of it. Many of the accused in the trials following 1956 asserted that they had not been subjected to physical abuse. (For instance, Ottó Bognár, who was heard as a witness during the Tóth trial.)[73] Moreover, the trial of Tóth and fellow defendants, in the presence of journalists from the West, was public, which would have made it much more difficult to keep mistreatment a secret. During the interrogation the accused had been staying in various cells, it would have been impossible to torture them without the entire prison finding out.[74] In light of all this, we may assert that no physical pressure was applied against Ilona Tóth.

One also hears quite often that the corpse was never identified, since the description does not match; in fact Jobbágyi and others assert that Kollár died only in 1981—on the basis of research done by attorney Frigyes Kahler, the head of the Main Section of Criminal Law in the Ministry of Justice under the Antall government.[75] There are various legends afloat about the survival of Kollár: a resident of Budapest reported that he knew Kollár from 1952–53, and thought of him as a nondescript vagrant. In 1960 he confronted Kollár with the role he played during the affair, and the latter replied that he was paid 10,000 forints by the authorities."[76] As regards the testimony of autopsy Dr. Vilmos Földes, "In his opinion what happened was that the lady doctor was called over to a dead man, hoping she could revive him. This failed. Nevertheless, this was enough to invent the theory of a murder. However astounding it may sound, it is possible that there was no dead man. For it is quite possible that Miklós Gyöngyösi and Ferenc Gönczi had indeed beaten someone quite hard, believed the man had died, took him out of the hospital and left him to his fate."[77]

Others have questioned whether there ever was a Kollár, hence no Kollár affair, or it was a matter of mystification. For instance, Sándor M. Kiss presents three Kollárs,[78] as a matter of disinformation. He is mistaken, however, in asserting that the relatives did not identify the corpse; his sister, brother-in-law, and cousin identified the corpse in the morgue on Szvetenai Street, between December 11 and December 18.[79] Yet, Dr. Loránt Tamáska, often cited by Gábor Jobbágyi and others, identified the corpse in question as definitely that of István Kollár. One uncertainty remains: Mrs. István Bak, Kollár's cousin, asserts that Kollár had sliced off the tip of his index finger with an axe, whereas this identification mark is not mentioned in the otherwise most detailed autopsy report. The work was apparently not thorough enough.

For the sake of demystification let us summarize what we know about Kollár. He was born on June 22, 1930 at Kiskunhalas,[80] his mother was Veronika Fodor, his father András Kollár. He was raised in poverty, cared for by his siblings, completed only six years of schooling. At least since 1951 worked as a stock clerk at the Magasépítés [High Rise] Company, and lived at the workers' hostel pertaining to that company on 24–26 Pillangó Street in the fourteenth district. Here he was known as a withdrawn, quiet person. From November 7, 1952, he performed his military service obligations with the secret police (ÁVH); he was discharged on November 82, 1955, as lance corporal, and returned to his former place of employment and residence. From October 23 to November 10 he stayed almost continuously with his sister Irén Kollár and bother-in-law, András Vári, who served with the ÁVH as a driver. Kollár was pointed out as a member of the secret police in front of the Parliament building but, when he displayed his work permit, he was let go.

After November 9 he would visit regularly his fiancée, Erzsébet Polgár, on Jenő Landler Street; he had been courting her, allegedly, for five years.[81] No evidence has turned up that he had been tracking anything or anybody, and even those who captured him could not say what made him suspicious. It is almost certain that he had no evil intentions, his tragedy was owing to his extreme simplicity. In spite of repeated warnings he still carried the picture taken in August 1956, on which he was dressed in his brother-in-law's ÁVH noncom uniform. Even though it seems absurd that someone should carry such damaging evidence on himself in those days, the suspicions entertained by Tóth and her companions were false. They killed an innocent man who was no danger to them. Two of his fellow workers came to his funeral, his belongings were turned over to András Vári by the superintendent of the workers' hostel.[82] After his release József Molnár visited Mrs. István Bak, Kollár's cousin, who told him about Kollár: "...he was innocent, István was not a member of any kind of military [or other armed] organization."[83] Kollár is also mentioned in other contexts.[84]

THE PROOFS

To elucidate the Kollár affair we need no post facto detective work, but rather investigate the causes, that is historical research and critical analysis. Who may have intended the trial and how? Were there other show trials in 1956? If so, which? If not, why just this one? What advantages did the powers hope to gain from a trial against a recent medical graduate? Why would they want to condemn innocent people when the country was full of "dangerous counterrevolutionaries?" How many innocent people had to be involved to construct a fake trial, and how could their discretion be ensured, to the grave? The character of the proceedings, its style, its tone—why did it differ so drastically from the trials of the former regime? Why did several persons recommend Tóth for mercy? Was it a glitch that the defendant in the third instance, Ferenc Gönczi, attacked the integrity of the judicial authorities at the trial?

All these questions have been avoided by the chorus of the so-called "civic national" forces which represent all those on the right of center who are opposed to the left-wing socialist-liberal alliance.

It becomes obvious from the records of the trial and from the specialized literature that the most outstanding feature of the police and state security apparatus in late 1956 is their state of disarray.[85] Moreover, it is obvious by now that the political theses which formed the basis of "restoration," were on a most insecure footing in December 1956.[86] The historian János M. Rainer summarized this as follows:

> Only a few weeks separate the ruling party and its fist, the state security agencies from the moment when János Kádár spoke of revolution and uprising....The first statement in December from the Hungarian Socialist Workers' Party, issued by Kádár and his coworkers, do not contain the same four causes, or the thesis of 'counterrevolution from the start,' that became the official and widespread version later on. It was the Soviet emissaries, including Malenkov, who composed the resolution, in other words, there were obvious uncertainties.

Below I quote Tibor Zinner regarding the nature of the reprisals after 1956, which corresponds completely to the results of my research over a period of thirteen years:

It cannot be said that these trials proceeded along the same lines as the earlier ones. Physical and psychological force, brutality and terror, witnesses who accuse one another, confessions describing atrocities are not what characterize this period....Of course, there have been beatings. But these did not serve the purpose of eliciting confession, but stem exclusively from the sadism of the interrogator. It is not the goal that sanctifies the means, the forcing of incriminating confessions is not the outcome of false ideas, but rather to force you to admit what you had done, and I will append my own explanation. There is a great difference. What matters is: what I believe to be a revolution, is considered by the investigators as a counterrevolution; when I talk to someone, when I discuss certain topics, the charge is now conspiracy. When I cheer someone, then it is considered a factor of instigation; in other words, the acts performed, the majority of the events of 1956 happened in the way they have been described in historical research, or as they sounded in the confessions; it is the attached commentary, the brutal marginalia which subvert these actions and cause tragedies.[87]

What need was there for fake charges in the case of Ilona Tóth; whose power was obstructed by an innocent, eminent medical graduate who enjoyed general appreciation of all those who knew her? According to Mária Rozgics "Her only crime was that she loved her fatherland, her calling and, perhaps, they could not forgive her for having been born on October 23. She had to die, because they wanted to prove to the world, through her, that the 'counterrevolution' of 1956 was nothing but robberies and killings committed by common fascist criminals."[88]
Mária Wittner agrees: "Ilona Tóth, who was the very symbol of purity, of virtue, of human decency, had to be besmirched by the muck they had devised during the trial....Ilona Tóth was born on October 23. This was an unforgivable sin in their eyes, even in retrospect. Ilona Tóth's virtue, purity, humanity only enhanced her sin. She had to be slandered and, through her, the revolution in its entirety."[89] It is clear that for these reasons there was no point in fabricating a fake trial.
Sándor M. Kiss and the historian Réka Kiss essentially agree:

...They could have done it—looking at events from their point of view—without adding any horror details." "What is formulated in the rationale for the death sentence is a particularly cruel murder that belongs in pulp fiction. So it was not enough that people had to die in the revolution. The revolution had to be besmirched—by a young woman who killed betraying her medical ethics.[90]

Of course, it was only with regard to the best known personalities that charges were invented[91]; against Imre Nagy it was the charge of "the group of Imre Nagy, against Maléter, it was responsibility for the siege of the Party headquarters on Köztársaság Square"—personalities whose reputation had to be besmirched at any cost by the Kádár regime. (But they did not indulge in fake self-confessions!) As for the politically insignificant medical graduate[92] the regime had no need to invent anything.

The problems involved in fabricating a show trial are presented convincingly by Tibor Zinner:

> There was simply no need to create a monster trial encompassing everything, to shock the international public. First of all because the organization of the emergency tribunal, and the condition of operation for the system of justice in general, would have run into serious problems. A group of professionals would have been needed for such proceedings. Those who had fabricated the great classical show trials until 1953 were no longer around. If they were, they could be found only with difficulty. There were no judges, nor a team of prosecutors who could be used for any dirty work....The old team no longer existed, whereas those who might get picked, would refuse....The other factor is: the international press may attend, but not the domestic press? If it is a show trial, it had to be effective primarily internally. To the outside world it did not matter yet, the borders were closed, at worst there may be another "twenty questions regarding Hungary" asked at the United Nations. It was necessary to intimidate people on the inside, and toward the Soviets, so that it may be said that the Soviet soldiers had come to sacrifice their life for something worth while a second time.[93]

The documentation is not complete; it includes many careless mistakes, many typographical errors. Réka Kiss and Gábor Jobbágyi see in this further proof that the proceedings were fabricated.[94] There are obvious omissions, however, when researching other trials as well. The legal briefs or some other key document may be missing. Presumably, in most cases, these documents were loaned out on a temporary basis, and never returned. But the records are not as incomplete as these authors would lead us to believe. Notwithstanding their assertion, we have the dossier for the appeal—some forty-seven pages long! Nor has the resolution dated November 21, 1956, which prescribed the initiation of an investigation against Ilona Tóth in the matter of murder, disappeared.[95]

According to Réka Kiss, "the dates may get mixed up perhaps, but it is difficult to confuse whether something happened in the morning or in the evening."[96] Memory, however, may vary significantly from individual to individual. But can one forget Ilona's physical condition at that time? Jobbágyi reaches the wrong conclusion also when he states, from the brevity of the investigation, that there was manipulation. In general the trials proceeded much faster in early 1957 than later. (Consider the defendants in the case of the Dudás and Szabó trial, in which the two accused were executed already on January 19, 1957.) His observation that the confessions of Gyöngyösi, Gönczi, and Molnár, contradict each other, and that of Tóth on any essential point, is also untrue.

Réka Kiss considers their confessions as having been largely manipulated. For proof she refers to articles in the contemporary press "of which we have no trace in the interrogations" as well as in the sentence, according to which Tóth did not confess to murder voluntarily but only when she saw that others were being accused of it. Thus the "records of the interrogation do not reflect reality by far."[97] The contemporary articles, mostly by László Szabó and István Pintér were, indeed, written with propaganda objectives in mind; obviously historiography designed to reveal the fact cannot be based upon them. It is clear, furthermore, that the judicial sentence would not make a good starting point, because the authorities in charge of reprisals could distort the confessions pretty much as they saw fit.[98]

Again, according to Réka Kiss, the show-trial nature of the proceedings is revealed in the fact that at the time of the trial all those who had been arrested in November and December 1956, and to whom Tóth was referring because they saw the corpse, or knew something about the Kollár affair, were not readily available. "Thus the story of the missing participants is a very important aspect, which we should resolve."[99] That answer is almost too simple; most of those arrested in 1956 who were not deemed dangerous were soon released, and many of them left the country. When the authorities became more self-confident, and their desire for vengeance increased proportionately, they could only regret that so many had slipped through their clutches.

According to Gábor Jobbágyi the accused were made to recite a memorized text. I quoted extensively from the confessions and the petitions to enable us to make comparisons with the typical show trials. In the case of the Rajk trial, what aroused suspicion is that they tried to match the parts to fit together perfectly.[100] The absurd black and white descriptions in some segments of texts, the situation reports were typical only of the Rákosi period. There is no trace of this in the trial of Ilona Tóth and her companions, and it is unimaginable—especially given the length of time available, to put together anything of the sort. But the content of the text demonstrated the same thing. In short: "It would be an absurd supposition that such prorevolutionary writings could be assembled by the detectives within the framework of a show trial."[101]

Some cannot accept the self-incriminating confessions as fact. Yet such confessions were quite common in the trials stemming from 1956, especially during the first period of reprisals. I already mentioned the similarity of the ideas of István Angyal and Ilona Tóth. This became apparent not only during the revolutionary days, but also in captivity. Both deemed that it was more important to reveal the facts than to resort to tactics, as most of their companions were doing. Moreover, both became disillusioned in prison, assessing the revolution more critically than earlier. Among the fellow defendants, Ferenc Gönczi and Csaba Matéffy likewise did not try to conceal their activities during 1956.

To make use of other than archival sources, the most important participants backed the account of the tragedy of Domonkos Street. The most authentic witness, József Molnár, reconstructed the events convincingly, without preconceived notions—as we have seen. József Gáli, moved by what had happened at the hospital, discussed the Kollár case

with his wife and closest friends before his incarceration,[102] and again
after his release. His fellow defendant, the writer Gyula Obersovszky,
played a major role in the dissemination of the myths; as late as 1993
he declared:

> Let us not forget Ilona Tóth was also a child of the times. She was
> brought up on Alexander Fadeyev's *The Young Guard* [Molodaya
> Gvardiya]. She could hardly have avoided its impact. Her role
> model was the merciless yet comradely and brave revolutionary,
> the Jacobin. She must have had two ids. On the one hand, the
> physician who saves lives, who nurses; on the other hand, the rev-
> olutionary, who dares almost anything for the sake of the cause.
> Such a character does not retract anything, even in court.[103]

After that Obersovszky wrote and spoke only of show trials.[104] The
implausibility of the charge was confirmed by a report from an agent
within the prison—Obersovszky told the Kollár affair as it happened,
without the show trial version.[105] Another report from an agent reveals
that Ilona's mother did not think the case was made up.[106] Nor do other
participants in the political resistance support the view, in their memoirs, that the trial was fabricated.[107] Moreover, several of the persons I
interviewed about 1956—among those who proved to be reliable—
mentioned that the Kollár affair was discussed among the political prisoners, but never as a concocted process.[108]

Thus the Kollár affair was based on facts, only the historical interpretation underlying the charges was made up: namely, that Hungary
was the setting for a counterrevolution, and the Soviet troops came to
liberate the country a second time.

The trial against Ilona Tóth and companions did include some
made-up elements. The most important of these was that a single trial
took care of three rather loosely related cases. By lumping the defendants together the government tried to demonstrate the social dangers
of "counterrevolutionary organization": two intellectuals, three university students, three manual workers, and three members of the lumpen
proletariat. This invention almost cost the life of two writers, Gyula
Obersovszky and József Gáli. The Kollár affair proved most handy for
the regime; it tried to use the trial to the greatest extent as exemplary

and for the purpose of spreading its own propaganda. The court proceedings were not as a rule held in public, yet the Western press was invited, as were the newsreels. In the Hungarian media the affair received extensive commentary far beyond any other affair, to make it clear to everyone that the legends of revolution and of freedom fight were false, what had happened was merely White Terror in action in Hungary. Moreover, the Kádár regime could appear as an advocate of freedom of speech and freedom of the press.

THE "CIVIC NATIONAL FORCES" AND THE CULT OF ILONA TÓTH

The petition filed by Ilona's half brother, Ferenc Tóth, to have the sentence annulled was rejected by the Supreme Court in October 1990. That body relied exclusively on the facts leading to the sentence of 1957. It recognized that the death of Kollár was related to the uprising, but "in no ways can the reasons [for the murder] be deemed justified in the case of the accused practicing the medical profession." This decision to reject surprised many, all the more so because in those years the overwhelming majority of those condemned on account of 1956 were rehabilitated. Actually, this was the third attempt.[109]

In May of 1992 Mária Wittner and Tamás Horváth, representing the organization of revolutionary veterans, the Pofosz, asked the Ministry of Justice to reexamine the Ilona Tóth affair. The minister, István Balsai, and the department head, Frigyes Kahler,[110] also spoke out on behalf of Ilona's innocence. In October 1992 Balsai requested the presentation of a review of the legal justifications from chief prosecutor Kálmán Györgyi,[111] who rejected the request in August 1994, saying the attached documents were insufficient. Yet the rehabilitation of Ilona Tóth was supported by an ever growing number of researchers and myth makers.[112] With the election victory of the right-of-center "civic national forces" in 1998, the Ilona Tóth affair became part of the political campaign: a documentary on the affair had its premiere,[113] a statue of Ilona was unveiled—with the participation of Minister of Justice Ibolya Dávid, Speaker of the House János Áder, and the chairman of the Fidesz Party, Zoltán Pokorni. From then on,

Ibolya Dávid and the hired writers were playing an ambiguous game. While they announced that the entire Kollár affair was made up from scratch, they introduced and passed a piece of legislation by means of their parliamentary majority in 2000 (Act 130), which made it possible to rehabilitate all those condemned for common crimes after the revolution.[114] On this basis the Municipal Court of Budapest could declare the death sentence of 1957 null and void. The justification: "The condemnation of Ilona Tóth, considering her identification with the goals and spirit of the revolution and of the freedom fight—came about as an act related to the revolution and its combats." This stood in stark contrast with the Ilona Tóth legends. The editors of the right-wing *Demokrata* and of the Fidesz Party daily, *Magyar Nemzet*, however, made it a point to omit the justification, and they even implied that the rehabilitation came about because of the show trial of 1957.[115] But if there had been a show trial, what need was there to rehabilitate all those who committed common crimes?

In the opinion of this author, rehabilitation could not have taken place on legal grounds, yet Ilona Tóth and her fellow defendants certainly deserve a place among the martyrs of the revolution, therefore we must be satisfied with the result achieved.[116]

NOTES

1. The Önkéntes Mentőszolgálat (ÖM) was established in October 24, 1957. Its founders were Dr. Miklós Lambrecht, Dr. Géza Jakó, and Géza Pech. First Lieutenant István Tóth, the later military commander of the hospital, started his service on October 26.
2. BFL, 165/57, Ilona Tóth jkv., 1957. II. 18. The historian Réka Kiss feels this confession was false, the result of manipulation by the authorities. Interview on MTV 2, September 2002.
3. BFL, 8005/58, Tóth jkv., 1957. VI. 12. Tóth was worried about the fate of Hungary even as a child. At age fourteen she wrote a poem observing the rules of versification in Hungarian:

   What became of you, proud nation of Árpád?
   What became of you, my nation, oh Hungary?
   Why have you laid down your sword from your hand?
   You never want war again?

Have you been frightened by the cowardly populace?!
Let it be your eternal shame, disgrace on you!
You who have defended it in turmoil, in catastrophe?
Do you let your home perish now?
Your eyes lowered, your hands shackled
Foreign hands are tilling your land
Strange magic has enthralled you
How long will you allow this situation?
Foreign nation is sacking your homes
And your weapons are not at the ready
Even if you have buried your pike of war
Let not rust corrode it
Wake up, Hungarian! Pin it to the tip of your lance
The banner of your glorious saint
Then you will be deserving of your ancestors
Do not feel discouraged, Hungarian
Your sword in hand, God be with you,
Because the fatherland is blessed when many hearts want....

György Ordódy, director, *Ki volt Tóth Ilona?* [Who Was Ilona Tóth] (Budapest: Unio Civilis-Hunnia, 1998). Until 1953 Ilona practiced fencing, swimming, and athletics. She was attracted to daredevil activities as well—interested in flying for sport—but was denied the doctor's permission to drop by parachute for being too light (she weighed a mere forty-seven kilos).

4. BFL, 8005/58, Tóth önv. 1957. VI. 10. The fourteen points refer to the October 23 demands of the university youths. For a sixteen-point version, see Appendix, pp. 187–189.
5. Mainly because of her meeting of October 30 with József Dudás, since she conceived a low opinion of him.
6. BFL, 8005/58, Tóth önv. 1957. VI. 10.
7. BFL, Tóth tárgy., 1957. III. 4.
8. BFL, Tóth tárgy., 1957. II. 18.
9. Ibid.
10. TH, V–142621, Tóth jkv., 1956. XI. 21.
11. BFL, Miklós Gyöngyösi ü., 1957. I. 8.
12. Eörsi, ed., *Angyal István sajátkezű vallomása*, pp. 138–39.
13. Endre Futacsi was summarily executed in the City Grove [Városliget] as a traitor on November 8.
14. "If it could have been proven that he was a traitor, it surely would have ended badly." In Eörsi, ed., *Angyal István sajátkezű vallomása*, pp. 138–39. "I did not extend my hand to Petruska when he left. I told him,

he is a traitor, and I will not shake your hand until the matter if completely cleared." In BFL, Tóth tárgy., 1957. VI. 11.
15. BFL, Tóth tárgy., 1957. II. 18.
16. "I was threatened by Ilona Tóth, she called me an ÁVH sergeant, she told me she will do away with me. One with a scarred face [Gönczi] pushed me so hard from the fourth floor that, had I not grabbed the banister, I would have died. I was afraid after that." In TH, V–142621, Mrs. József Turcsányi tk., 1956. XI. 20.
17. TH, V–143522, and HL, 284/58, Károly Fehér jkv., 1958. I. 31., and II. 21; TH, V–143522, and HL, 284/58, Erzsébet Kovács tk., 1958. I. 30.
18. BFL, Tóth tárgy., 1957. II. 18.
19. "If Kollár had carried a work pass, he would not have gotten murdered," testified Gönczi. In BFL, 1957. III. 4.
20. BFL, Gyöngyösi ü., 1957. I. 8.
21. BFL, Tóth jkv., 1956. XII. 29.
22. BFL, Gyöngyösi ü., 1957. I. 8.
23. BFL. Gáli jkv., 1956. XII. 29; BFL, Gáli, tárgy. 1957. III. 4.
24. The mood of distrust became widespread among all resistance groups, resulting in several deaths around the city, in addition to the Futacsi case already mentioned. The victims were simply shot, therefore these instances, although mentioned in several death penalty cases, did not become sensations.
25. BFL, Tóth tárgy., 1957. II. 20; TH, V–142621/1, Veszprémi jkv., 1957. XII. 7. 1956.
26. BFL, Tóth jkv., 1957. II. 18.
27. Ilona Tóth claimed that they entered the office, but Gönczi chased them out in no uncertain terms. Gönczi denied this.
28. This is intimated in the account by Tibor Missura as well. See OHA, no. 346, "Tibor Missura," 1991, pp. 85–87. Missura heard about the Kollár affair from a stranger, when under arrest between December 7 and 14. He was also told that the person was together with the doctor Ilona Tóth, and saw her mop the floor. (The stranger could only have been Veszprémi, who indeed pretended to be a physician on occasion.)
29. BFL, Gáli tárgy., 1957. III. 6. At this time Ilona Tóth said at the trial: "Since Gáli dared to speak—the only one [among the writers]—I must conclude that he is the most courageous, or the sharpest observer."
30. In 1986–87 Gyula Obersovszky recalled (erroneously) that the two of them had spoken to Ilona Tóth: "...son, the Hypocratic oath, is not your concern....It has its own....It should be resolved some other way." OHA, no. 96, "Gyula Obersovszky," 1986–87, p. 437.
31. BFL, Gáli tárgy., 1957. III. 6. Obersovszky said something similar. BFL, Obersovszky tárgy., 1957. II. 28; OHA "Obersovszky," p. 437.

32.   BFL, Gáli tárgy., 1957. III. 14, 1957.
33.   TH, V–142621, 1956. XI. 19.
34.   BFL, Mrs. Pál Fazekas and Éva Török tárgy. 1957. III. 18.
35.   BFL. Tóth tárgy., 1957. II. 20. Ilona knew First Lieutenant Sándor Kár-
       páti from the university; he too was arrested later and sentenced to five
       years in prison.
36.   BFL, Tóth tárgy., 1957. VI. 11.
37.   BFL, Tóth tárgy., 1957. II. 20.
38.   BFL,. Tóth tárgy., 1957. II. 26.
39.   TH, V–142621, Tóth jkv. December 29.
40.   TH, V–142621, Tóth jkv., 1956. XII. 21.
41.   BFL, Tóth tárgy., 1957. II. 20. She added: "My responsibility is not
       diminished by the fact that I had not yet taken the oath...when I said
       that I was not yet a certified physician, I said that only to calm myself.
       This Kollár affair did happen, to my misfortune."
42.   BFL, Tóth tárgy., 1957. II. 26. In his memoirs István Eörsi wrote about
       the jail rumor, according to which Gönczi had declared at the trial, that he
       committed no crime. He fulfilled his duty by killing Kollár because, as a
       political official, he had learnt, and even taught, that traitors must be exe-
       cuted, since the interest of the community comes ahead of the life of an
       agent. It would have been unprincipled on his part if he did not apply in
       practice what he professed to his subordinates. That was when the prose-
       cutor interjected that Kollár was not a member of the ÁVH, he was wear-
       ing someone else's clothing on the picture. "In that case I am a murderer
       and deserve to die." "And if the uniform had been his?" "Then I did the
       right thing." In István Eörsi, Emlékezés a régi szép időkre [Remembering
       the Good Old Days] (Budapest: Napraforgó Kft., 1988), pp. 73–74.
43.   BFL, Letter from Gyöngyösi to the chairman of the Presidential
       Council.
44.   In contrast to the assertion by Ildikó Hankó ("Tóth Ilona védelmében"
       [In defense of Ilona Tóth], Demokrata, no. 45 (2000): 20–21.
45.   In the building of the hospital on Domonkos Street.
46.   Obersovszky and Gáli, the fifth and sixth defendants in the trial, peti-
       tioned Prime Minister János Kádár on June 25, 1957. Among other
       things Gáli wrote: "Mr. Prime Minister! In your person we have a man
       at the helm of the government whose unjust imprisonment was the rea-
       son I wrote my drama entitled Szabadsághegy [Freedom Mountain] I
       tried to evoke your fate in the tragic story of János Bojtár....I wrote it
       in 1954–55, but it remained in the drawer of my writing desk for over
       one year."
47.   Perhaps it is no wonder that there are some who prefer this sort of
       myth. For instance, erstwhile council chairman Ferenc Vida. In Jenő

Faragó, "Perbe fogott ítélet. Interjúkötet Vida Ferenccel" [A sentence on trial. Interviews with Ferenc Vida], manuscript, pp. 26, and 116.

48. Sándor Polgáry. "Nemzedékek" [Generations], manuscript, 1986.

49. Matild B. Tóth was not Mrs. Biszku, as some historians believe, but Mrs. Braunstetter.

50. The *Manchester Guardian* was also appreciated by George Orwell in the course of his research work for *Homage to Catalonia*....

51. Paul Karlsson, *Dömd pa förhand: Ilona Tóth-processen i Budapest 1957* [Doomed from the Start. The Ilona Tóth Trial in Budapest 1957] (Viken: Eremit-press, 1983).

52. Reference is to Zoya Kozmodenskaya, a female partisan, who posthumously was awarded the Hero of the Soviet Union medal. It is not yet clear to what extent the "populist-nationalists" like this argument. Karlsson's volume is often mentioned, but not quoted by them.

53. Letter by the son of János Kardos; Gyula Obersovszky, *Tóth Ilona, a magyar Jeanne d'Arc* [Ilona Tóth, the Hungarian Jeanne d'Arc] (Budapest: Codex, 1999), p. 103.

54. Mária Rozgics, "Drótozott kézzel, arccal lefelé" [With hands wrapped in wire, eyes downcast], *Demokrata*, no. 45 (2001): 16–18. "Véd- és vádlott egyaránt áldozat" [Defender and accused are both victims], *Magyar Nemzet*, December 14, 1998.

55. *Magyar Fórum*, no. 39 (1992), note by the editors.

56. Anna Párdi, "Fehér lobogó oktoberi balladán" [White banner on a ballad from October], *Magyar Fórum*, no. 43 (1992): 122. Frigyes Kahler added his views at the end of the article: "I don't believe the story about the aggressive informer. There is no need to enhance the horrors artificially."

57. VIP, "Miután letartóztatták, szabadlábon gyilkolt?" [After her arrest: did she murder while free?], *Reform*, October 22, 1992, p. 29. This article simply forges the content of the confessions.

58. OHA, no. 415, "Károly Antal Németh," 415, p. 344. Even the editor of the popular history journal *Rubicon*, Borbála Juhász, was not able to resist the influence of the myths, although the quote below leads us to suspect strongly that she had not even seen the primary sources: "The circumstances of the alleged murder are extremely confused, the undercover member of the police had been practically beaten to death by two members of the insurgent group. They took the dead body to the twenty-four-year young woman commander, overstressed from work, living off caffeine tablets; she later never denied the murder (euthanasia) attributed to her. Of course, we must examine the words of the author of the petition for mercy, facing the death penalty, with a serious critical analysis of the sources." In "1956. Mégis kinek az

emlékezete?" [Whose memory should count?], *Rubicon*, no. 6 (2001): 36–40.

59. At the trial Gönczi stated: "I am not religious, I have become convinced that there is no God, because if there were, I would not be standing here." In BFL, Gönczi jkv., 1957. II. 20.

60. They were on the tracks of an anonymous person from 1957. The nameless author tried to convince Matild B. Tóth, that Ilona Tóth was innocent, the murderers being her two companions. PIL, 290. f. 108. ö. e., dossier 67. If we examine nothing but the actions, then Gönczi would be the primary perpetrator, Ilona Tóth would be next, and Gyöngyösi in third place. Even that would not be quite fair because "Piri" played the decisive role in determining "the guilt" of Kollár.

61. On the same grounds, we may challenge any trial stemming from 1956 as unjustifiable to a greater or lesser extent.

62. Report by András Kő, *Magyar Nemzet*, December 7, 2001.

63. BFL, Dr. Földes Vilmos tk., 1957.

64. BFL, Országos Bírósági Vegyészeti Intézet, 1957. I. 8.

65. BFL, Tóth tárgy., 1957. II. 20.

66. Of course, from a legal point of view it does matter whether Ilona Tóth stabbed Kollár to death, or whether she thrust the knife into a dead body. The significance, however, has been exaggerated; in this same trial an attempt to murder was considered sufficient for the death penalty and execution of Ferenc Kovács.

67. The historian Sándor M. Kiss asserts the opposite as regards the tactics and strategy of Tóth's defender, János Kardos. See "Tóth Ilona tragikuma" [The tragic predicament of Ilona Tóth], *Magyar Nemzet*, April 27, 2002. He does not elaborate.

68. Gábor Jobbágyi. "Ténymegállapítás: mindkét oldalt néma talp" [Stating of fact: the sole is unresponsive on both sides], *Magyar Nemzet*, February 5, 2002. By the way, I have been unable to locate this expert opinion.

69. Verbal communication by Dr. György Frigyesi, 2002.

70. Report by János Adonyi Stancs, *Köztársaság*, no. 1 (1993).

71. Rozgics, "Drótozott kézzel, arccal lefelé," no. 45 (2001): 17.

72. OHA, no. 429 "József Molnár," 1992. On page 77 Molnár responds to two direct questions categorically that no one laid a finger on him in prison. As far as he knows, the others were not harmed either, p. 88.

73. BFL, 3308/57.

74. Among the defendants in the Tóth trial, István Eörsi met Gyöngyösi, Csaba Mátéffy, Ferenc Kovács at the Markó Street jail. He asserts "the topic of torture was never even raised." Moreover, the defendants in the show trials from the 1953 period were all isolated from the rest, when worked upon.

75.   In response to my inquiry, Kahler told me that the sources were to be found in the Office of the Chief Prosecutor of the capital and the Ministry of Justice, and consented to using him as reference. These agencies, however, informed me that they held no records pertaining to the Ilona Tóth case.
76.   Szilvia Zimber, "A Tóth Ilona-dossié lapjai" [The pages of the dossier pertaining to Ilona Tóth], *Pesti Hírlap*, October 24, 1995.
77.   Report by András Kő with Gábor Jobbágyi. *Magyar Nemzet*, December 7, 2001.
78.   M. Kiss, "Tóth Ilona tragikuma." Sándor M. Kiss argues, as a result of over one year of research, that nothing can be known for certain, and adds to the mystification. He does not reveal his sources, thus his statements cannot be verified.
79.   BFL, Mrs. István Bak and András Vári tárgy., 1957. III. 14.
80.   The persons who compiled the *White Book* indicate Kelebia as Kollár's birthplace (vol. 3, p. 140). The editors of this publication from the Kádár period did a great service to the fabricators of myth by their inexpert elaboration, their inexactitudes and mixing up of the data.
81.   From the contradictory confessions of Polgár, the fiancée—for in those days she was in contact with other men as well, and she married very shortly after Kollár's death—several persons think of this as proof of show trial.
82.   BFL, Confessions by Mrs. István Bak, Mihály Karsai, Demeter Rádai, András Vári. Report by István Szentgáli.
83.   OHA, "Molnár," p. 56. In his childhood Molnár was raised by Mrs. Bak for a while.
84.   At the trial "Sándor Torácz and fellow defendants" there are several references to this. See TH, V–143522, and HL, 284/58. According to Sándor M. Kiss and Réka Kiss, Torácz received the death penalty also because of the fictional Kollár murder. Report on Duna TV, October 22, 2002. This is out of the question. Torácz was a commander of a group of insurgents, the main reason for the reprisals against him.
85.   "There is the notion, that they began to come to their senses having been unconscious, a favorite jargon used by the security forces....If the Russians are not around, they cannot kick the ball...it was the Soviets who arrested the bulk of the people, they are the ones who decide on the most basic issues...." Tibor Zinner's personal communication, 2003. The disarray of the agencies is also demonstrated by the fact that "counterrevolutionaries" who were later deemed dangerous were released en masse, and by the fact that they often acted at cross purposes.
86.   Duna TV, October 22, 2002.

87. Personal communication by Zinner, 2003.
88. Rozgics, "Drótozott kézzel, arccal lefelé."
89. Report by Zsuzsa Halas, *Vasárnapi Újság*, online, October 24, 2000. Mária Wittner mentions the same two causes in her book. See Wittner, *Ellenőrizve* [Passed] (Budapest: Magyar Ház, 2002), p. 106.
90. Duna TV, October 22, 2002.
91. I can only assert this much, with a clear conscience, about the trials held in Budapest, because I have conducted no research on trials in the country. Tibor Zinner, legal historian, stated in his personal communication (2003): "I have yet to encounter a trial stemming from 1956 that may be described as a show trial in the classical sense of the term."
92. My debating partner on Duna TV, on October 22, 2002, Réka Kiss described this as an "assertion with a question mark," but she never gave an explanation.
93. Zinner, personal communication.
94. Gábor Jobbágyi, *A néma talp. (Tóth Ilona, az orvosi kar mártírja)* [The Silent Sole—Ilona Tóth, the Martyr of the Faculty of Medicine] (Budapest: Püski, 2002). The author had already published the full text in the February, March, and April 2002 issues of the *Magyar Szemle*. I pointed his mistakes out to him long before the book was published, and I even sent him the records, at this request. He thanked me for it in the copy dedicated to me, yet he did not feel prompted to correct the mistakes.
95. The attorney János Kardos also pointed out the mistakes in dates, and these were allowed.
96. Duna TV, October 22, 2002.
97. Ibid.
98. It is interesting that the most enthusiastic defenders of the procedure refer most often to this sentence—including Dr. Péter Kende. See "Szobor egy gyilkosnak?" [Statue for a murderer?], *Népszabadság*, April 22, 2002.
99. Duna TV, October 22, 2002.
100. Béla L. Szász, *Minden kényszer nelkül* [Without the Use of Force] (Budapest: Európa-Historia, 1989).
101. Sándor Rávász, "Idusról idusra" [From ides to ides], *Beszélő*, no. 12 (2001): 18.
102. Communication by Vera Káldor and István Eörsi.
103. Report of János Adonyi Stancs, *Köztársaság*, no. 1 (1993): 15. Also, "It is my conviction that the vigilance inculcated in people in the period played a major role. There is no forgiveness, there is no excuse, the traitor has to be eliminated. Peruse the *Young Guard*, and those films." In OHA, "Obersovszky," p. 439. There is no mention of any show trial in this interview.

104. Obersovszky, *Tóth Ilona, a magyar Jeanne d'Arc.*
105. TH, 36/60, Report April 17, 1960, "Benjámin Hercegh and fellow defendants."
106. TH, V–144984, Report by agent assigned to Mrs. Ferenc Tóth. "Mrs. Ferenc Tóth and fellow defendants."
107. The physician Tibor Missura saw no indication of a show trial, nor did the physician Vera Káldor or the engineer Gyula Bagó, a former fellow defendant. The physician Mikós Lambrecht was dubious about the official version: "For it did not jibe at all that a woman doctor in internship would resort to such primitive and brutal methods...." His opinion may be summarized as follows: "I knew only what I read in the papers. I had to extract the truth by reading between the lines and then one may surmise that somewhere there was some validity to the official version." See OHA, no. 109, "Vera Káldor,"1987; OHA, no 375, "Gyula Bagó," 1992; OHA, no. 192, "Miklós Lambrecht," 1988–89. The former cell mate, the programmer Csaba Mátéffy: "Look, I don't understand either, but do not ask me about this, because all I can do is guess. And you are not interested in what I guess or don't guess. These were extraordinary circumstances, extraordinary times, extraordinary actions." In OHA, no. 314, "Csaba Mátéffy," 1991, pp. 81–82. He felt that the monster trial, the choice of defendants constituted the kangaroo court. See ibid., pp. 46, 183, and he is quite right about that. Both Lambrecht and Mátéffy offered logical answers.
108. Communications by Péter Czajlik, Endre Ebinger, Pál Kabelács, Mihály Nagy, Géza Pásztor, János Puchert, László Schmidt, István Szigetvári. See also István Eörsi, *Emlékezés a régi szép időkre*, pp. 73–74.
109. Her former schoolmates and girl friends formed the Ilona Tóth Circle of Friends (TIBK) in 1989, fighting for the declaration of martyrdom. That same year the circle petitioned the minister of justice for rehabilitation. It was rejected with the argument that the petition had not been filed by a relative. At the same time and independently, at the request of Ferenc Tóth as a representative of the Committee for Historical Redress, the attorney Alajos Dornbach, launched a procedure which was turned down by the Supreme Court. See letter of Ferenc Tóth to Dr. Péter Polt, in Wittner, *Ellenőrizve*, p. 108.
110. It is clear from Ferenc Tóth's letter to Polt, ibid., p. 109, that an unpublished essay by Pál Gyenes in 1991 "included hitherto undisclosed data that Frigyes Kahler, a department head at the Ministry of Justice at that time, found the data pertinent and used it to advocate the reopening of the trial proceedings."
111. According to the letter by Ferenc Tóth, the TIBK requested the support

of the president of the republic on the basis of the study by Gyenes. President Árpád Göncz forwarded it to the chief prosecutor.

112.   The historian and sociologist Pál Gyenes does not belong in this group; he has been researching the topic most conscientiously since the change of regime. For three years he has been promising that he will prove in his monograph, in detail, that the Kollár affair led to a fake trial. See *Magyar Hírlap*, November 16, 2000.

113.   Ordódy, *Ki volt Tóth Ilona?* *"Magasabbak az egek a földnél"* [Who was Ilona Tóth? "The Skies Are Higher than the Earth"], The work, which reminds us of the propaganda movies produced by the Party, has been reviewed by the this author in the 1999 yearbook of the 1956 Institute.

114.   Finally the parliament approved it by a large majority.

115.   It is interesting that one of the leading advocates of the show trial version, Mária Wittner, published the document in its entirety in her book, without wasting a single word on this contradiction. Attorney Gábor Jobbágyi is likewise most silent about this in this essay, although his summary includes a serious misrepresentation: "Thus Ilona Tóth and her companions were legally exonerated." (Jobbágyi, *A néma talp*, p. 8). In fact, the exoneration of Gyöngyösi and Gönczi was never even contemplated.

116.   There are several, even nowadays, who identify completely with the sentence handed down in 1957, seeing and presenting Ilona Tóth and her companions as simply common murderers. The best known among them is the journalist Dr. Péter Kende, who used nothing but the sentence from 1957 in his pertinent article, in spite of the fact that this genre is far from constituting the most reliable source. The authorities necessarily always present the infinitely simplified picture, as reflected in Dr. Kende's article.

PÉTER MANSFELD

"I wanted to stir up some trouble...."

Péter
Mansfeld

József
Blaski

Rezső
Bóna

László
Furka

Attila
Egei

CHILDHOOD

The Mansfelds were originally from Vienna, the family having moved to Pest in the nineteenth century.[1] Péter Mansfeld was born on March 10, 1941. In 1945 the male members of the family— father, uncle, grandfather—were taken for "malenkiy robot" [in Russian, a little work] by the Soviets and the grandfather never returned.[2] His father was a hairdresser, managing his own shop until 1946. He had one employee, and his wife also worked in the business as assistant hairdresser. Following the Communist nationalization of privately-owned businesses, the couple settled in a cooperative shop. They separated in 1951, and got divorced two years later.[3] With his sister, ten years older, and his brother, four years younger, Péter stayed in his mother's care. "I finished fifth grade with an 'unsatisfactory' in the school on Medve Street, I had to take a make-up examination to get into the next grade. I continued my studies in Balkány, in a reform school."[4] He continued as an apprentice turner at the Mátyás Rákosi vocational school at Csepel.[5] In the contest for the "best vocational student in the trade" he came in second: "...the machines, the equipment, messing with gizmos were the essence of his life."[6]

Péter had a wide range of interests: raising rabbits, playing soccer, martial arts, but best of all driving vehicles. He learnt to drive at the Iron and Metalworks of Csepel. In 1956 he was transferred to the MÁVAG [Hungarian State Iron and Machinery Works]. "I used to read sometimes, especially crime stories, but also the youth paper *Ifjú Gárda* [Young Guard]."[7]

During the revolution, at the time of the armistice negotiations, he went to Széna Square and joined the armed group there. The commander of the insurgents, János Szabó (alias "Uncle Szabó") sent him away at first, with his friend and later codefendant Rezső Bóna, as being too young. Nevertheless, he became the driver and messenger later on, although he could not have had a driver's license. Besides acting as messenger, he delivered weapons, reams of paper, and medicine. He went to Széna Square daily, but slept at home. He was not a conscious revolutionary—it would be difficult to imagine such a person at age fifteen and a half—but Uncle Szabó did make a lasting impression on him. He took no part in the fighting that broke out on November 4.

The following day he was busy collecting weapons. He and his friends collected a total of one machine gun, five or six submachine guns, fifteen drum magazines, thirty hand grenades, large numbers of fuses and ammunition, distributing these among each other and hiding them in case another revolution broke out.

In spite of what is commonly believed, in the course of 1957 it never even occurred to Mansfeld to resist with arms or politically. He got transferred to the Magyar Optikai Művek [Hungariam Optical Works] (MOM) where he continued his apprenticeship. He appropriated from there, and from his former workplace, MÁVAG, a number of generators, drills, and other tools or objects, to the value of 3 or 4,000 forints (two month's average salary). From August 4 he and his friends carried out a whole series of thefts, altogether about 30,000 forints worth.[8]

He and his companions were arrested on October 4; he noticed while driving their "borrowed" car that they were being chased and, to shake off his pursuers, Mansfeld made a sudden turn, into a tree. Three days later, however, he escaped from police custody, and continued to steal until the middle of the month, when he was rearrested. He spent three and a half months in custody during the investigation. The time he spent there, and everything he learnt from his fellow inmates were a defining moment in his life, and he became an irreconcilable enemy of the regime until his death, even though the circumstances were not that unfavorable to him. On January 29, 1958, he was sentenced to one year in jail, which was suspended for a three-year period of probation. In other words, he was released, and he was forgiven at his workplace, since he was "an intelligent, hard-working boy who learnt easily."[9]

THE "GANG OF TERRORISTS"

In late 1957 Mansfeld became close friends with the skilled worker József Blaski, who was three years his senior. When he ran away from police custody, he sought out Blaski; and the latter offered to hide him in his apartment, but Mansfeld did not accept the offer. Instead he spent the nights in a haystack on the Rózsadomb in Buda, and his food was brought to him by his younger brother.[10]

On February 15, 1958, Blaski and Mansfeld decided that they would undertake joint actions. They considered the various means of acquiring funds. The best method, in their opinion, was to carry out armed robberies, with the help of a stolen getaway car. Their hidden machine pistols were not good enough for the purpose; they needed pistols, which they could acquire by disarming cops and workers' security guards. Their plan was to make use of the identity cards and uniforms in the process of attacking post offices.[11]

That same day they tried to appropriate a Pobeda [Soviet-made vehicle]. Mansfeld was unable to get the car started, but they removed the documents they found inside the vehicle and a certificate that entitled the owner to free gas....The next day they took out of the cellar of a ruined garage the machine pistols and the magazines that Mansfeld had hid there in a professional manner.

During their first conversation, Blaski had already mentioned that they needed more help. On November 16 Mansfeld also met, by accident, his former friend and classmate, the semiskilled worker Rezső Bóna, and told him, at his apartment (his parents being absent), what they had in mind. In addition, there was the vocational student László Furka, a year younger than they, whom Mansfeld had not yet met. It turned out that Bóna too was considering the formation of a group, to distribute leaflets. Mansfeld had no objections to this, but he noted that he would need Blaski's consent. Furka announced that at the time of the revolution he had collected some leaflets, and those could be duplicated.[12] Bóna asked Mansfeld if he could be admitted into the band, and recommended Furka, adding that he knew the latter well, and could vouch for him. Mansfeld agreed to their participation, They discussed the possibility of disseminating the leaflets with the car Mansfeld was to steal. Bóna and Furka were assigned the mission of procuring a typewriter.[13] Bóna was under threat of court action for appropriating food stamps, therefore he had decided to leave the country shortly, and Furka would have gone along.[14]

The next day, the morning of the 17th—again as a result of a chance encounter, for Mansfeld did not feel like going to school that day—he recruited another old friend into the group, Attila Egei, who was two years younger, and still in secondary school. This time Mansfeld was able to take off in a Warszawa (a Polish-made copy of the Pobeda) stationed in front of the Ministry of Foreign Affairs, which he parked off the beaten track on a side-street on the Rózsadomb. In the afternoon Blaski and Mansfeld manufactured a license plate from a broken piece of gutter. To ensure peace for themselves they decided to paint a Soviet number on the plate, but eventually gave up on the idea, because the primer paint took too long to dry. Instead, they went on a voyage of discovery in the neighborhood. They decided it would be possible to disarm the policeman stationed in front of the Austrian Embassy, since traffic was rather sparse in the area. Blaski asked Mansfeld to teach him to drive, so that he may escape to the West even on his own, or save the others, should Mansfeld get hurt during one of their operations.[15] The group met at the school on Medve Street, at half past six as planned. Blaski and Mansfeld arrived with the vehicle, bringing their machine pistols. Blaski did not know the new recruits, or just barely, but raised no objection to their participation. All five boarded the car, and began cruising on the Buda side. Mansfeld was keen on demonstrating his driving skills, plus they had to discuss their plans.

The dissemination of leaflets was not discussed, then or later. The two leaders had arrived with specific plans, to be carried out; in any case, Blaski was cool to the idea of political resistance, even though he had reported for duty, in October 1956, with the National Guard, at the twelfth district police station, since that was where his brother-in-law was serving. He stayed there, after the revolution, as aide to the police until January 14, when he was decommissioned, since he had not done his military service.

Neither was László Furka driven by political considerations. As he later confessed: "[Mansfeld] had plenty of money, without having to work, as a result of the crimes committed, and lived well. I did not like my trade, I don't like to work. And I felt this would be the easiest way to make a living....What Péter Mansfeld told me grabbed my imagination, and I decided to join the band, if possible."[16]

Mansfeld, on the other hand, since his days under investigation in jail, had become a determined enemy of the regime and, in addition to his devotion to gang activities, he was driven by the desire for vengeance for the reprisals under Kádár, and the desire to revive the revolution. His most important task would be the liberation of his brother-in-law, the teacher János Virág, who had been sentenced to five years in jail for revolutionary activity. Allegedly, he was thinking of attacking the headquarters of the Prosecutors' Office and the liberation of Pál Maléter as well, and planned to elect the legendary soldier as their leader.[17]

Next to Mansfeld it was Rezső Bóna who experienced most adventures. He had taken part in the demonstrations of October 23, 1956, and had joined the group at Széna Square. After the occupation of the Second District Party Committee's offices, he played a role in burning brochures and books found there. On November 22, 1956, he left the country and ended up in Switzerland. He lived in barracks or monasteries, then, with two companions, "borrowed" a boat. They crossed into France with the rowboat, climbed a mountain, but were soon stopped. Since they refused to join the Foreign Legion, they were returned to Switzerland, where all three were jailed for six days for stealing, fighting and brawling. In January 1957 Bóna returned to Hungary; in the summer of 1957 they reported at the American and French Embassies for duty with the Foreign Legion.[18] He was expecting his arrest at any minute for defrauding of the sickness benefit program at the Waterworks Enterprise.

In 1956, both brothers of Attila Egei were on medical duty on Széna Square; Attila also visited the base of the insurgents. After the revolution he distributed leaflets. According to his account, once he joined the Mansfeld band, there was no more talk of leafleting, only of obtaining handguns for every member: "we will rob a post office, and use the money and the weapons to escape the country."[19]

Blaski and Mansfeld meant to recruit enough men for the band to load three cars comfortably. They planned to arm everyone with the handguns obtained from police and paramilitary guards. Mansfeld and Bóna felt it was important to launch a fresh revolution. Once they had launched it, most assuredly others would join. "We must not fear spending some time in jail, because the regime is bound to change, and we will be the heroes, they will bow to us" they insisted, according to their fellow defendants.[20]

On February 17, 1958, at 7 P.M. they stopped their vehicle about seventy meters from the Austrian Embassy. Mansfeld proposed that all five go over to disarm the guard, but Blaski argued that would make it too obvious, and suggested that the plan be carried out by three of them, while the other two stood on guard, and whistled in case of danger. Bóna, however, chickened out of the assignment,[21] nor did Egei volunteer, so they were posted next to the vehicle as watch. When they reached the cop, Mansfeld would inquire about a street as they had agreed, then Blaski would pull out the automatic hidden in his coat: "Hands up!" Master Sergeant Elek Vekerdi went for his pistol, but when Furka shouted at him too, he did not try to resist. Mansfeld took his service weapon, his badge, the ammunition, and loaded the weapon. Then they escorted him to the car, but since Bóna had signaled the arrival of a passer-by, they asked Vekerdi to lower his hands.

Mansfeld drove the vehicle toward Budakeszi; the sergeant was surrounded by the pistol-toting Blaski from behind, Furka on one side, Bóna in front. Egei sat next to Bóna. They took the policeman's identity card. At that point Blaski informed him that their original plan had been to kill him, but seeing that he has two children, they decided to spare his life. The gang had decided beforehand to eliminate the policeman, but probably none of them were keen on that outcome. It is possible, of course, that if the man had resisted, they would have used their weapons but, as it happened, they were mostly showing off. When another car passed them, Blaski shouted: "this is our car, they are taking the other policemen out!" By which he meant to imply that they were a well organized gang, the task of which was to round up all police. Mansfeld asked the sergeant major whether he had seen in the movies newsreels, numbers four and six, showing the train robbery carried out by their comrades.

Bóna asked him if he was Hungarian. When the man said yes, they responded that they too were Hungarian, and they were gangsters. Bóna then asked the man about his activities during the revolution: how many did he have arrested or executed? Upon his non-committal answer, Egei tried to find how long had he been a cop and had he hurt anyone with the "Kádár sausage?" Vekerdi defended himself saying he did not even have a billy club. Then they bugged him with further questions, why would he not rather work in a factory, where he could earn better money?[22] Finally Blaski offered him a cigarette, shook his hand, and let him go, telling him that should he finger them, they would kill him along with his family. They instructed him to tell everyone he was attacked by bandits wearing masks. The badge was not returned, and he was not allowed to see the license plate.

The other actions were postponed until the next day. On the 18th, early in the afternoon, the car was not where they had left it, but its location was marked. Then Mansfeld and Blaski took a Mercedes belonging to the Ministry for Heavy Industry. They went to visit a former fellow inmate of Mansfeld who lived in the borough of Újpest, for automatic weapons. He was not at home, and the relatives told them the police had been looking for him as well. They met Bóna and Egei; it was then they found out that Furka was no longer with them, because he was afraid of the consequences.[23] They drove all around town, looking for a cop or a security guard, but could not find a location appropriate for an attack. A policeman tried to stop them, and they were pursued by police on a motorbike. Blaski and Bóna got ready to fire, while Mansfeld gave the engine full gas and sped through a red light, shaking off the police. They left the car inside a park in Buda, deeming further use of it too risky. They dispersed, but Mansfeld found Blaski and Bóna and told them the police was already on their track. First they went to Blaski's place; he instructed his wife to tell the cops he is away on a trip.

Then, at Mansfeld's suggestion they went to look up the wife of a former cell mate, József Kalló, on Lukács Street, to "mete out justice." For the woman had reported her husband to the police for collecting photos of 1956, in order to shack up with a military officer once her spouse was arrested. The others accepted Mansfeld's opinion that they must do away with the ratting woman—"the enemy"—and with the officer. They even contemplated raping the woman.[24] They planned to break into the apartment by means of their police badge, and then use the apartment to hide from the police. Who knows how serious they were; probably no more serious than in their plan to do away with the policeman—but we cannot know for sure, for unexpectedly they found the former cell mate at home. Mansfeld told him the story of the stolen pistol, and also that the police was looking for them, but said nothing about the purpose of their visit. Kalló invited them to stay over, but they did not because Mansfeld did not trust him: he might call the police once they fell asleep.

Then they tried to steal another Pobeda. Mansfeld was able to open the car's door with his dagger, but could not start the car. Then he tried another car, but Blaski warned him it might be a police vehicle.[25] They began to feel cold sitting in a park for an hour or two, and went over to the Turkish bath, where Mansfeld knew of an abandoned room. They slept there until the morning. Then Mansfeld noticed a group of police looking for them in the vicinity. During a moment when they felt safe, they fled to the courtyard of the neighboring building, but the detectives noticed them. They ran toward the bank of the Danube, then towards the Árpád Bridge. Blaski told some of them to drop behind somewhat. Mansfeld and Bóna, however, were soon captured, while Blaski fled by streetcar. At the Fishermen's Bastion on Castle Hill, he buried his pistol and the ammunition, then went to the Southern Railway Station. Here he was supposed to meet up with his wife, but two policemen grabbed him in front of the ticket counter and took him into custody.

IN JAIL, UNDER INVESTIGATION

With the arrest of Blaski the whole "band of terrorists" was behind bars. László Furka and Attila Egei had been arrested already the night before in their apartment. József Blaski was the only one among them who was over seventeen. Mansfeld and Egei were locked up in the same cell, Blaski next door. The detectives had hidden microphones on both sides. Egei told Mansfeld that Blaski will probably hang. As expected, they shouted to each other across the walls, especially after Blaski's cell-mate was taken out for interrogation. According to the prognosis of Mansfeld he would get three to four years, Blaski three. Blaski shouted back: "so long as it's not ten!"[26] According to Blaski they used a nail to drive a hole through the wall on both sides and conversed through that hole.

All of them had prison plants assigned to them, and not just anyone: they were former cops and counterintelligence agents, for whom extracting information was child's play.

According to the report of the agent assigned to Blaski, he felt it had been a mistake not to discuss what to confess beforehand, and he was hoping Mansfeld would have the opportunity to coach the others.[27] According to another report Bóna was wondering "how they could manage to make Mansfeld keep quiet."[28]

The agent observing Egei noted, among others: "I am sure if we had prepared the affair better, we would have been able to eliminate a couple of traitors by now. We should not have let this one go, but do away with him, and bury him deep, where they would look for him in vain, he would be asking for no bread. The series of car thefts was foolish as well, because we merely drew attention to ourselves; we stole three cars in six days, including cars from the ministries. Five teens riding in a car, a ministry car at that, with automatic weapons—that can only lead to fall."[29]

In his solitude, his hopeless situation, Péter Mansfeld demonstrated incredible courage and fortitude. From the moment of his arrest he felt certain that he would manage to escape somehow. First he contemplated knocking out his detective with an iron bar he broke off his cot, then escape with the man's identity card and weapon. This plan required extensive preparations for days on end, especially breaking the iron rod in two, since it was too long. He had to keep an eye on the guard. The cell mate reported everything. The detectives worked out all sorts of combinations so that their spy would not get caught: they took Mansfeld to the photographer, where he was forced to remove his coat in which he had hidden the iron rod. One policeman "accidentally" stumbled on the rod. This happened on Mansfeld's seventeenth birthday. His examiner, First Lieutenant István Fenyvesi, asked him what he meant to do with that piece of iron. "I declare that I refuse to answer the above question," was the answer. The next question resulted in Mansfeld protecting his cell mate: "My cell mate did not know that I had removed an iron rod from my cot, and I broke it into two."[30] Indeed, the person would have been punished for failing to report. Mansfeld was condemned to five days in solitary confinement, in an unlit cell. After his release from that cell, he told the his cell mate agent, how bad it had been in the dark, but "he would tell the interrogator it was all right to show that he was not intimidated."[31] Indeed, as the agent reported, "Mansfeld is often undisciplined, and the guards have to reprimand him."[32]

The plant in the cell continued to be on his guard. Once Mansfeld engaged in autocriticism, saying "that he had been too hasty in setting up this group, he did not believe the fellows would get frightened so easily, that they would betray one another so quickly once they are in trouble."[33] Although there was not much tactics in Mansfeld's confessions, he tried to ascribe the initiative and the overall leadership in organization to a fictional József Schoherin, but the attempt was doomed to failure: "Mansfeld tries to mislead his detective with the spy story he invented."[34]

The young man did not get depressed when he failed to escape in March, during a visit to one of the crime scenes. "The next time it will work."[35] Mansfeld tried his best to save his friends on the outside. He preserved his sunny disposition, until the moment his interrogator told him that his brother-in-law, János Virág, "will be done in."[36] (Actually, that was never even contemplated.)

The informer warned his employers that Mansfeld was planning to escape during the visits to the sites, but in vain. The events of April 30 are related credibly by both sides.

Earlier...I made confessions to the effect that I had hid weapons in the cave on Barlang [Cave] Street and in the mushroom cellar on Vérhalom Street...in order that they may take me there, and I can escape. I knew the terrain and I knew the detectives would not be able to follow me....My confession was not true, I just said for the sake of escape. I had two plans. One was to jump down into a cavern at the entrance to the cave on Barlang Street, where the detective would not be able to follow me. This plan of mine did not work because since I last visited the place, it had been reconstructed, I was not familiar with the new environment, so I gave up the plan. My other plan was to escape from the mushroom cellar on Vérhalom Street. After we descend into the cellar I would crawl out through one of the vents, since I knew there were ladders installed. The person renting the cellar did not stay there, so First

Lieutenant Fenyvesi had to go and fetch him in a vehicle. I went to
the top of the cellar with the captain escorting me, the photographer and a woman. Here I decided that I would jump down the side
of the cellar, a drop of about 4 meters, hide out in the vicinity, then
move to the cave on Barlang Street, and hide there....When First
Lieutenant Fenyvesi returned with the owner of the cellar, everyone was focusing on them. I took advantage of this moment to
remove the leash on my hand, and stuck the belt back again into the
knot. I suddenly jerked the belt loose from the hands of the captain,
and began to run. The photographer reached after me and caught
the sleeve of my lumberjack. I lost my balance and fell through a
ditch about four meters deep, when I realized that my left arm was
broken.

Then I ran toward Borbolya Street, and the yard of number
seven (which is our house); I ran across to Apostol Street, when I
noticed that there was a policeman standing at the corner. So I ran in
the opposite direction, down Gülbaba Street, and entered the Hospital of the Sisters of Mercy to ask for first aid. A policeman asked for
identification, but I said I had none, that I had left it at home. I
explained to him that I had a quarrel with my friends who wanted to
beat me, I jumped from a second story window, and broke my left
arm. The cop acknowledged what I told him, and reported to the
police station of District II, that I was given first aid. From the hospital I was taken for surgery to another on Karolina Street. This was
where I was captured....My plan had been to steal a vehicle from the
Italian Embassy on Borbolya Street, and proceed to Sásd or Sárbog-
ard to my father's relatives place. Once I broke my arm, I had to give
up this plan. I planned to go to the Gellért Hill after receiving first
aid, and hide somewhere near Villányi Road, until my arm healed....
I was told that my mother shouted after me twice as I was running
down Gülbaba Street.[37]

The police account stated the following:

Lt. Szűcs caught only the edge of his clothing, but could not
hold him back. After Mansfeld jumped Captain Izer took out his
weapon and was getting ready to shoot. In the meantime Mansfeld

began to run along the stone wall. Thus the vines on the stone wall concealed Mansfeld from the view Captain Izer. He ran after Mansfeld on the stone wall or the roof of the cellar, jumped when the wall came to an end, caught his foot in the vines and fell. In the meantime Mansfeld ran across the yard next door toward Borbolya Street, and jumped across into a garden at the end of another house.

Then Captain Izer fired two shots at Mansfeld but, since Mansfeld jumped into the deeper garden, he missed. Captain Izer continued to run after Mansfeld, and saw him exit from 9 Borbolya Street toward the garden. By the time the captain reached the spot, he had lost track of Mansfeld. Then he fired another shot to indicate his whereabouts to the comrades. When the other comrades reached there, we searched the gardens of the two houses, the annexes and the cellars. Mansfeld escaped at 1540 hours. Then the brigade returned to the station immediately, and Captain Izer reported the escape to his superior.

We understand the reasons for the escape as follows:

1. Knowing Mansfeld's behavior and his intentions to escape, we went to the spot with insufficient manpower. Thus the location was not duly secured.

2. In spite of the environment at the cave, on the way to the mushroom cellar, we failed to use handcuffs.

3. Captain Izer was careless when Mansfeld disconnected the leash from his hand.[38]

4. Following his failed escape, Mansfeld grew suspicious. He asked the agent in the cell how could the detectives have found out about his plan to escape, when only the two of them knew. The reply was that the guards had probably overheard them.[39]

JÓZSEF BLASKI AND COMPANY

On September 13, 1958, prosecutor János Götz was ready with his indictment, and the case of the "band of terrorists" came in front of the People's Tribunal of the Municipal Court.

All of the defendants admitted the charges and all pleaded guilty, as they had during the preliminary investigation. They were also unanimous in acknowledging that they had not been harmed or subjected to duress during the investigation.

Little was said about their actions in 1956, but a lot about the two-part accusation regarding conspiracy to commit murder. No one denied the facts regarding the case of Vekerdi and Mrs. Kalló, as already presented here. It was mainly the intent to kill, the "counterrevolutionary" motivation, and the identity of the "gang leader" that were the focus of the interrogations.

From every point of view Blaski and Mansfeld were the ones most in trouble, to about the same degree. It was clear that they were the leaders, and they participated in both attempts at murder. Blaski was already an adult, but Mansfeld appeared to be the more dangerous "counterrevolutionary."

Blaski was the better tactician to the end; he denied what could be denied, even during the investigation: "I am not aware of the killing of the policeman, or of the plan to this effect. I would never admit it, even if all my fellow conspirators did so. I only admit that, had the policeman resisted, or had he attempted to escape, then we would have killed him, in accordance with the original plan. It is true that I talked about his children, but that was not the reason we let him go."[40]

During the trial Mansfeld tried to fend the blame from Blaski,[41] probably because he felt that Blaski was in greater danger, and honor among thieves required it. "Blaski said that he knew of places where we could take the policeman; I noted that would not be enough, we have to do away with him, otherwise he will denounce us. I said, when we reached the cliff, we would order him to advance, while I would shoot him from behind....I talked to Blaski at the Ságvári Grove, behind the vehicle; at that point Blaski disagreed with me, that we should not kill the cop, while I and the others were of the opinion that kill him we must. At then end of the conversation I told Blaski, okay, let it be the way you propose."[42]

In the case of Mrs. Kalló, Blaski also denied that he wanted to kill or commit rape. In this instance he was backed not by Mansfeld but by Bóna.[43]

In both cases the prosecution could rely only on the self-incrimination of the accused. Sergeant Major Vekerdi harbored no ill will and probably spoke the truth: "I declare that in the car nothing was said about killing me, [they even mentioned] that I would not be harmed."[44]

József Kalló had no idea about the real purpose of the young men's visit, so the court gained little information from him.

It is obvious that the boys bragged in front of one another. This proved to be the case with Vekerdi. According to the logic of the charges the life of Furka was also in grave danger because, in the evening of February 17 they were talking about next day's meeting, one of the leaders said: "whoever does not show up will get a bullet in his head."[45] Mansfeld was the champion by far, when it came to boasting: Mansfeld also told us about his friends who rob trains....He showed us a piece of paper listing the ones he wanted to liquidate."[46] "He said, he would eliminate every cop who crossed his path."[47] "He [also] talked about disarming Soviet soldiers. He would expand to the whole country the stealing of motor vehicle, the robberies."[48] Thus the most serious charges would never have been even mentioned, had the accused not been children without experience.

As regards giving orders, Blaski tried in vain to escape, shifting the main responsibility to Mansfeld; the others tended to view Blaski as the leader. The most factual assessment came from Mansfeld: "There was no understanding among us as to who would lead the band. Basically, it was I and József Blaski who took turns."[49]

As for the political charges Mansfeld always asserted Blaski's "innocence"—albeit unsuccessfully. "Of course, along with procuring arms, we should have produced leaflets as well, to form a counterrevolutionary group. I would like to point out that József Blaski had no knowledge that the band was formed with a counterrevolutionary objective."[50]

From the beginning Blaski's tactics were to demonstrate that he was suffering from a mental illness. He even had proof that as a child he had fallen on his head from a great height, and was under the treatment of a physician for two weeks. Once he suffered from an "attack of rage," attacking the guards, kicking and hitting them, while shouting: "Murderers! Scoundrels! We will meet again on the outside, and I will take care of you then!" Three of them overcame him, probably beat him up, gave him a shot in the emergency medical room, and put him in a strait-jacket. During a day in court all of a sudden he began to shout: "Don't lie! Don't lie, I did not attack the order of the state! I did not organize!" The chair of the tribunal had him escorted out for a while.

Then the court declared its decision based on the opinion of specialists: there is no sign of mental illness in the case of Blaski. Nevertheless, the tactic had some effect because Blaski was declared of very limited mental capacity, thanks in part to the cleverness of his lawyer.

Mansfeld continued his renitent behavior and tried increasingly to antagonize the court and the prosecutor. The most clearcut example of this was the expert opinion of the pair of doctors, László Balassa and Endre Kelemen:

> In answer to a question he tells that he was with the Széna Square group, next to Uncle Szabó...."I wanted to stir up some trouble, let the policeman go to work where he belongs, in the factory." He talks in the most cynical tones: if the trouble did not happen he would not mind if people were to lose their life, because they are hanging people every day anyway. During the entire examination he behaved superciliously and cynically, speaking rigidly about his counterrevolutionary concepts, refusing to admit the incorrectness of his actions to the least degree.[51]

Mansfeld annoyed his judges by making it clear he was proud of his past at the Széna Square: "I swore to Uncle Szabó....that I would defend my country to the end of my life." To the politically inspired questions he would answer: "I cannot tell you what was Uncle Szabó's ultimate goal. I went to him, because everyone did....The goal of the counter-revolution is to overthrow the revolutionary government formed in 1945....I am aware of the sentence meted out to Uncle Szabó."[52]

On November 17 the Chief Prosecutor György Matsik maintained the charges against all six defendants.

> I wish to stress that the defendant in the second instance gave a clear answer to the question of the people's tribunal, what is the counterrevolution. The principal defendant wanted counterrevolu-tion and not money, as he pretends....The accused are a great dan-ger to society, striving for the restoration of the capitalist system. I wish to stress, that in this criminal affair we must look at the fact that all the defendants are children of working class families, in a different light; they must be viewed as traitors to their class. These

are not misguided people, but conscious counterrevolutionaries....Moreover, I wish to stress that, when it comes to politics, there are no minors or adult defendants. We must administer the most Draconian measures against them in the sentencing.

He recommended the death penalty for both Blaski and Mansfeld, and long jail sentences for the others.

In his last words, Blaski said (among other things): "My only objective in sticking with the defendant in the second instance was to procure money, I insist 100 percent....It is possible that the other accused considered me their leader, but I was not the one, it was Péter Mansfeld, in whose hands I was but a means....I request, on the basis of the aforesaid, that insofar as I do not feel guilty, the Council of the People's Tribunal should not condemn me."

The bloodthirsty speech of prosecutor Matsik frightened even Mansfeld, but not enough to stop protecting his friend: "indeed my companion, the defendant in the first instance, did not know what we wanted to accomplish. We committed our acts as a consequence of the influence of the counterrevolution. It was only during the investigation that I found out who Uncle Szabó really was. I ask the court to consider my youth, and I would like to work, if I am not sentenced to death."

On November 21, 1958, the council presided over by Béla Guidi, voted 2 to 1 for "life" in the case of both accused. Although people's judge István Horváth agreed with the recommendation of the prosecutor, people's judge István Menráth also felt that a sentence for life was sufficient. Guidi was even more soft-hearted. He would have sentenced both Blaski and Mansfeld to fifteen years in jail "because the defendants had a spark of humanity in them, and they had avoided committing murder." Since the council took three different stands, chairman Guidi joined Menráth's recommendation. Furka was sentenced to three years, Bóna to eight, and Egei to four years in jail.

The Council of the People's Court of the Supreme Court discussed the appeal of the state on March 19, 1959. In his speech the prosecutor Zoltán Borsi sustained the appeal in the case of all the defendants.

The facts are stated correctly....The defendants definitely did not form a band of robbers. They had political goals....The court in the first instance, however, made a mistake in deciding the sentence. The defendants were consistent and resolute. In the case of the defendants in the first and second instances I initiate the most severe sentence, in the case of the others a sentence that is proportionately more severe.

In his last words Mansfeld changed his confessions altogether:

I never told Egei what our intentions were, nor that he should come; he came of his own volition. We never intended to kill the policeman, I had no intention of pushing the vehicle over the cliff. We never wanted to kill Mrs. Kalló and the officer, we only needed to acquire the policeman's cap. Bona invited me upstairs to his apartment. I had no mind to organize. Furka spoke about leaflets, asking me what life was like at the Markó Street jail.

On this occasion he asserted that the detectives did use force.

I was held in solitary confinement, in darkness, for seven days, because I refused to admit things at the police station. It is certain that the detectives told my companions to say we wanted to kill a policeman. I did not admit to everything. At the court I was allowed to look at the documents for no more than ten minutes, and only with my hands shackled. I had to sign the report on the investigation without reading. I had not said, at the original trial, that we wanted to kill the policeman. I did not organize a group.

Mansfeld was probably hoping for a fresh trial. In the remainder of his speech he tried to elicit some sympathy from the court, something he had never done before.

In 1950 my parents got divorced. I was institutionalized. I became a turner, even received an award for my work. In October 1956 I happened by the Széna Square. Uncle Szabó kissed me and hugged me, and said, "we need such young ones." I did not know on whose side was I fighting. I was confused. I was afraid of the death sentence, that is why I tried to escape. If I get out of jail, I want to work in my trade. The inmates in prison during my first sentence were a bad influence on me. It was mainly they who interpreted the events of the counterrevolution to me.

Bona's lawyer even asked, why he had not spoken this way earlier. "I could not think clearly at the trial," he answered.

The council headed by Vágó, however, proved merciless. "[At the original trial], the arguments regarding the degree of punishment, in the case of the second defendant Péter Mansfeld, were mistaken. This defendant was the spiritual and practical ringleader of the organization, of the series of thefts and lootings. He was usually in the forefront even during the execution of the crimes. In addition to the extreme severity his crimes, and in spite of his relatively young age, he represents a high degree of danger to society." He had been punished before, but that had no positive impact. He initiated the murder of Mrs. Kalló. "In view of all this the Council of the People's Court of the Supreme Court finds that we cannot expect that even a longer jail sentence would have an educational impact. Therefore, with regard to him, we argue that a measure of complete prevention, the meting out of the most severe punishment, was justified for the sake of the protection of society at large."

Bona's jail sentence was raised to ten years.

Mansfeld requested mercy and a new trial. The Council of the People's Court, as was the custom in those days, transformed itself into a Mercy Council. Its members were Tibor Vágó, council president, and the people's judges, József Győre, Sándor Keresztes, Sándor Szabó, István Varga. They voted unanimously against mercy.[53]

It is clear that the reason for their ruthlessness cannot be found in the nature of the charges. The judges simply could not bear that Mansfeld dared to challenge them, even in his totally hopeless situation.[54] Thus he must have appeared incorrigible, an unremittent "counterrevolutionary" in their eyes.

The sentence was carried out on March 21, 1959, eleven days after Mansfeld's eighteenth birthday.

Bóna was released in 1964, Blaski in 1963, the others in the course of 1960 or 1961.

THE "CIVIC NATIONAL FORCES" AND
THE CULT OF MANSFELD

The extent of the reprisals after 1956 became public knowledge during the change of regime. The greatest indignation was elicited by the execution of the barely eighteen-year old Péter Mansfeld. Although several articles were published in 1989 regarding the actual facts, the legends that evolved during the period of the party-state, without the sources, proved lasting. More recently the tragedy of Mansfeld has been used by the "civic national forces"[55] for political purposes, for instance by Viktor Orbán, Hungary's prime minister in 1999–2002.

"The young ones had to await adulthood in the jails to make it possible to hang them thereafter....The silence which surrounded the civic political forces becomes ever deeper....The Hungarian people did not wish to chose between good socialism and bad socialism, but demanded a return to civil society."[56]

Reprisals against Mansfeld were not meted out for his acts in 1956, except perhaps indirectly. He was condemned overwhelmingly because of his acts in 1958, even though the authorities tried to make it sound like a "counterrevolutionary" affair. Moreover, the authorities did not have to wait two years to come up with a death sentence, because on July 15, 1957, Directive 34 with force of law came into effect, enabling the handing down of the death sentence to minors.

There were no "civic political forces"[57] in 1956, hence they could not demand a return to civil society.

NOTES

1. Communication by László Mansfeld. Csaba Kósa, *"Alhattál-e, kisfi-am?"* [Could You Have Slept, My Son?] (Budapest: Kósa és Társai , 1996), pp. 11–12; Csaba Kósa, *Tizenhárom perc* [Thirteen Minutes] (Budapest: Kósa és Társai, 1999). The contents of the two books are identical.

2. Communicaton from Mrs. János Virág, Mansfeld's sister (report by Károly Martinko, *Vasárnapi Újság*, online). Mrs. Virág added that her brother was shocked.

3. "Unfortunately my husband began to drink, before 1945, so I was

forced to leave him....He was jailed twice, even though his parents
were decent folk," said Mrs. József Mansfeld as witness. In BFL,
8084/58, and 2541/75, 1958. XI. 11. "He escaped from the grip of the
Soviets. God gave him back. But he was taken away by his restless-
ness...his nature....In 1949 he packed and left home.·He had been
thinking about it for a long time....History conspired against him, he
felt. So he punished us for it. But I believe he punished himself, first of
all." According to Mansfeld's younger brother, Péter Mansfeld: "My
father lives, but where, I don't know....My father liked to drink, and
gambled...he was caught and punished several times," confessed Péter
Mansfeld at the trial. In Kósa, *"Alhattál-e, kisfiam?"* p. 11
4. BFL, Péter Mansfeld tárgy., 1958. X.
5. The siblings followed their parents' trade. "Everyone in the family
became a hairdresser, but he was not interested in the trade" said László Mansfeld. In Kósa, *"Alhattál-e, kisfiam?"* p. 10.
6. Communication by László Mansfeld in Kósa, *"Alhattál-e, kisfiam?"*
pp. 13–14. His mother said: "What I know is that my son had some
kind of automobile invention, which he took to the factory....There he
received the bronze medal as 'outstanding worker.'" BFL, Józsefné
Mansfeld tvall., 1958. XI. 11. According to the tale of his friends, he
could assemble a car from parts, all by himself.
7. BFL, Mansfeld tárgy., 1958. X. 30.
8. According to Mansfeld's confession, he stole a car on twenty-two
occasions in 1957. See BFL, Mansfeld jkv., 1958. II. 20. His fellow
defendants knew this too.
9. TH, V–144222. Péter Mansfeld körny. tan. His mother testified: "We
made a promise to the Court of Justice for Minors that the family will
gather, and decide what measures to take to change our son's behavior." BFL, Mrs. József Mansfeld tvall., 1958, XI. 11.
10. BFL, István Holecz jkv., 1958. II. 22; and BFL, József Blaski jkv.,
1958. II. 20.
11. According to Mansfeld's testimony, Blaski's purpose, in addition to
escaping, was to make the two armed organizations nervous. "He anticipated that after such actions there would be more policemen patrolling
the streets, and thus it would be easier for him to move around in uniform. Moreover, he anticipated that in the evening and at night the
members of the above armed bodies will not dare to go out on the
street. Then his plan to escape to the West could be carried out more
easily." BFL, Mansfeld jkv., 1958. II. 22. According to Mansfeld's testimony Blaski wanted to escape from Hungary, because he had an argument with his wife. Although Blaski corroborated this testimony, it is
possible that they had prearranged the account.

12. Furka knew that these leaflets—which were no longer topical—had been found and discarded by his mother; he only wanted to create trust among the friends. BFL, Furka László jkv., 1958. II. 27.
13. Mansfeld made this claim during the trial, but Bóna denied it.
14. BFL, Mansfeld jkv., 1958, II. 24; BFL, Furka jkv., 1958. II. 27, 1958. Hence it seems Mansfeld was the only one of the four who wanted to stay in Hungary.
15. BFL, Mansfeld jkv., 1958. II. 20, and 22. According to Mansfeld's testimony the next morning they drove to Érd, and he began to instruct them.
16. BFL, Furka jkv., 1958. III. 8, and VI. 13.
17. TH, Report by the prison agent assigned to Furka, 1958. II. 3.
18. "Those days we read books about Tarzan. We thought we would join the Foreign Legion, escape from there, go to the jungle, and live the way Tarzan had." BFL, Rezső Bóna jkv., 1958. III. 28.
19. BFL, Attila Egei jkv., 1958. II. 21. According to Mansfeld, Egei also communicated plans about leaflets. BFL, Mansfeld jkv., 1958. II. 27.
20. BFL, Furka jkv. 1958. II. 22; BFL, Bóna jkv., 1958. III. 3. Allegedly Mansfeld had proposed that they should move to a cave, but this idea was rejected by Blaski and Bóna saying, "we don't want to become cave dwellers, we have apartments." BFL, Bóna jkv., 1958. III. 3.
21. "I said, I was afraid, I had never done anything like this, I don't dare go there. Mansfeld said he had never done such things either, but there is no need to be afraid, it can be done quickly. 'You too will get used to it, because next time you will have to be there.'" BFL, Bóna jkv., 1958. III. 3.
22. BFL, Elek Vekerdi tk., 1958. V. 5.
23. Bóna visited him already on the evening of the 17th and told him. "Then Bóna said, I should not be scared because, if there is danger, we will go to the American Embassy, they will take us in and give us asylum." BFL, Furka jkv., 1958. VI. 13. During the trial Furka was accused of having chickened out because they did not kill the cop.
24. "Péter Mansfeld raised the possibility that, if the woman is pretty, all three of us would rape her before killing her," claimed Bóna. BFL, Blaski and Bóna jkv., 1958. V. 27.
25. BFL, Blaski jkv., 1958. II. 25.
26. TH, Report on conversation overheard, 1958. II. 20.,
27. TH, no date.
28. TH, V–144222/3, no date.
29. TH, V–144222/4, jel., 1958. III. 26.
30. BFL, Mansfeld jkv., 1958. III. March 3.
31. TH, Report by a prison agent, 1958. II. 27.

32. TH, Report by a prison agent, 1958. III. 27.
33. TH, Report by a prison agent, 1958. III. 5. There is no doubt that the two youngest boys, Furka and especially Egei, revealed everything.
34. TH, Report by prison agent,1958. II. 27.
35. TH, Report by prison agent,1958. III. 27.
36. TH, Report by prison agent, 1958 III. 26.
37. BFL, Mansfeld jkv., 1958. V. 5.
38. TH, Report by Captain Lajos Izer and First Lieutenant István Fenyvesi, 1958. IV. 30.
39. TH, Report by prison agent, 1958. V. 2.
40. BFL, Blaski jkv., 1958. III. 7.
41. The same can be said about Bóna. This statement applies mostly to the last segment of the trial proceedings. In the first days there were even confessions: "As the police were looking for us at the Török bath, you were cleaning your pistol, so that, should they come near, you will shoot." BFL, Mansfeld tárgy., 1958. 10. 30. He did not even conceal that Blaski, when the police were pursuing them on motorbikes, had his pistol prepped, and warned Bóna to be ready for firing.
42. BFL, Mansfeld tárgy. 1958. X. 28. The quote also underscores the statement of the former defendants, that Mansfeld received the most severe punishment because "he was intent on disculpating all of us from the charges." This statement must be viewed as an act of piety. See György Hintsch's documentary film, Irgalmatlanul [Without Mercy] (Budapest: Forgatókönyv Alapítvány, 1994). This applies only to testimony about Blaski. Mutually damaging confessions were often heard.
43. BFL, Mansfeld tárgy., 1958. X. 30.
44. BFL, Elek Vekerdi tvall., 1958. XI. 7.
45. BFL, Attila Egei tárgy., 1958. XI. 3.
46. BFL, Bóna jkv., 1958. II. 25, and 28.
47. BFL, Furka jkv., 1958. VI. 13.
48. BFL, Furka jkv., 1958. III. 8. 1958.
49. BFL, Mansfeld tárgy., 1958. X. 30.
50. BFL, Mansfeld tárgy., 1958. X. 28.
51. BFL, 1958. X. 10.
52. BFL, Mansfeld tárgy., 1958. X. 30.
53. In the trials resulting from 1956, Tibor Vágó issued ten death sentences. The peoples' judges sitting alongside had an even greater share of the reprisals meted out under Kádár. Speaking on a program hosted by György Kőbányai in 1989, Vágó recalled the trial as follows:

    Conspiracy did take place, as defined by the law, the conspiracy to commit murder....The fact is [that they merely removed the pistol of the policeman] yet in those days the procedure was legal. It must be remembered that the council was made up of four people's judges, and one chief judge. Theses people's judges were imbued with their sense of obligation to the movement. We must also remember the climate of the period. Cases were decided by majority vote.

In response to the journalist's question, he did not deny that as chief judge he could have sealed his dissenting vote in an envelope, but he refrained from doing that: "It would have served no purpose, it would not have helped. The Ministry of Justice also reviewed the legality of the sentence at the time. The sentence was legal, but extremely strict by today's standards." "Did you feel it was fair?" "I said it was too strict, and what is too strict, is not a good sentence." In "Az ítélet túl szigorú volt" [The judgment was too severe], *Mai Nap*, November 26, 1989.

54. This is confirmed in Vágó's recollections from 1989. "He was a forceful, stalwart young man." In ibid. Defense lawyer Tibor Gárgyán, on the other hand, declared: "Mansfeld responded casually....He did not follow my instructions....He testified this way out of a desire to appear brave and heroic." In Hintsch, *Irgalmatlanul*.

55. We have in mind the right-wing, extreme right-wing, conservative politicians, intellectuals and their followers, who claim to represent the "national side" since 1990.

56. *Új Magyarország*, October 24, 1994, pp. 1, and 4.

57. The right-wing politicians in Hungary also describe themselves as "civic," quite confusingly, without any justification.

THE "BÁSTYA" GROUP

László
Hegedűs

Lajos
Szabó

György
Ivicz

József
Nagy

János
Karászy

Béláné
Vancsó

Ferenc
Forgács

Imre
Mécs

The defeat of the Hungarian Revolution of 1956 by force of arms did not mean all resistance had come to an end; some social groups continued to organize. Since these groups did not abdicate the basic goals of the revolution, they confronted the new/old regime both within the country and from abroad. The resistance with the greatest impact was that of the workers' councils, but the activities of the intellectuals and of the political parties were also significant.

Moreover, there were groups which conspired almost completely without expectation of success, isolated from society at large. Because of their hopeless endeavors they were subjected to more severe reprisals than the participants of other, better known organizations. Once captured, many of their members were executed. Such was the fate of the group formed at the Central Military Hospital of Budapest, later renamed the "Bástya" [Bastion] group.

Unlike the better known groups, the "Bástya" was made up of members of diverse social strata. It included the apprentice butcher, the semiskilled mechanic, the woman bus conductor, as well the university student, the doctor, the military officer and the architect. Most of them belonged to the twenty to twenty-eight age group, and almost every one of them had been brought up under compounded disadvantaged circumstances.

POLITICAL RESISTANCE AT THE CENTRAL MILITARY HOSPITAL

In November 1956, by the time the Soviet forces had almost completely defeated the revolution, the Central Military [Honvéd] Hospital became a hotbed of resistance. The physicians, staff and members of the makeshift rescue teams working under the command of Colonel Dr. György Radó protested against the Soviet intervention, against the deportation of young people to the Soviet Union, eventually against the transfer of Imre Nagy and associates to Romania. They blamed the casualties on the recently formed Kádár cabinet. They stood for "a free, independent, socialist and truly democratic Hungary." They demanded the inclusion of Imre Nagy and Pál Maléter in the government, the use of the Kossuth coat of arms, and the traditional army uniform.

They issued a call for a general strike. They wrote leaflets in foreign languages, to inform the public in the West and ask for United Nations support, as well as leaflets in Russian: "Soviet soldiers! You are not fighting against fascists! Do not shoot at the people of Hungary, the Hungarian workers and peasants!" "We are not fascists, we do not want a government of the landowners or of the bourgeoisie. We want a free and independent Hungary." They printed the leaflets in the name of the "Uprising of the Revolutionary Youth." Most members were fully aware of how hopeless armed struggle would be, and disapproved of its continuation. They did assume that the government would be inclined to compromise at the impact of pressure coming from below, thus leading to true consolidation.

At the beginning the leaflets were prepared by those volunteer rescue workers and nurses from the days of October and November who were lodged at this hospital. The most active among them was the sixteen-year-old Mrs. Lajos Molnár (née Veronika Szatmári), conductor for the bus lines, who had been taking care of the wounded already during the siege of the Radio Broadcasting building. There was also József Borsodi, hauler in the mines by trade, who became a volunteer medic during the revolution. Also involved was László Hegedűs, a volunteer for the Red Cross, a second-year student at the Institute for Physicians' Aides, who had a worker's permit assigning him to this hospital, and his friend Tamás Korniczky, the x-ray technician on the neurology ward. Thanks to Borsódi, they were joined by Lajos Szabó, a skilled mechanic at the Danuvia firm, formerly of the Corvin group, who had been a Party member between 1945 and 1953. The physicians of the hospital, György Radó and Captain Dr. László Iván, read and often edited or completed the text of the leaflets, and placed paper, mimeograph machine at the disposal of the group.

A surprise check by Soviet and Hungarian law enforcement on November 8 or 9 jeopardized the operations of the group. They were in the midst of reproducing a flyer, when one of them became aware of the raid. They destroyed the flyers in feverish haste, while Radó treated the visitors to coffee and drinks.

THE MYSTERIOUS LIAISON

Around November 10, Lajos Szabó met up with a former comrade in arms, the electrician György Ivicz, who became impressed with the illegal activities conducted at the hospital. It occurred to them to draft the former commanders from the Corvin Passage, but they failed in that endeavor. A few days later Ivicz called on Szabó and promised help for his group. He announced that he was in touch with Pál Maléter and his troops fighting in the Bakony Mountains,[1] then read out a slip of paper containing the names of other military commanders and the location of their units.[2] He offered to become the liaison between Maléter and Szabó. The group would undertake combat assignments under the guidance of the "central command," and would have to extend its activities to the entire city.

From the moment of the appearance of this mysterious liaison the nature of the organization changed. On November 20 and 21, Szabó called a meeting in the hospital neurology ward, with the participation of Ivicz and the flyer designers—about eight or ten individuals. Another comrade in arms from the Corvin group came along, the apprentice butcher József Nagy, who was already involved in the distribution of flyers. (The hospital directors did not attend the meeting, but made it possible for the "visitors" to enter.)

Ivicz repeated the nature of his mission, his contacts with Maléter, and the need to expand the operations. He explained how this could be done: in order to minimize the chances of getting caught, the members of the operation should not know about one another. He announced that he would take care of the transport of weapons, once the commanders set the date for launching the attack. He warned those members of the group who already had weapons to be cautious, the fighting must not start without his instructions. He stressed the need for an arms depot.[3]

Then they formed new units—some were already in existence—and decided their functions. Lajos Szabó, József Borsodi and József

Nagy would organize the groups of resistance by municipal district, to simplify the distribution of weapons. Mrs. Molnár was designated as the liaison between the groups, Hegedűs and Korniczky would continue to print flyers, Szabó was in charge of their distribution. Szabó[4] was also in charge of reporting on the results, and he would inform the members of the time of the next meeting. The participants took on cover names, the use of which was mandatory. Surprising as it may sound, no one in the group voiced any doubts; in other words, they had no inkling of the arrest of Minister of Defense Pál Maléter by his Soviet hosts at Tököl.[5]

Szabó and József Nagy drafted the law student Mária Lévai, whom they knew from the Corvin group, and through her the university student Imre Mécs. Their task was first of all to win over the students. József Nagy was most assiduous in organizing, although he warned everyone he talked to about the dangers, and told them that traitors will be punished by death.[6] Hegedűs, the leader of those at the hospital, was in touch with the Béla Békési group of medical students, known as the "Bagoly" [Owl] group, who were staying at the Clinic No. 2 for Women and who were also engaged mostly in distributing flyers.

Late in November or early in December Szabó called for another meeting since Ivicz, the alleged messenger did not show, his promise notwithstanding. Those in attendance reported on the tasks accomplished. Only the section in charge of producing flyers could show any real accomplishment,[7] the others were merely boasting. It was decided that everyone would continue their work, keep Szabó informed of what they had done, and he would forward the information to the "central command" under Maléter.

On December 6, Air Force First Lieutenant János Karászy, former insurgent, who at this time formally belonged to law enforcement, joined the conspiracy. He took part in the organization work with enthusiasm, and offered to recruit insurgents from the southern districts of the city. It is strange that Karászy who was an officer on active duty and an old acquaintance of Maléter—they has fought together as partisans in World War II—also believed that his former commander was still fighting with his troops in the Bakony Mountains. József Nagy, however, was beginning to have enough of all the mystery surrounding the "central command," and called another meeting for mid-December.

Then he challenged Szabó to explain his role and provide specific evidence of Maléter's "central command." Szabó, however, had no information to communicate; he could only refer to the liaison Ivicz, of whom there was no trace. The participants agreed that they must find out the facts, to avoid unnecessary risks. Nagy and Szabó were entrusted with the fact-finding mission. The outcome would determine whether they would remain under the guidance of the "central command" or create their own independent command. They confirmed or defined their tasks, and the new members took on aliases. At the end of the meeting, after the participants sang the national anthem, they took an oath of loyalty. In his confession during the investigation Nagy recalled the text of the oath as follows:

I, XY, swear that I will be loyal to the organization and its goals, and will not reveal the identity of the leaders and its members, no matter what tortures I am subjected to. I will carry out the orders and instructions issued by the leader of the organization and obey them without ado. I also swear that as long as there is a single Soviet tank on Hungarian soil, I will not lay down my arms. I swear that I will promote the independence of Hungary with all my strength.

I swear that I will not aid any kind of capitalist or imperialist venture in Hungary. Should I be untrue to my oath, let me be struck by the ire and vengeance of my comrades and God. If I find out that my best friend or brother or sister has betrayed the organization, I will report to that effect to the leader, and I will know no pity with regard to the traitors. Let God be my witness.'[8]

The oath was the brainchild of Nagy and Karászy, and they wrote the text, perhaps with the help of others. Nagy read it out, the others repeated it standing, and confirmed their oath by signing their name, (a few new recruits were attending as well; among the more important ones were the dispatcher, Mrs. Béla Vancsó, who recorded the minutes by shorthand, and the architectural engineer Ferenc Forgács).

WITHOUT CENTRAL COMMAND

The next meeting was held on December 26, in the same apartment. The reports by Nagy and Szabó dissipated all remaining illusions—there was no central command; Ivicz, the alleged liaison, who had misguided the group, left Budapest and found a job in Miskolc (We do not know what his motives were. Was he a pathological liar? Was he playing a practical joke? In any case, he contributed significantly to the serious tragedy that was to affect him as well). The representatives of the Military Hospital—Hegedűs, Korniczky and Ferenc Halkrant—noted what they had heard from Major Dr. László Iván, namely that Maléter was being held in the prison on Fő Street. Once again the contact with the hierarchy and the issue of armaments came up, namely the notion that groups belonging to the "Maléter Party" should be contacted across the country. At Karászy's suggestion, the participants decided that he and Korniczky should travel to Vienna and enter in contact with General Béla Király and the Social Democratic leader, Anna Kéthly, who were considered legitimate leaders.

They decided to name their organization "Bástya." József Nagy was elected commander in chief, Karászy[9] his deputy, Szabó the political leader—earlier they considered him the overall leader—and Nándor Tóth as staff commander. Karászy nominated his acquaintance, Ferenc Forgács, as "D" officer—meaning he was in charge of internal affairs within the group. The two of them elaborated a strategy for armed combat: occupation of the broadcasting stations, the telephone central, the railways, the media, disarming all military and police units, occupation of the barracks. First they would take prisoner all those who knew the effectives of the armed forces, their order of battle, their station, those who knew where the revolutionaries were being held, and who would be freed immediately. The operations would be elaborated district by district, under the direction of unit commanders; thus, according to the rules of conspiracy, contacts would be limited to the liaisons. The plan was studied and endorsed by Lajos Szabó and József Nagy.[10]

Once again they appointed the local commanders and the other officers. It must be emphasized that the functions remained merely nominal, to the end.[11] Nagy delineated the objectives: the independence of Hungary, preventing a Horthyist restoration, free elections, a democratic form of state.[12] Karászy briefed the group about the structure he elaborated and the specific tasks of the units.[13] There were, however, no more than a handful of personnel to execute these ambitious plans,[14] without any financial base whatever.

The unification of all the resistance group operating across the country was also suggested. The first step along those lines was a given, since three members of the "Bagoly" group of medical students were in attendance.[15] Nagy advocated fusion, but when it came to defining the chain of command, an intense debate ensued. The university students felt they were intellectually more developed, hence more fit for leadership, but according to the spokespersons of the "Bástya" group the leadership role behooved the workers. Ultimately they only agreed on keeping in touch.[16]

The representatives from the hospital also wanted rules, since they had reservations about the activities of the "Bástya" group.[17] From then on they preferred to conspire with the medical students.[18] At the end of the meeting, the new recruits took a make-up oath of loyalty. Hegedűs and company, who had been absent, subscribed to the oath only after extended tergiversation. The "cell from Óbuda" became increasingly isolated from the rest.[19]

A day or two later Karászy and Korniczky left for Vienna. The latter joined the representatives of the "Bagoly" group who also made it to Vienna, but finally opted to emigrate, and settled in England. Karászy returned early in January, and reported on his unsuccessful trip: Király and Kéthly were not staying in Vienna, the exile organizations were not receptive, they could not expect help from any quarters. There were, however, foreign informants who offered to cooperate. The members of the group, however, were almost unanimous in rejecting this kind of contact, because it did not match their objectives: "we are not traitors." They did not know that Karászy had entered into contact with two members of the staff of the British Embassy even before his departure. The British assured him of their support, and he gave them military data in exchange (Mrs. Vancsó was translating, in the presence of Forgács).[20] Karászy concluded his report by adding there was no sense in continuing the fight, the group had to be disbanded, the records pertaining to the conspiracy had to be destroyed.[21] His words astounded everyone, for they had been expecting good news. Some even refused to accept Karászy's stand, and even questioned whether he had been abroad. The air force officer, however, was able to show bills, receipts, tickets.

COLLAPSE

Nagy and Szabó were of the opinion that one should not run scared, the conspiracy must continue.

Soon, however, they were forced to change their opinion. Szabó was beaten up by the police, and locked up for a few days; other members of the group were sought at their respective apartments. Now the leaders of the organization released everyone from their oath and, on January 24, started to shred the minutes, and other records, hide the weapons (the lone machine pistol, a few hand grenades and a pistol) and the ammunition.

The extremely risky armed organizing process ended without accomplishing anything.The last activity of the "Bástya" group was carried out by their section at the Military Hospital; a stencil machine was transferred at great risk to the Women's Clinic No. 2, where the "Bagoly" group continued to print the serial *Élünk* [We Are Alive] even after the arrest of Gyula Obersovszky and friends.

Among the members of the group Mária Lévai, János Karászy, László Iván and, as we have already mentioned, Tamás Korniczky, fled abroad. József Nagy, who also intended to escape, was rounded up on February 22 in Pécs.[22] He was in the process of writing a letter to Imre Mécs, who had helped the others to escape, when the police broke into the apartment of his host. He meant to throw the letter into the lit stove, but missed. At this juncture he received a sentence of only eight months, for attempt to flee.[23]

One of the leaders of the section from the borough of Óbuda, József Borsodi, denounced the group—more precisely Mrs. Lajos Molnár, Captain László Iván, and Lajos Szabó—at the third district police headquarters.[24] That was when the authorities decided to redouble their efforts at investigation. Their task was made easier by an agent working in the German Federal Republic who made the acquaintance of Karászy. The letter of Forgács, which he was about to send to Karászy

in England in code, was intercepted by the police, due to the vigilance of the postal services.[25]
The arrests started in April. The one who squealed was released and the investigation against him was halted, in spite of his involvement in the movement.[26] As a result of the judicial proceedings József Nagy, Lajos Szabó, János Bárány[27] and György Ivicz were executed on Feb-ruary 18, 1959; indeed, former armed insurgents had no chance for mercy. On appeal the death sentences of Ferenc Forgács, and Imre Mécs, were commuted to life. The others received sentences ranging from one year to life.

NOTES

1. This legend spread across the country, and even abroad. One version went thus:

    The news is that general Pál Maléter was liberated by the insurgents soon after November 4. The liberation happened without the need to resort to force: a Soviet colonel and a Soviet political commissar were exchanged for Maléter. Since then Maléter is leading the partisans forces in the Bakony and Vértes Mountains. Soviet officers and military units, armed to the teeth, sided over to the insurgents and constitute the backbone of Maléter's army in the Bakony. These honorable Soviet soldiers are more determined than even the most determined Hungarian insurgents. The partisans are well supplied in the mountains of Pilis. They have large quantities of canned food supplies, hidden in various places, unknown to most; the supplies of preserved food items would allow them to hold out for at least one year. The local population supplies them with fresh food regularly, in the most ingenious ways. They have sufficient military equipment, primarily ammunition, and can cope with the most massive Soviet attack, if necessary. (In OSA, no. 266/57.)

2. According to another version, György Ivicz spoke of Béla Király and his unit in the Bakony Mountains, amounting to 50,000 effectives (Lajos Szabó, önv. 1957, 23 July 1957, BFL, TH). According to József Nagy, commander Maléter had 14,000 troops under his command, General Szabó another 16,000 fighters in southern Hungary, Colonel

Bata was leading resistance in northern Hungary with 17,000 troops, while General Béla Király was fighting with 14,000 armed men in the Bakony. See BFL, György Ivicz jkv., 1957. V.16; TH, György Ivicz jkv., 1957.

3. According to Lajos Szabó and József Nagy, Ivicz spoke of transporting explosive mines and TNT, and was looking for a chemical engineer to help in the project.

4. According to Szabó's confession, everyone agreed to armed organizing except for Hegedűs and himself; the two of them felt the support of the workers' councils and strikes would be more conducive (BFL, jkv. July 12, 1957, BFL, TH). Hegedűs felt that Szabó was hesitant when it came to armed organizing, and only the ones from the hospital—Korniczky, Halkrast and himself—felt it was unnecessary to shed blood. See Lajos Szabó jkv., 1957. VI. 20; TH, Lajos Szabó jkv., 1957. VI. 20.

5. In 1989 Imre Mécs remembered the event as follows:

...we tried to create a great network to include legitimate formations from the revolution, but not illegal formations. In addition to irrepressible rage, we were prompted by lack of information. Western broadcasts, with some exceptions, were whipping up our justified passions with irresponsible newscasts, spreading disinformation...namely that there are insurgent groups in the Bükk mountains, the Gerecse, the Bakony...and that Maléter would descend from the Bakony to liberate Budapest...A defeated nation always seeks refuge in legends, and these legends often provide the strength for the struggle...expressing the sensations, the yearnings of the people....And we too believed, because we wanted to believe. In Országos Széchenyi Könyvtár [National Széchenyi Library] (hereafter OSZK), Interview with Imre Mécs, 1989.

6. The attempt to recruit must have taken the most varied forms: "I was playing soccer with my friends in the field at the corner of Vezér and Egressy Streets when József Nagy joined us in the match, and it was after that, in the evening, that he asked me to join the band." BFL, Endre József Nagy, tk; TH, Endre József Nagy.

7. László Hegedűs recalls that they disseminated three types of flyers, in almost 3,000 copies. BFL, László Hegedűs jkv., 1957. V. 28; TH, László Hegedűs jkv., 1957. V. 28.

8. BFL, József Nagy jkv., 1957. VII. 25; TH, József Nagy jkv., 1957. VII. 25. According to the recollection of Lajos Szabó, historical models

were part of the oath: "We are fighting in the spirit of the freedom fighters of 1848." BFL, József Nagy jkv., 1957. VII. 28; TH, József Nagy jkv., 1957. VII. 28. According to Nándor Tóth there was also something about the thousand-year-old fatherland, the spirit of the great ancestors, Rákóczi and Kossuth, moreover "we will defend the people's democracy and the power of the workers, we do not need the capitalists, the industrialists, the counts, or those who do not keep their oath, let the curse of the ancestors strike them down." BFL, Nándor Tóth jkv., 1957. VI. 19; TH, Nándor Tóth jkv., 1957. VI. 19.

9.   In the eyes of some, Bagoly was leader in name only, in reality it was János Karászy. Lajos Szabó described József Nagy as follows: "easily led, somewhat fanatical, does not have a clear line of ideas" BFL, Szabó jkv., 1957. VII. 10; TH, Szabó jkv., 1957. VII. 10. Mécs thought of him as "a naïve child...." BFL, 8016/58 Imre Mécs tárgy., 1958. V. 6. Szabó judged Karászy as follows: "He had a police identity card. He had military knowledge about the entire country, and nothing frightened him, as he says. He proposed and accepted to carry out an action at the meetings of the MSZMP: an explosive planted in a flowerpot would do the trick." BFL, Szabó, önv., 1957. VII. 22; TH, Szabó, önv., 1957. VII. 22.

10.   BFL, Nagy jkv., 1957. VII. 25; TH, Nagy jkv., 1957. VII. 25. Nagy also confessed that they began collecting data even earlier. Karászy obtained the battle order of the police units, whereas Hegedűs and Korniczky got information regarding the air force from an hospitalized officer. They entrusted the records to Mrs. Vancsó, and destroyed them in January 1957. There was talk even earlier that, with the help of Karászy's identification card, they could make copies thereof, but desisted when Bárány got arrested.

11.   Perhaps the following excerpt from the confession of Lajos Szabó describes the movement best: "District XIII. I was the commander. There was no deputy. There were no members." BFL, Szabó jkv., 1957. VI. 27; TH, Szabó jkv., 1957. VI. 27.

12.   According to the testimony of József Nagy and Mrs. Béla Vancsó, the organization intended to enter into negotiations with the Kádár government, and would have confronted it with arms only if he refused to negotiate. BFL, Nagy jkv., 1957. VII. 25; TH, Nagy jkv., 1957. VII. 25; BFL, Mrs. Vancsó jkv., 1957. VI. 5; TH, Mrs. Vancsó jkv., 1957. VI. 5.

13.   According to Lajos Szabó, Karászy suggested the creation of cells of ten members each. The central command would have been made up of the group leaders. Their task was to learn to use weapons, but Szabó complemented this with the idea of initiating political training.

Their political discussions were mainly about the "mistakes" of the past twelve years of the Communist regime. BFL, Szabó jkv., 1957. VI. 27; TH, Szabó jkv., 1957. VI. 27. József Nagy, however, recalled that the district units would have been divided into units of fifty. The leaders of these would have been appointed by the district commanders. BFL, Szabó jkv., 1957. V. 20; TH, Szabó jkv., 1957. V. 20.

14.   The effectives reported by the district commanders suggest something different: District III, 200 to 250; District XIII, 150 to 200; District XIV, 100; District VIII, 800; District XXI, 1000 to 1200, Districts XIX and XX , 250 to 300 each. BFL, Szabó jkv., 1957. VI.27. 1957; TH, Szabó jkv., 1957. VI. 27. The total effectives, according to the reports of the group leaders, were 5,000 to 8,000. BFL, Szabó jkv., 1957. V. 20; TH, Szabó jkv., 1957. V. 20.

15.   Béla Békési (alias "Bagoly"), József Rácz, and Erneszt Kovács.

16.   BFL, Hegedűs, jkv. 1957. VI.10; TH, Hegedűs, jkv. 1957. VI. 10. Hegedűs was the one who brought the two groups together. He talked to Békési about the work of the "Bástya" group, but by then he realized that "they were muddle-headed, stubborn, power-tripping." Békési thought of including them into his group, then he would be able to define their mission. Hegedűs also talked about his contacts with the "Bagolys" to Lajos Szabó and company. At first they approved of the chance to meet them, but later they felt the university boys liked to order them around.

17.   The organizational rules were the idea of Hegedűs and Korniczky, because they felt that Lajos Szabó and his friends were undisciplined and were not even able to follow their own unwritten rules. In their introduction they stressed the fight for the cause of freedom, the need for unity, whereas unity could only be assured by organization and structure, hence the need for rules. At the top of the organization there would be a congress, formed by members or leaders of underground groups in the counties and urban centers . Ground rules determined the function of the congress. In case of an uprising, the committees of the capital, of the counties, and of urban centers in the counties would subject themselves to the National Central Committee; the committees in turn would be in charge of directing the activities of towns other than the official urban centers and of the cells in the villages. The district committees would influence the cells at the level of the industrial plants. The ground rules defined the mode of relations between individual groups, by means of liaisons. Anyone who believed in the idea of an independent Hungary was eligible for membership in the groups. The document also mentioned dues and discipline within the organization. After the presentation Lajos Szabó rejected it, saying "there is no

need," but Békési and Iván liked the idea. BFL, Hegedűs, jkv., 1957. VI. 17. 1957; TH, Hegedűs, jkv., 1957. VI. 17.

18. Békési told Hegedűs, that "he did not care for the ideology of our organization." He allegedly also mentioned that they had good contacts in the West, there were 15,000 U.S. dollars available to them in Vienna for expenses of organization, their task was intelligence gathering in Budapest. BFL, Szabó jkv., 1957. VII. 10; TH, Szabó jkv., 1957. VII. 10.

19. According to his confession, József Borsodi was replaced on December 17, because he was assessed as not serious, someone who does not carry out his tasks. BFL, József Borsodi jkv., 1957. VII. 6; TH, József Borsodi jkv., 1957. VII. 6. Vilmos Kramolis replaced him. Szabó also attended the meeting of the group from the borough of Óbuda on December 14. As it turned out, he was distrustful with regard to Kramolis, who had served with the AVH at the rank of corporal. He vowed to shoot him down, if his suspicion proved correct. See ibid.

20. According to the confession of Mécs, Karászy claimed in his report that he had rejected the approaches of British intelligence. BFL, Mécs jkv., 1957. VI. 28; TH, Mécs jkv., 1957. VI. 28.

21. As Mécs recalled, Karászy advised everyone to leave the country, and announced that he himself was going to do that. Mécs jkv., 1957. VI. 25; TH, Mécs jkv., 1957. VI. 25.

22. It is interesting to note that Nagy intended to escape not out of fear of getting caught, but because of the military draft call for the following day.

23. Szabó found out about this, yet did not give up on the conspiracy; he talked Mrs. Molnár to join the KISZ [Communist Youth League], for tactical reasons. BFL, Mrs. Lajos Molnár, jkv., 1957. V. 2; TH, Mrs. Lajos Molnár, jkv., 1957. V. 2.

24. "In February of 1957 József Borsodi called on our subdivision, because he was asked to do so by the reconnaissance unit of the third district police." By then Borsodi was a member of the Party and a leader in the KISZ. BFL, Police report jkv., 1957. VII. 2; TH, Police report jkv., 1957. VII. 2; BFL, Borsodi jkv., 1957. VI. 5; TH, Borsodi jkv., 1957. VI. 5. "In mid-January he denounced the members of the organization at the law enforcement offices of the third district, and the District Police Headquarters." The authorities knew nothing about the organization before then. BFL, Note by the prosecution, 1957. VII. 23; TH, Note by the prosecution, 1957. VII. 23.

25. Forgács and Mrs. Vancsó were gathering information for Karászy: all three were in contact with British intelligence.

26. "In such cases the law ensures impunity to the person making the

denunciation....Release must be ordered urgently and the investigation must be halted." BFL, Note by the prosecution, 1957. VII. 23; TH, Note by the prosecution, 1957. VII. 23. Even though Borsodi was accused of serious charges in the confession, to the effect that he had contemplated terrorist acts, such as the bombing of the water tower on Margaret Island and of the Csepel Railway Bridge. These plans were opposed by Lajos Szabó, who received the most severe sentence nevertheless. BFL, Mrs. Molnár jkv., 1957. V. 2; TH, Mrs. Molnár jkv., 1957. V. 2.

27. He played a much more important role during the revolution, since he was the commander of a significant group.

APPENDIX

Resolution Adopted by the Students of the Technical University of Building and Construction Industry on October 22, 1956

Minutes of the October 23, 1956, Meeting of the Central Committee of the CPUSSR [Excerpt]

Report by Mikoyan and Suslov to the Central Committee of the CPUSSR, from Budapest, October 24, 1956 [Excerpt]

Declaration of the Soviet Government, October 30, 1956 [Excerpt]

Minutes of the October 31, 1956, Session of the Central Commitee of the CPUSSR [Excerpt]

Minutes of the November 1, 1956, Meeting of the Central Committee of the CPUSSR [Excerpt]

RESOLUTION ADOPTED BY THE STUDENTS OF THE TECHNICAL UNIVERSITY OF BUILDING AND CONSTRUCTION INDUSTRY ON OCTOBER 22, 1956

The following resolution was drafted on 22 October 1956, at the dawn of a new period in Hungarian history, in the Assembly Hall of the Technical University of Building and Construction Industry [in Budapest] as a result of the spontaneous motion by of several thousand of the Hungarian youth who love their Fatherland:

1. We demand the immediate withdrawal of all Soviet troops in accordance with the provisions of the Peace Treaty [of 1947].

2. We demand the election of new leaders in the Hungarian Workers' Party at the low, medium and high levels, by secret ballot from the ranks upwards. These leaders should convene the Party Congress within the shortest possible time and elect a new central body of leaders.

3. The government should be reconstituted under the leadership of Comrade Imre Nagy; all criminal leaders of the Stalinist-Rákosi era should be relieved of their posts at once.

4. We demand a public trial in the criminal case of Mihály Farkas and his accomplices. Mátyás Rákosi, who is primarily responsible for all the crimes of the recent past and for the ruin of this country, should be brought home [from Russia] and placed before the tribunal of the people.

5. We demand general elections in this country, with universal suffrage, secret ballot and the participation of several parties for the purpose of electing a new national assembly. We demand that the workers should have the right to strike.

6. We demand a reexamination and readjustment of Hungarian-Soviet and Hungarian-Yugoslav political, economic and intellectual

relations on the basis of complete political and economic equality and of nonintervention in each other's internal affairs.

7. We demand the reorganization of the entire economic life of Hungary, with the assistance of specialists. Our whole economic system based on planned economy should be reexamined with an eye to Hungarian conditions and to the vital interests of the Hungarian people.

8. Our foreign trade agreements and the actual figures in respect of reparations that can never be paid should be made public. We demand frank and sincere information concerning the country's uranium deposits, their exploitation and the Russian concession. We demand that Hungary should have the right to sell the uranium ore freely at world market prices in exchange for hard currency.

9. We demand the complete revision of norms in industry and an urgent and radical adjustment of wages to meet the demands of workers and intellectuals. We demand that minimum living wages for workers should be fixed.

10. We demand that the produce delivery system should be placed on a new footing and that produce should be used rationally. We demand equal treatment for peasants farming independently.

11. We demand the reexamination of all political and economic trials by independent courts and the release and rehabilitation of innocent persons. We demand the immediate repatriation of prisoners of war and of civilians deported to the Soviet Union, including prisoners who have been condemned beyond the frontiers of Hungary.

12. We demand complete freedom of opinion and expression, freedom of the press and a free radio, as well as a new daily newspaper of wide circulation for the MEFESZ [League of Hungarian University and College Student Associations] organization. We demand that the existing "screening material" should be made public and destroyed.

13. We demand that the Stalin statue—the symbol of Stalinist tyranny and political oppression—should be removed as quickly as possible and that a memorial worthy of the freedom fighters and martyrs of 1848–49 be erected on its site.

14. In place of the existing coat of arms, which is foreign to the Hungarian people, we wish the reintroduction of the old Hungarian Kossuth coat of arms. We demand new uniforms for the Hungarian army worthy of our national traditions. We demand that March 15

should be a national holiday and a day of rest and that October 6 should be a day of national mourning and a school holiday.

15. The youth of the Technical University of Budapest unanimously express their complete solidarity with the Polish and Warsaw workers and youth in connection with the Polish national independence movement.

16. The students of the Technical University of Building and Construction will organize local units of MEFESZ as quickly as possible, and have resolved to convene a youth parliament in Budapest for the 27th of this month (Saturday) at which the entire youth of this country will be represented by their delegates. The students of the Technological University and of the various other universities will gather on Gorkij Avenue before the Writers' Union headquarters tomorrow, the 23rd of this month, at 2:30 P.M., whence they will proceed to Bem Square (Pálffy) Square to the Bem statue, on which they will lay wreaths to signal their sympathy with the Polish freedom movement. The workers of the factories are invited to join in this procession.

MINUTES OF THE OCTOBER 23, 1956, MEETING OF THE CENTRAL COMMITTEE OF THE CPUSSR
[Excerpt]

In attendance: Bulganin, Kaganovich, Mikoyan, Molotov, Pervukhin, Saburov, Khrushchev, Suslov, Brezhnev, Zhukov, Furtseva, Shepilov. Regarding the situation in Budapest, and Hungary in general.

(Comrades Zhukov, Bulganin and Khrushchev)

Report by Comrade Zhukov: Demonstrations in Budapest by a hundred thousand....According to comrade Khrushchev the troops have to march into Budapest. Comrade Bulganin seconds Khrushchev's proposal, the troops have to march in.

Comrade Mikoyan: The movement cannot be controlled without Nagy, that would make it more cost effective for us as well. He has doubts concerning the marching in of troops. What can we lose? Let the Hungarians bring about order on their own. If our troops march in, we will spoil the matter for ourselves. Let us take political measures first, and send in the troops only after that.

Comrade Molotov: If we use Nagy we merely undermine Hungary. In favor of marching in.

Comrade Kaganovich: The government is being overthrown. Comparisons with Poland do not apply. In favor of marching in.

Comrade Pervukhin: In favor of marching in.

Comrade Zhukov: In favor of marching in. Let a member of the Central Committee travel there. A state of war must be declared in the country, institute a curfew.

Comrade Suslov: The situation is not the same as in Poland. In favor of marching in.

Comrade Saburov: In favor of marching in, to restore order.

Comrade Shepilov: In favor of marching in.

Comrae Kirichenko. In favor of marching in. Comrades Malinin and Serov should be sent to Budapest.

Comrade Khrushchev: Nagy must be included in the political action. But let us not appoint him prime minister as yet. Let Mikoyan and Suslov travel to Budapest.

REPORT BY MIKOYAN AND SUSLOV TO THE CENTRAL COMMITTEE OF THE CPUSSR, FROM BUDAPEST, OCTOBER 24, 1956
[Excerpt]

In Buda, people gathered in small groups were calmly watching our columns of vehicles drive by—some seemed preoccupied, others greeted us with smiles. The roads leading to the city, and the streets within the city were jammed with Soviet tanks and other Soviet materiel.

In addition to the Soviet formations Hungarian patrols are also visible. While there was calm on the Buda side, on the Pest side there was continuous shooting between the bridge and the building of the Ministry of Defense, and from there to the building of the Central Committee, between single provocateurs or small groups of provocateurs on the one side and our own machine gunners and automatic riflemen. Our own troops were firing more, responding with volleys to single shots....Our impression is that comrade Gerő in particular, as well as other comrades, have overestimated the strength of the adversary, and underestimated their own forces.

DECLARATION OF THE SOVIET GOVERNMENT, OCTOBER 30, 1956
[Excerpt]

For the sake of ensuring the mutual security of the socialist countries, the Soviet government is ready to examine the issue of Soviet troops stationed on the territory of the socialist countries participating in the Warsaw Pact. In this regard the Soviet government stands on the general principle that Soviet troops are stationed on the territory of any member state of the Warsaw Pact on the basis of an agreement, and only with the consent of said state....

The Soviet government, along with all the people of the Soviet Union, deeply deplore that the events of Hungary had led to bloodshed.

At the request of the Hungarian government the Soviet government agreed to allow Soviet military formations to march into Budapest in order to assist the Hungarian People's Army and the Hungarian police in restoring order inside the city. Considering that the continued stationing of Soviet formations in Hungary may serve as an excuse for increased confrontation, the Soviet government has given instructions to the military command to withdraw the military formations from Budapest as soon as the Hungarian government agrees to the move. At the same time the Soviet government is prepared to negotiate with the government of the Hungarian People's Republic and the governments of other member states of the Warsaw Pact regarding stationing Soviet troops in Hungary.

The defense of the socialist achievement of the people's democracy in Hungary is the principal and sacred obligation of the workers, peasants and intelligentsia, and the entire working population of Hungary.

MINUTES OF THE OCTOBER 31, 1956, SESSION OF THE CENTRAL COMMITTEE OF THE CPUSSR
[Excerpt]

Information regarding discussions with Gomułka on the Polish and Hungarian situation.

(Khrushchev)
The discussion was about the meeting with Gomułka (near Brest) on the Hungarian situation. Regarding Hungary comrade Khrushchev presents the envisioned plans. The earlier assessment must be reexamined, the troops must not be withdrawn from Hungary and Budapest, we have to take the initiative in order to restore order in Hungary. If we were to withdraw from Hungary, this would only hearten the American, British and French imperialists. They would view this as signs of weakness on our part, and launch attacks. [By withdrawing] we would only be showing the weakness of our position. The Party would not understand us in this case. In addition to Egypt, we would hand Hungary over to them. We have no other choice.

Zhukov, Bulganin, Molotov, Kaganovich, Voroshilov, Saburov are in agreement. If this stand is backed, if we are in agreement, we must consider the next steps. It must be said that we took the initiative, but now there is no government. What line should we follow? We must form a provisional revolutionary government (led by Kádár).

[Yet] it would be best, if he were to remain a deputy prime minister. Let Münnich be the prime minister, minister of defense, and of the interior. We would invite this government, let us say, for negotiations regarding the withdrawal of troops, and resolve the issue. If Nagy agrees, let him be deputy prime minister. Münnich asks for our help, we give help, and restore order. To be discussed with Tito. Inform the Chinese comrades, the Romanians, the Bulgarians. There will be no major conflict.

Comrade Saburov:...Our move would justify NATO.

Molotov: Yesterday's decision was half-hearted....

Comrade Furtseva: What is to be done next? We have been patient, but now matters have gone too far. We must act to ensure our victory.

Comrade Pospelov: We must use as justification: we cannot allow it [socialism in Hungary] to be repressed.

Comrade Shvernik: The proposal of Comrade Khrushchev is correct.

MINUTES OF THE NOVEMBER 1, 1956, MEETING OF THE CENTRAL COMMITTEE OF THE CPUSSR [Excerpt]

In attendance: Voroshilov, Bulganin, Kaganovich, Mikoyan, Saburov, Suslov, Brezhnev, Zhukov, Shvernik, Furtseva, Pospelov, Konev, Serov.

Regarding the situation in Hungary. Mikoyan, Comrade [Suslov]: The demand for the withdrawal of the troops has become general. The anti-Soviet mood has grown.

Comrade Mikoyan: Under the present conditions it is would be more correct to back the existing government. We would achieve nothing by resorting to force. We must undertake negotiations. [let us wait] ten to fifteen days. If the power continues to weaken, then we can decide what to do. We must not allow Hungary to leave our camp. Let us not quarrel with the army. If the situation becomes stabilized, then we can decide whether to withdraw the troops. Let us wait ten to fifteen days, back this government. Once there is stabilization, matters will improve.

Comrade Suslov: The political situation is unstable. The danger of a bourgeois restoration is quite real. The situation will become clear in the next few days. The events are spontaneous, evolving without control from the Party. There is schism within the Hungarian Workers' Party, and the dissension has spilled into the street. I don't believe that Nagy organized the uprising, but his name has been used. There is no assurance that this government can hold on to power. Only with an occupation force can we ensure a government on our side.

Comrade Serov: The uprising has been carefully prepared. Nagy was in touch with the rebels. We must take forceful measures. We must occupy the country.

Comrade Bulganin reports on the resolution of October 31, 1956 and on the discussions with the Chinese comrades.

Comrade Bulganin: The international situation has changed. If we take no measures, we lose Hungary.

Comrade Konev: Budapest is under the control of the rebels. Anarchy prevails. Reactionary forces are dominant. The solution is to occupy the country.

Comrade Kaganovich: The discussion has been complicated. The stand of the Chinese is that we should not withdraw our forces. Objectively speaking, the movement is strongly reactionary. The Party does not exist. We must not wait long. The forces of reaction are on the move, whereas we are [not].

Comrade Furtseva: They are afraid that we might hand over Hungary.

Comrade Zhukov: There is no reason to reassess the resolution of October 31, 1956. He does not agree with Comrade Mikoyan that we must back the existing government. Decisive action must be taken. Arrest all the scoundrels. Disarm the counterrevolution....

Comrade Suslov: Now the situation is clearer. The honorable ones [i.e. the supporters of the intervention] have to be identified and separated.

MAPS

Budapest

Legend:

1. Estern Railway Station
2. Western Railway Station
3. Southern Railway Station

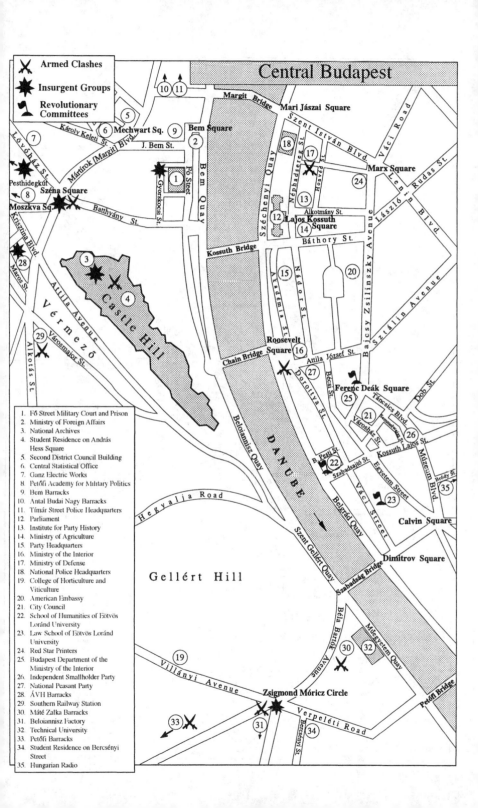

Central Budapest

Legend:
- ✗ Armed Clashes
- ✦ Insurgent Groups
- Revolutionary Committees

1. Fő Street Military Court and Prison
2. Ministry of Foreign Affairs
3. National Archives
4. Student Residence on András Hess Square
5. Second District Council Building
6. Central Statistical Office
7. Ganz Electric Works
8. Petőfi Academy for Military Politics
9. Bem Barracks
10. Antal Budai Nagy Barracks
11. Tímár Street Police Headquarters
12. Parliament
13. Institute for Party History
14. Ministry of Agriculture
15. Party Headquarters
16. Ministry of the Interior
17. Ministry of Defense
18. National Police Headquarters
19. College of Horticulture and Viticulture
20. American Embassy
21. City Council
22. School of Humanities of Eötvös Loránd University
23. Law School of Eötvös Loránd University
24. Red Star Printers
25. Budapest Department of the Ministry of the Interior
26. Independent Smallholder Party
27. National Peasant Party
28. ÁVH Barracks
29. Southern Railway Station
30. Máté Zalka Barracks
31. Beloiannisz Factory
32. Technical University
33. Petőfi Barracks
34. Student Residence on Bercsényi Street
35. Hungarian Radio

Map labels:
- Margit Bridge
- Mari Jászai Square
- Mechwart Sq.
- Bem Square
- Marx Square
- Lajos Kossuth Square
- Roosevelt Square
- Ferenc Deák Square
- Calvin Square
- Dimitrov Square
- Zsigmond Móricz Circle
- Castle Hill
- Gellért Hill
- DANUBE
- Moszkva Sq.
- Széna Square
- Pesthidegkút
- Szechenyi Quay
- Kossuth Bridge
- Chain Bridge
- Szabadság Bridge
- Petőfi Bridge
- Várkert
- Villányi Avenue
- Verpeléti Road
- Hegyalja Road

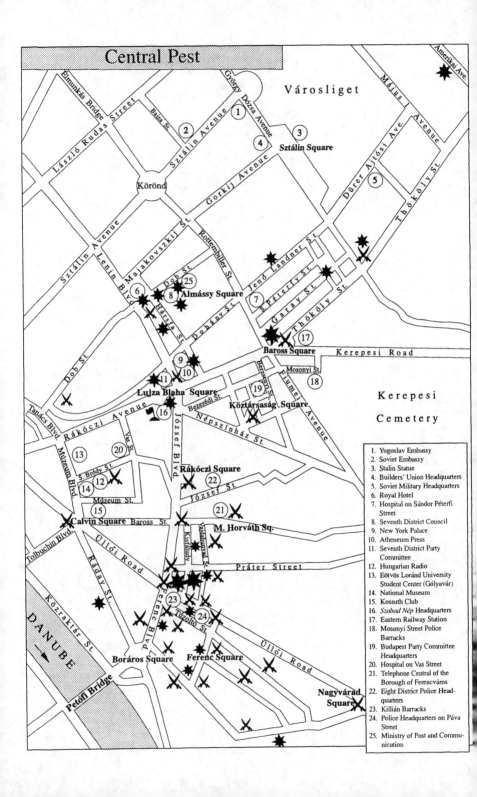

Central Pest

Várossliget

Sztálin Square

Körönd

Almássy Square

Baross Square

Kerepesi Road

Lujza Blaha Square

Köztársaság Square

Kerepesi

Cemetery

Rákóczi Square

M. Horváth Sq.

Calvin Square   Baross St.

Práter Street

Üllői Road

DANUBE

Boráros Square   Ferenc Square

Nagyvárad Square

Petőfi Bridge

Streets and avenues: Elmunkás Bridge, László Rudas Street, Baiza St., Sztálin Avenue, György Dózsa Avenue, Gorkij Avenue, Máius 1 Avenue, Amerikai Ave., Dürer Ajtósi Ave., Thököly St., Sztálin Avenue, Lenin Blvd., Majakovszkii St., Rottenbiller St., Jenő Landner St., S Péterfy St., Garay St., Thököly St., Dob St., Hársfa St., Dob St., Dohány St., Mosonyi St., Bezerédi St., Fiumei Avenue, Tanács Blvd., Rákóczi Avenue, Vas St., József Blvd., Népszínház St., Múzeum Blvd., S Bródy St., József St., Múzeum St., Tolbuchin Blvd., Ráday St., Üllői Road, Kisfaludy St., Vadahuzyai St., Ferenc Blvd., Tűzoltó St., Köztraktár St.

1. Yugoslav Embassy
2. Soviet Embassy
3. Stalin Statue
4. Builders' Union Headquarters
5. Soviet Military Headquarters
6. Royal Hotel
7. Hospital on Sándor Péterfi Street
8. Seventh District Council
9. New York Palace
10. Atheneum Press
11. Seventh District Party Committee
12. Hungarian Radio
13. Eötvös Loránd University Student Center (Gólyavár)
14. National Museum
15. Kossuth Club
16. *Szabad Nép* Headquarters
17. Eastern Railway Station
18. Mosonyi Street Police Barracks
19. Budapest Party Committee Headquarters
20. Hospital on Vas Street
21. Telephone Central of the Borough of Ferencváros
22. Eight District Police Headquarters
23. Killián Barracks
24. Police Headquarters on Páva Street
25. Ministry of Post and Communication

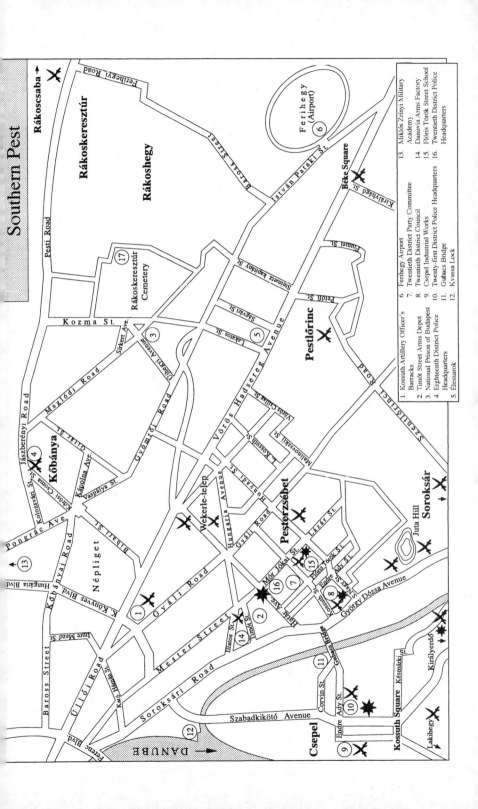

Southern Pest

Rákoscsaba →

Fenyheyi Road

Rákoskeresztúr

Rákoshegy

Pesti Road

Feri h e g y
(Airport)
6

Béke Square

Pestlőrinc

Kozma St.

Rákoskeresztúr
Cemetery
17

3

5

Kőbánya
4

Néplige t

13

1

Pesterzsébet

Soroksár

Csepel

Kossuth Square

9

12

DANUBE →

Szabadkikötő Avenue

1. Kossuth Artillery Officer's Barracks
2. Timót Street Arms Depot
3. National Prison of Budapest
4. Eighteenth District Police Headquarters
5. Élessarok
6. Ferihegy Airport
7. Twentieth District Party Committee
8. Twentieth District Council
9. Csepel Industrial Works
10. Twenty-first District Police Headquarters
11. Gubacs Bridge
12. Kvassa Lock
13. Miklós Zrínyi Military Academy
14. Danuvia Arms Factory
15. Flóris Török Street School
16. Twentieth District Police Headquarters

INDEX

ABOUT THE AUTHOR

LÁSZLÓ EÖRSI is a fellow of the 1956 Institute, Budapest, and a recognized authority on the 1956 Revolution. He is a specialist of the history of the uprising in Budapest. His books in Hungarian include: *The Confession of István Angyal by His Own Hands* (1991); *The Insurgent Group of Tűzoltó Street in the Revolution* (1993); *Ferencváros 1956* (1997); *1956 in the Thirteenth District* (1997); and *The Corvinists 1956* (2001).

BOOKS PUBLISHED BY THE CENTER FOR HUNGARIAN STUDIES AND PUBLICATIONS

CHSP Hungarian Authors Series:

No. 1. *False Tsars.* Gyula Szvák. 2000.

No. 2. *Book of the Sun.* Marcell Jankovics. 2001.

No. 3. *The Dismantling of Historic Hungary: The Peace Treaty of Trianon, 1920.* Ignác Romsics. 2002.

No. 4. *The Soviet and Hungarian Holocausts: A Comparative Essay.* Tamás Krausz. 2006.

CHSP Hungarian Studies Series:

No. 1. *Emperor Francis Joseph, King of the Hungarians.* András Gerő. 2001.

No. 2. *Global Monetary Regime and National Central Banking. The Case of Hungary, 1921–1929.* György Péteri. 2002.

No. 3. *Hungarian-Italian Relations in the Shadow of Hitler's Germany, 1933–1940.* György Réti. 2003.

No. 4. *The War Crimes Trial of Hungarian Prime Minister László Bárdossy.* Pál Pritz. 2004.

No. 5. *Identity and the Urban Experience: Fin-de-Siècle Budapest.* Gábor Gyáni. 2004.

No. 6. *Picturing Austria-Hungary. The British Perception of the Habsburg Monarchy, 1865–1870.* Tibor Frank. 2005.

No. 7. *Anarchism in Hungary: Theory, History, Legacies.* András Bozóki and Miklós Sükösd. 2006.

No. 8. *Myth and Remembrance. The Dissolution of the Habsburg Empire in the Memoir Literature of the Austro-Hungarian Political Elite.* Gergely Romsics. 2006.

No. 9. *Imagined History. Chapters from Nineteenth and Twentieth Century Hungarian Symbolic Politics.* András Gerő. 2006.

No. 10. *Pál Teleki (1874–1941). A Biography.* Balázs Ablonczy. 2006.

No. 11. *The Hungarian Revolution of 1956. Myths and Realities.* László Eörsi. 2006.